THE
PERSONAL
FINANCE
CALCULATOR

How to Calculate the Most Important Financial Decisions in Your Life

ESMÉ FAERBER

McGraw·Hill

New York   Chicago   San Francisco   Lisbon   London   Madrid   Mexico City
Milan   New Delhi   San Juan   Seoul   Singapore   Sydney   Toronto

Library of Congress Cataloging-in-Publication Data

Faerber, Esmé.
    The personal finance calculator: how to calculate the most important
financial decisions in your life / by Esmé Faerber.
        p.   cm.
    Includes bibliographical references.
    ISBN 0-07-139390-0 (pbk. : alk. paper)
        1. Finance, Personal—Mathematics.   2. Investments—Mathematics.
    3. Calculators.   4. Business mathematics.   I. Title.
    HG179.F34   2003
    332.024'001'51—dc21   2002013682

1 2 3 4 5 6 7 8 9 0   DOC/DOC   1 0 9 8 7 6 5 4 3 2

ISBN 0-07-139390-0

Interior design by Robert S. Tinnon
Interior illustrations by Randy Miyake

This publication is designed to provide accurate and authoritative information in regard to the
subject matter covered. It is sold with the understanding that neither the author nor the publisher
is engaged in rendering legal, accounting, or other professional service. If legal advice or other
expert assistance is required, the services of a competent professional person should be sought.

From a Delaration of Principles jointly adopted by a
Committee of the American Bar Association
and a Committee of Publishers

McGraw-Hill books are available at special quantity discounts to use as premiums and sales
promotions, or for use in corporate training programs. For more information, please write to the
Director of Special Sales, Professional Publishing, McGraw-Hill, Two Penn Plaza, New York, NY
10121-2298. Or contact your local bookstore.

This book is printed on acid-free paper.

Contents

PART TWO
Managing Your Personal Wealth—Debt

FINANCIAL CALCULATOR:

PART THREE
Managing Your Personal Wealth—Investments

FINANCIAL CALCULATOR:

PART FOUR
Planning for Your Future

FINANCIAL CALCULATOR:

Acknowledgments

THE PREPARATION OF THIS BOOK WAS greatly facilitated by many people at the McGraw-Hill Publishing Company. Most notably, I am grateful for the support of Stephen Isaacs and Kelli Christiansen. Rena J. Copperman and Linda Gorman provided superb editorial assistance and were a pleasure to work with. I am especially appreciative of their help.

My husband Eric and our children Jennifer and Michael were patient and supportive, for which I am especially grateful.

Introduction

I HAVE ALWAYS WANTED TO WRITE A book that would be different from every other book on the market. There are no basic money management books that provide the tools and resources to determine and quantify answers to personal financial situations and most people's pressing financial problems. There are countless personal finance books on the market, but many do not address how to quantify the specifics of each situation to make the decisions that will help you achieve your financial objectives and attain financial freedom. To get answers about a specific issue, you would have to consult a textbook on the subject, which might not be tailored to the problem facing you. Most people have never had any formal money management education, and this holds true for many of the current business graduates from four-year college and university programs. *The Personal Finance Calculator* was written to bridge this gap and provide you with a practical set of tools you can use not only to solve your financial problems but also to better manage your financial affairs.

Financial decisions form the basis of much of what we do in our lives. Poorly thought out personal finance decisions can at best cause great anxiety and at worst lead to bankruptcy, whereas well thought out, sound financial decisions can lead to a prosperous lifestyle. Now more than ever, we need to understand the complexities of our financial circumstances to make sound decisions. We are confronted by countless financial decisions in our daily lives, and this book provides a format to assist you in most, if not all, of your decision-making. Fifty-two different financial calculators provide you with the opportunity to take charge of your own financial affairs. Each financial calculator has one or more worksheets with step-by-step instructions to assist you in determining your answers to each of the financial questions.

The financial tools in this book are arranged into four parts:

1. Assessing your current wealth
2. Managing your debt
3. Managing your investments
4. Planning for your future

Using the financial calculators in each section, you will be able to:

- Determine how much money you have, how much you owe, and how to better control your finances
- Use the time value of money calculations to make better financial and investment decisions
- Formulate a plan to manage your debt by using credit wisely
- Figure out how much your debt is costing you and how to choose the least costly form of financing
- Determine whether you should buy or rent a house
- Determine whether to buy, finance, or lease a car.
- Set investment objectives, make asset allocation plans, and measure the returns on different investments
- Determine your needs in retirement

The financial tools presented in this book allow you to work through these and other personal financial problems that you are likely to encounter in managing your personal finances. Most personal finance decisions involve choices, and making the right choice most of the time involves more than intuition and guesswork. By working through the different calculations, you will be able to make informed decisions, which in many cases may save considerable amounts of money over time. Keep in mind, however, that decision-making is an ongoing process that will affect your current and future choices.

Each of the financial tools in the four parts can be read and used individually, except for those calculations involving the time value of money. Read the sections on the time value of money, simple interest, compound interest and future value, present values and annuities (sections 4, 5, 6, 8, and 9) first for an understanding of the subject matter before attempting to use any of the calculations. Understanding the basis of present and future values is helpful in determining the price of a bond. Similarly, understanding annuities can assist you in the calculation of a monthly mortgage payment and the determination of a mortgage schedule. There are many software programs and financial calculators that can assist you in your calculations, obviating the need to crunch numbers with pen and paper. Reading the text can help you determine what figures to punch into these programs.

By successfully managing your personal finance decisions, you will manage and increase your wealth.

PART ONE
ASSESSING YOUR
CURRENT WEALTH

How to Determine
Your Net Worth

*N*ET WORTH IS SYNONYMOUS WITH your wealth at a single point in time. It is the starting point for financial planning and indicates your capacity to achieve your financial goals. Your net worth can be ascertained by drawing up a personal balance sheet, as shown in Worksheet 1.1. The process consists of three steps:

1. List your assets (items of value that you own).
2. List your liabilities (amounts that you owe to others).
3. Subtract your liabilities from your assets; the difference is your net worth.

This relationship is shown below:

Items of Value − Amounts Owed = Net Worth

In other words, if you sell all your assets and use the money to pay off all your debts, what is left over is your net worth.

Assets

Assets are arranged in order of liquidity; that is, the ability to convert them into cash without losing much in the conversion. The most liquid are at the top of the list and include cash, checking accounts, money market securities, and money market mutual funds.

WORKSHEET 1.1 How to determine your net worth

Assets

Cash	$ _____
Checking account balance	_____
Savings accounts/money market funds	_____
Certificates of deposit	_____
Current value of savings bonds	_____
Cash surrender value of life insurance	_____
Cash surrender value of annuities	_____
Market value of investments	_____
Mutual funds	_____
Stocks	_____
Bonds	_____
Other	_____
Market value of IRA/Keogh pension/profit sharing/401K	_____
Market value of house/real estate	_____
Investment property	_____
Other	_____
Automobile(s)	_____
Household furniture/appliances	_____
Jewelry/precious metals	_____
Collectibles	_____
Loan receivables	_____
Other	_____
Total assets	$ _____

Liabilities

Credit card balances	$ _____
Bills outstanding	_____
Auto loan balances	_____
Taxes due	_____
Mortgage loans	_____
Total liabilities	$ _____
Net worth (assets minus liabilities)	$ _____

Step 1 List all items of value starting with cash, investment assets, the current value of your house, and possessions.

Step 2 List and total all liabilities.

Step 3 Subtract total liabilities from total assets.

Determining the value of your stocks, bonds, and mutual funds is easy. The prices can be found in the financial pages of a newspaper or obtained from brokerage and mutual fund statements.

Determining the current value of pension funds may be more difficult if the pension fund provides amounts of future income to be received. This means that for this type of plan, you would need to determine the present value of the plan. The human resources or benefits department of your company can provide this information.

If the cash surrender values of your whole life insurance policies and annuities are not shown on the latest statements you receive, call your insurance agent for this information.

Your home is likely to be your largest asset, so its value should not be over-inflated or underinflated. The figure that you are looking for is the current market value; that is, what someone would be willing to pay for your house. Generally, the cost of the property is not particularly relevant if you have owned your house for a long period of time. The most recent selling prices of houses similar to yours in your area are a good indicator of the likely market value of your house. Real estate brokers can also provide you with an estimate of the value of your house.

The value of cars can be obtained from used car price guides such as the *N.A.D.A. Official Used Car Guide* and the *Kelley Blue Book* (www.kbb.com). These guides can be found in most public libraries, or you can obtain the price of your car from your bank, which should have copies of these guides.

Household furniture, clothing, and personal effects should be more conservatively valued so as not to overstate their value. In an actual sale of these items, you might get far less than the estimated values.

Add the estimates of the value of all the items that you own and you will have the total of your assets.

Liabilities

Begin by listing your most current debts, such as utility bills, telephone bills, and others. Next, list the balances outstanding on your credit card debts and loans.

For most people, a home mortgage is their largest single debt outstanding. The amount to include is not the original amount of the loan but the current outstanding balance. The reason is because a part of the monthly payments made to the lender over the duration of the mortgage reduce the outstanding balance of the loan. The current outstanding balance of the loan may be obtained directly from the lender or from mortgage statements from the lender. You can also determine the balance yourself. See the financial calculator in section 20, which explains how to determine your mortgage balance.

Add up all the amounts owed to others and you have the total of your liabilities.

Net Worth

Your net worth is the difference between the totals of your assets and liabilities. In other words, if you sold all your assets for the values stated and paid off all your debts, the amount left over would be your net worth. Your net worth should not be thought of as cash to be spent. Rather, it is a measure of a person's financial position as of the date of the personal balance sheet.

Can your net worth be a negative number? Yes, this is possible. If you have more debt than total assets, you are technically insolvent. A continuation of this position may make it difficult for you to pay off all your debts on a timely basis, which could necessitate a declaration of bankruptcy.

Why Is Determining Net Worth Important?

Determining your net worth is the first step in financial planning and assessing your financial wealth. Net worth changes on a daily basis, so it is not a good idea to focus on these changes, as net worth is not cash available for use. Rather, net worth is a yardstick for comparing the changes in your financial position over a period of time. An increase in net worth over a period of time is a favorable trend, and a decrease in net worth is a reduction in wealth.

There are a number of ways to increase net worth:

- Appreciation of assets (for example, a rise in the value of stocks, bonds, mutual funds, and real estate).
- Reducing liabilities. This also reduces the amount of interest payments made to service the debt.
- Increasing your income, such as through salary and wage increases and increases in investment income.
- Reducing the amount spent on living expenses.

The importance of increasing net worth is obvious, but the addition of assets may not always increase your net worth. This is especially true for depreciating assets, such as automobiles, computers, stereo equipment, and the like. Investment assets could also lose some of their value, as in the stock market decline of 2000–2002. Paying off liabilities will also increase net worth if assets remain the same.

Creating a personal balance sheet will assist you in tracking your personal wealth over time and enable you to see relationships among the balance sheet items. The relationship between liquid current assets and current liabilities indicates the relative ease or difficulty in paying upcoming debts. This evaluation ratio is the *current ratio* and is determined as follows:

$$\text{Current Ratio} = \text{Current Assets} \div \text{Current Liabilities}$$

For example, if a person has $10,000 in liquid current assets and $5,000 in current liabilities, the current ratio is 2. This means that for every $1 in current debts, there is $2 in liquid assets. Generally, most current debts are repaid from liquid current assets such as cash, savings accounts, and money market funds. In the event of unemployment or insufficient liquid current assets to cover current debt, longer-term investment assets would need to be liquidated to pay off the debt.

The other significant relationship between balance sheet items is the *debt ratio*, which is total liabilities divided by net worth:

$$\text{Debt Ratio} = \text{Total Liabilities} \div \text{Net Worth}$$

For example, if a person has $100,000 in total liabilities and a net worth of $200,000, the debt ratio is 0.5.

By setting aside more money for savings and investment assets each month, you will increase your worth. In general, if total current liabilities and total liabilities are reduced over time, your net worth will also improve and this will be indicated by a lower debt ratio.

FINANCIAL CALCULATOR #2

How to Determine a Cash Inflows and Outflows Statement

ONE GOOD REASON TO DRAW UP A cash inflows and outflows statement is to see where your hard-earned money has gone. Many people complain that they earn large sums of money, but they never have anything left over. Recording their expenditures is a first step to taking control of their financial affairs. Because earnings and living expenses also influence net worth, this statement, also known as an income statement, shows that change. The income statement shows actual income and expenditures over a period of time, whereas a balance sheet shows financial position at a single point in time. There are three easy steps to creating an income statement, as shown in Worksheet 2.1.

1. List income received during the time period.
2. List expenditures made during the time period.
3. Determine the surplus/deficit of income over expenditures.

WORKSHEET 2.1 Determine your statement of cash inflows and cash outflows for the period _____, ended _____

Income (cash inflows)

Gross salary/wages		_____
Payroll taxes	_____	
Federal income taxes	_____	
State income taxes	_____	
FICA tax	_____	
Minus total payroll taxes		_____
Net salary/wages		_____
Interest/dividend income		_____
Gain on the sale of stocks/ bonds/investment bonds		_____
Tax refund		_____
Receipts from pension/ retirement plans		_____
Gifts/grants		_____
Alimony/child support receipts		_____
Other		_____
Total income		$ _____

Expenditures (cash outflows)

Auto expenses		_____
Food		_____
Telephone & utilities		_____
Medical & dental expenses		_____
Entertainment/recreation		_____
Donations		_____
Gifts		_____
Other		_____
Rent/mortgage payments		_____
Credit card payments		_____
Loan payments		_____
Insurance premiums		_____
House maintenance/repairs		_____
Total expenditures		$ _____
Cash surplus/deficit		$ _____

Step 1 List all sources of income for the period.
Step 2 List all the cash payments made during the period.
Step 3 Subtract expenditures from income. Cash surplus is positive and a deficit negative.

Step 1: List All Sources of Income

List all sources of income for the period of the income statement (one month, three months, six months, or one year). Income from wages and salaries is generally received net of payroll tax withholdings. In other words, taxes are taken out of your gross income, leaving you with income after taxes. Some forms of income are paid gross of taxes (in other words, no payroll taxes are withheld). If these sources of income are large, you would need to estimate the quarterly federal and state tax payments that you need to make. Quarterly tax payments are made to avoid the possibility of being assessed penalties for underestimating your federal and state taxes at the end of the tax year.

The main source of income for most people comes from what is earned from their occupations in the form of salaries, wages, self-employment income, and commissions. Other sources of income include bonuses, interest, dividends, rent, alimony and child support payments, income from Social Security, gains on the sale of assets, and gifts and inheritances. All sources of income should be included in order to make the income statement complete and accurate.

Step 2. List All Expenditures

Expenditures show where cash flows have been spent. The types of expenditures to include in the income statement will depend on the complexity of your financial affairs. Major categories of expenditures should be listed, but it is not necessary to account for every penny spent. By reviewing checkbook records and credit card statements and performing the more difficult task of tracing cash payments, you can easily develop categories of expenditures. By adding the payments made in each category, you will have a fairly accurate account of where your money has gone.

Certain expenditures are fixed; that is, they remain the same each month or year. Examples are rent, mortgage payments, life insurance premiums, and child care payments.

Variable expenditures are payments and expenses that change from month to month, such as food, clothing, medical, dental, gas, and auto expenses; telephone and utility payments; household operating expenses; contributions; and recreational expenses.

Step 3: Determine Whether There Is a Surplus or Deficit of Net Cash Flow

When income exceeds expenditures, there is a surplus. When expenditures exceed income, there is a deficit. Funds to cover a deficit can come from savings or a loan, both of which decrease net worth. A surplus represents an increase to net worth if the amount is used to increase savings, acquire additional assets, and/or pay off debt.

What an Income Statement Can Tell You

The income statement shows whether you have been successful in living within your income. If the amount saved is negligible or there is a deficit, you should review where you can make changes to your income and expenditures.

Income is difficult to increase in the short term, although it can be done; for example, by taking a part-time job. Longer-term income can be increased by establishing yourself in your profession, finding a better-paying job, or changing careers. The latter alternative should be deliberated carefully before any moves are made.

Expenditures are also difficult to reduce, but variable expenditures are easier to cut than fixed expenditures. For example, it may be easier to reduce recreation, summer vacation, and/or entertainment expenses than necessary living expenses, such as food, mortgage, auto, and utility expenses.

By going through the process of compiling an income statement, you can see where money has been spent and where you need to reduce expenditures, if necessary. The income statement is not only an important tool in helping to understand current spending patterns, it also assists in formulating a budget.

How to Formulate a Budget

"Cheshire Puss," Alice began . . . "would you please tell me which way
I ought to go from here?"
"That depends," said the cat, "on where you want to get to."

LEWIS CARROLL, *Alice in Wonderland*

A BUDGET IS A PLAN FOR HOW YOU INTEND to spend your money during
the coming month, months, or year. It is an integrated statement based
on details of your income statement and balance sheet for the past month,
months, or year and a reflection of your financial goals. It expresses what you
would like to achieve in terms of spending and savings in the future.

A budget can assist you in determining whether:

- You are living within your income limits
- Your current spending patterns are satisfactory
- You are saving and investing sufficient amounts to satisfy your financial goals
- You need to make changes in order to satisfy your financial goals

A suggested budget format is shown in Worksheet 3.1. You can use this
as a model for your own budget sheets, or you can make several copies to allow
you to project your budget for several months into the future. There are many
personal finance software programs, such as Quicken and Microsoft Money,
that make it easy to compile a budget using your personal computer.

A budget can be drawn up in six easy steps:

1. Estimate your future net income for the period of the budget.
2. Determine your expected expenditures during the period of the budget.

WORKSHEET 3.1 How to develop a budget

	Income	Budgeted	Actual	Variance
Step 1 List expected income from all sources for the period.	Net salary	_____	_____	_____
	Business profit (Net)	_____	_____	_____
	Dividends/interest	_____	_____	_____
	Capital gains	_____	_____	_____
	Gifts received	_____	_____	_____
	Total income	_____	_____	_____
Step 2 List all expected expenditures for the period.	**Expenditures**			
	Food	_____	_____	_____
	Clothing	_____	_____	_____
	Utilities	_____	_____	_____
	Mortgage/rent	_____	_____	_____
	Home maintenance/ repairs	_____	_____	_____
	Medical/Dental	_____	_____	_____
	Auto loan	_____	_____	_____
	Auto expenses	_____	_____	_____
	Insurance payments	_____	_____	_____
	Real estate taxes	_____	_____	_____
	Recreation/ entertainment	_____	_____	_____
	Vacation	_____	_____	_____
	Donations/gifts	_____	_____	_____
	Child care payment	_____	_____	_____
	Other	_____	_____	_____
	Total	_____	_____	_____
Step 3 List all expected amounts to fund goals.	**Goals**			
	Emergency fund	_____	_____	_____
	New car	_____	_____	_____
	Savings–investment	_____	_____	_____
	Retirement fund	_____	_____	_____
	Total	_____	_____	_____
Step 4 Determine whether there is a deficit or surplus.	**Surplus/deficit**			
	Income less expenditures	_____	_____	_____
	Cash deposit/ withdrawal	_____	_____	_____

Step 5
Record actual income and expenditures to determine variances.

Step 6
Evaluate whether changes in spending and savings are necessary.

3. Determine what you expect to spend to fund your personal goals.
4. Determine whether there is a surplus or a deficit.
5. Record your actual income and expenditures.
6. Evaluate whether changes in spending and saving are necessary.

Step 1: Estimate Your Future Income

Estimated income includes all anticipated receipts of money, such as future salary, estimated profits (or losses, which are deductions from income) from a business, bonuses, commissions, interest, dividends, rent, gains, tax refunds, loans, and other sources of income.

Wages, salary, and/or partnership/corporate income should be included net of payroll taxes. Payroll tax deductions can be shown in the income section or the expenditure section. An example of these deductions is shown in Figure 3.1. Mr. X is expecting a 5 percent increase in salary for the coming year and Mrs. X expects her business income to be $36,000 for the coming year. The expected gross income for Mr. X is shown, along with the deductions withheld to give his net monthly income. Payroll tax withholdings are the amounts deducted by an employer from employees' paychecks to pay their taxes. The amount of income earned and the number of exemptions filed by the employee on Form W-4 determines how much is withheld for federal income taxes.

Self-employed workers receive income that is not subjected to payroll tax withholdings. This does not mean that they do not have to pay taxes on this income. The tax laws require such taxpayers to estimate their tax liability and pay it in quarterly installments by April 15, June 15, September 15, and January 15 for the tax year. The amount of these payments depends on a person's total income from all sources, deductions, exemptions, and credits, which determine taxable income.

Mrs. X estimates that her monthly gross budgeted income will be $3,000. Mrs. X would have to make quarterly estimated tax payments to the U.S. Treasury on this business income and, depending on the requirements of the state in which she lives, to the state as well.

FIGURE 3.1 Budgeted monthly income for Mr. and Mrs. X

	Budgeted annual	Actual annual	Budgeted monthly	Actual monthly
Salary Mr. X	$54,000	_____	$4,500	_____
Less withholdings				
Federal income tax	(4,800)	_____	(400)	_____
Social security tax	(3,348)	_____	(279)	_____
Medicare tax	(783)	_____	(65)	_____
State tax	(1,512)	_____	(126)	_____
Net salary	**$43,557**	_____	**$3,630**	_____
Business profit Mrs. X	$36,000	_____	$3,000	_____
Less estimated taxes				
Federal tax	(3,000)	_____	(250)	_____
State tax	(1,008)	_____	(84)	_____
Net business profit	**$31,992**	_____	**$2,666**	_____

Income from sales commissions may be difficult to estimate, as they may be irregular or seasonal. Being conservative by underestimating budgeted income may be prudent in order to avoid overspending and, consequently, having to dip into cash accounts.

Step 2: Determine Your Expected Expenditures

The second step is to estimate all expenditures during the period of the budget. Certain expenditures such as rent, mortgage, and auto loan payments are fixed in amount and do not vary from month to month, whereas other expenditures such as food, clothing, and utilities do vary in amount from month to month. Anticipating these variable expenditures with accuracy may be difficult. The purpose of budgeting is not to put you in a straitjacket in which you cannot maneuver. On the contrary, its purpose is to provide you with flexibility in your financial planning so you can achieve your financial goals.

Step 3: Determine Your Financial Goals

In order to set aside money for your financial future, you need to estimate the expenditures that go toward your savings and investments. Financial goals vary from person to person over time. Some financial goals are:

- Saving for an emergency fund
- Increasing savings and investments
- Buying a new car
- Paying off a loan
- Buying a house
- Buying a larger house
- Saving to fund children's education
- Providing retirement income
- Saving for annual vacations

Some of these are short-term goals while others are longer term. It is often easier to concentrate on the short-term goals and neglect longer-term goals. By assigning priorities to each of the goals and quantifying their cost, you can determine the amount of savings needed to fund them. Figure 3.2 contains an example of Mr. and Mrs. X's goals and the amounts needed to achieve them.

Column 1 shows the estimated amount of money needed to fund each goal, while column 2 lists each goal's priority. Buying new furniture is the lowest of Mr. and Mrs. X's priorities. Column 3 shows when the expenditures will be needed. For example, they hope to buy a new car in 12 months; be able to fund their children's education in 15 years (180 months); retire in 30 years (360 months); and buy new furniture in two years (24 months).

FIGURE 3.2 Mr. and Mrs. X's personal financial goals

Goals	(1) Estimated cost	(2) Priority	(3) Time needed (mos.)	(4) Monthly amount	(5) Monthly amount using time value of money
New car	$24,000	1	12	$2,000.00	$1,972.65
Children's college fund	100,000	2	180	555.56	343.46
Retirement fund	600,000	3	360	1,666.67	597.30
New furniture	5,000	4	24	208.33	202.41
				$4,430.56	$3,115.82

Column 4 shows the monthly amount needed to finance each goal, calculated as follows:

Monthly Amount = Estimated Cost ÷ Time Needed

In order to have funds to buy a new car for $24,000 in a year's time, Mr. and Mrs. X will need to save $2,000 a month for the next year. If they were to fund all their goals, they would need to save $4,430.56 per month.

The astute reader is apt to disagree on that amount and argue that the Xs will need to save less per month due to the fact that the monthly amounts will be invested, which will earn a return. That is correct. Assuming a conservative rate of interest of 3 percent for short-term goals and 6 percent for longer-term goals, Mr. and Mrs. X would need to save $3,115.82 per month to fund all four goals (column 5). See the time value of money calculator (section 4) to determine how to calculate these amounts.

Realistically, however, Mr. and Mrs. X would have to save more than the amount in column 5 to fund all their goals because of two factors: income taxes and inflation. Mr. and Mrs. X will have to pay taxes on their interest income and inflation will push up future prices.

Step 4: Determine Whether There Is a Surplus or a Deficit

If budgeted amounts for income exceed expenditures, there is a surplus. Expenditures and the amounts needed to fund personal goals added together equal the total expected expenditures. It is a good idea to incorporate goals into a budget so that monthly or periodic income is set aside to address them. When projected income exceeds projected expenditures, there will be additional amounts of cash, which can then be added to savings/investment plans or used to pay down liabilities.

When projected expenditures exceed projected income, there is a deficit. This means additional amounts will have to be withdrawn from savings/investment plans to pay for these additional expenditures. In such a case, it may be necessary to review projected expenditures and reduce some of them, or look for ways to increase projected income.

Step 5: Record Actual Income and Expenditures for the Period Budgeted

Actual amounts earned and spent are not always the same as those projected. By recording the actual amounts and comparing them with the budgeted amounts, you can immediately see the differences, called variances. Spending more than a budgeted amount for one item can be offset by spending less than the budgeted amount for another item.

Similarly, if actual income exceeds actual expenditures, there is a surplus, which means additional cash. The opposite is a deficit, which means that cash will have to be withdrawn from cash savings or other assets in order to pay for the deficit spending.

Step 6: Evaluate Whether Changes in the Budget Are Necessary

If there are large variances, or your surplus/deficit is not what you would like, you need to analyze your budget. Examine the variances and study where the amounts spent are greater than the budgeted amounts. For example, if your actual utility bills are consistently greater than the amounts budgeted, then you need to either reduce your utility usage, if possible, or increase the amount budgeted for this item. When you increase planned spending, you will need to find items where you can make corresponding cuts to compensate for the increases. If you don't, the amounts set aside for personal goals or savings will be reduced.

There are certain expenditures over which you have some degree of control. These are your variable expenditures, such as entertainment and miscellaneous expenses. Entertainment and food are the most common areas of overspending, particularly when they involve eating out at restaurants. By contrast, fixed expenditures such as rent, mortgage payments, taxes, and insurance premiums cannot be easily trimmed without undue consequences.

Deficit spending may be more difficult to remedy when you have already reduced many of your unnecessary and variable expenditures. It then becomes more difficult to cut essential spending items. If spending still exceeds income after revising spending amounts, you need to reevaluate your entire budget. Perhaps you have created too tight a straitjacket for yourself. Revise your goals and set aside amounts to attain them before allocating the rest of your income to your expenditures. You may need to prioritize your expenditures to see which are necessary and which can wait.

The purpose of a budget is to help you plan the use of your resources so that you can fund your goals and set aside more of your money to savings. Following your budget will help you achieve what you want most from your resources.

FINANCIAL CALCULATOR #4

Time Value of Money and What It Can Do for You

THE *TIME VALUE OF MONEY* is one of the most important concepts in personal finance decision-making. Money does not have the same value over time due to the fact that it earns interest. Consequently, a dollar today is not the same as a dollar in the future even if it is the same physical dollar bill note that is presented. Investing that dollar today yields an amount greater than the dollar in the future. Put another way, the rate of interest is the bridge that links present and future values. Similarly, a dollar expected in the future can be discounted at the rate of interest to yield a present value, which is less than a dollar.

The time value of money is equally important in decision-making with regard to annuities, which are a series of payments as opposed to a single payment. Suppose you win the lottery and you are given the option of receiving $50,000 a year for 20 years or taking a lump sum now of $623,110.52. What should you do? If you can earn more than 5 percent on your investment, you should take the lump sum of $623,110.52. If you are not able to earn as much as 5 percent, you are better off taking the $50,000 per year for 20 years. Bear in mind that this decision is based solely on the time value of money and that taxes have not been considered. In real life, this would be the first step; then you would look at the differential taxes involved with each alternative to come to a decision as to whether to take a lump sum now or receive a series of payments into the future.

The impact of the time value of money is dependent on the following three factors:

1. The amount of money
2. The annual rate of interest
3. The length of time

No doubt you are familiar with these factors from your school days when you used them to determine the simple interest on an amount of money. These same factors are also used in the determination of future values and present values, using compound interest and discount rates, respectively. The financial calculators that follow this section show you how easily these amounts can be determined.

Another way to look at the time value of money is to view it as an opportunity cost. Spending rather than saving means lost interest. What you could have earned on that money has been lost. It therefore becomes important to know the interest rate on all your savings and investments to determine whether you should be saving or spending your money. Worksheet 4.1 is helpful in

---

WORKSHEET 4.1 Determine the interest rates on your savings

Accounts	Amounts	Annual Rates of Interest
Checking account	_____	_____
Savings account	_____	_____
Savings account 2	_____	_____
Certificate of deposit	_____	_____
Certificate of deposit 2	_____	_____
Money market fund	_____	_____
Money market fund 2	_____	_____
Treasury bills	_____	_____
Treasury bills	_____	_____
Bonds	_____	_____
Bonds	_____	_____
Bonds	_____	_____
Stocks	_____	_____
Stocks	_____	_____
Bond mutual funds	_____	_____
Stock mutual funds	_____	_____
Other	_____	_____
Other	_____	_____
Total	_____	_____

determining the trade-off between savings and spending. Determining the rate of interest that you can earn on different investments makes it easier to compare your alternatives—to save or to spend. The financial calculators that follow will help you determine the future values of these investments using the time value of money.

FINANCIAL CALCULATOR #5

Simple Interest and How to Calculate It

THE MOST BASIC METHOD OF CALCULATING INTEREST is the *simple interest* method. The other, more common method of calculating interest is the compound interest method (described in section 6).

Interest is the cost charged or payment made for the use of money. The simple interest method calculates interest on the principal only without any compounding. In other words, the interest earned is not used to earn further interest.

The elements used to determine simple interest are the *principal,* the *rate of interest,* and the *length of time* that the principal is invested or borrowed. The formula for simple interest is as follows:

Interest = Principal Amount × Annual Interest Rate × Time Period

or

$$I = P \times R \times T$$

For example, $2,000 deposited for two years at 5 percent per annum would earn $200 in simple interest ($2,000 × 2 × 0.05). The total amount received at the end of two years would be $2,200, the principal amount plus the interest.

WORKSHEET 5.1 How to calculate simple interest

Principal amount   P   _____
Annual interest rate   R   _____
Time period of deposit or loan   T   _____
Simple interest = P × R × T

    = _____ × _____ × _____
    = $ _____

The following example illustrates simple interest earned when the amount is deposited for less than a year. A principal amount of $2,000 is deposited in a certificate of deposit at an annual rate of 6 percent for six months. The interest is $60 ($2,000 × 0.06 × 6 ÷ 12).

The rate can be expressed in decimal form or as a fraction (0.06 or 6 ÷ 100, respectively). The time is shown in months (6 ÷ 12). It can also be expressed in days (360 per year, used by banks, or 365 days). Worksheet 5.1 provides the framework for you to calculate simple interest on a deposit or loan.

FINANCIAL CALCULATOR #6

Compound Interest and How to Determine Future Value

COMPOUND INTEREST DIFFERS FROM simple interest in that interest is paid not only on the principal but also on the accumulated interest, assuming that the interest is left to accumulate. The greater the number of periods for which interest is calculated, the greater the accumulation of interest earned on interest plus interest earned on the principal.

The formula for compound interest is expressed as follows:

$$\text{Future Value} = \text{Principal } (1 + \text{Interest Rate})^n$$

$$FV = P (1 + i)^n$$

where

FV = Total future value (principal plus total compound interest)
P = Principal (amount invested)
i = Interest rate per year or annual percentage rate
n = The number of periods at the interest rate

To illustrate the difference between simple and compound interest, assume that $100 is invested at 5 percent per year for three years and the interest is not withdrawn. If compounded annually, the compound interest earned would be $15.76, while the simple interest earned would be $15, as shown in Figure 6.1.

The principal amount of $100 is used to determine the interest in the simple interest method, whereas compound interest uses the principal plus the accumulated interest from the previous year to calculate the interest for the next year. Thus, when given a choice between investing in a simple interest or compound interest account, you would choose compound interest, assuming risk and all other factors are the same.

FIGURE 6.1 Simple interest versus compound interest

	Simple interest	Compound interest
Year 1	$100 × 5%; FV = $105.00	$100.00 × 5% = $5.00; FV $105.00
Year 2	$100 × 5%; FV = $110.00	$105.00 × 5% = $5.25; FV $110.25
Year 3	$100 × 5%; FV = $115.00	$110.25 × 5% = $5.51; FV $115.76
Total interest = $15.00		**Total interest = $15.76**

FV = Future value

There are easier ways of determining the compound interest than by going through this tedious calculation: for example, by using a formula and pen, paper, and a calculator; using financial tables; using a financial calculator with time value of money keys; or using a personal finance software program. Most of these methods for calculating future values are described in the following pages. First, however, an important aspect of the compounding process needs to be noted, and that is that compounding is not always done on an annual basis. Banks and savings and loan associations may compound their accounts on a semiannual, quarterly, daily, or continuous basis.

For example, if $10,000 is invested in a certificate of deposit (CD) for five years at 6 percent compounded semiannually, there are 10 six-month periods earning 3 percent each period. Similarly, if this same CD is compounded quarterly, then there are 20 three-month periods earning 1.5 percent each period.

The formula below includes modifications to take into account nonannual compounding periods:

$$FV = P(1 + i \div m)^{mn}$$

where

FV = Total future value at the end of n periods
P = Principal or original amount invested
I = Annual compound interest rate
m = The number of times compounding occurs during the year
n = The number of years of compounding

Using Financial Tables to Determine the Future Value

Future values can be determined by using the compound sum of $1 table found in Appendix A. You may find it helpful to know how the values in the table are computed.

TABLE 6.1 Determining the future value of $1

Year	Formula	Future value
1	(1 + 0.02)	$1.02
2	1.02 (1 + 0.02)	1.04
3	1.04 (1 + 0.02)	1.061

Assume that $1 is invested at 2 percent compounded annually for three years. Table 6.1 shows the accumulated values.

The future value amounts in the right column in Table 6.1 are found in the compound sum of $1 table in Appendix A under the 2 percent column, the first three rows indicating the first, second, and third investment periods. Worksheet 6.1 illustrates how to determine the future value using financial tables.

An example on page 27 illustrates the ease of using financial tables to determine the future value.

WORKSHEET 6.1 How to determine the future value using financial tables

$$FV = P \, (1 + i \div m)^{mn}$$

FV = _____ (_____) ——
FV = _____ (_____)
FV = _____

Step 1 Insert values into the formula.
Step 2 Find the row with the number of periods (mn) that the principal will be invested in Appendix A.
Step 3 Find the column with the interest rate for the period (i ÷ m) that the principal will be invested in Appendix A.
Step 4 The intersection of the row and the column locates the factor.
Step 5 Multiply the factor by the principal. The product is the future value.

How much money will you have if you deposit $2,000 in an account yielding 8 percent interest compounded quarterly for 10 years?

$$FV = P(1 + i \div m)^{mn}$$
$$FV = 2,000(1 + 0.08 \div 4)^{(4 \times 10)}$$
$$FV = 2,000(1 + 0.02)^{40}$$
$$FV = 2,000(2.208)$$
$$FV = \$4,416$$

Using a Financial Calculator to Determine the Future Value

Future value calculations can also be made using a financial calculator. With a financial calculator it is easy to solve time value of money calculations if you have any three of the four variables. The exact steps depend on the type of calculator. Most financial calculators use the following format, but if there are deviations consult your calculator's manual.

Worksheet 6.2 shows the step-by-step use of a financial calculator to determine the future value.

The previous problem can be solved using a financial calculator. What is the future value of $2,000 invested at 8 percent compounded quarterly for 10 years?

Step 1 Key in quarterly payments instead of the default mode of annual or monthly.

Step 2 Key in 40 as the number of payments into *N*.

Step 3 Key the interest rate of 8 percent into *I*.

Step 4 Enter the principal, $2,000, into the *PV* button.

Step 5 Press the *FV* button to calculate the future value, which is displayed as $4,416.08.

WORKSHEET 6.2 How to determine the future value using a financial calculator

Most financial calculators have the following keys:

N = Total number of compounding periods or payments

I = Interest

PV = Present value

FV = Future value

PMT = Annuity payment or receipt

Step 1 Key the number of compounding periods per year (annual, semiannual, etc.) into the calculator program.

Step 2 Key the number of payment periods for the investment into the N button on the calculator.

Step 3 Key the interest rate into the I button.

Step 4 Key the principal into the PV button.

Step 5 Press the FV button to calculate the future value.

Using a Computer to Determine the Future Value

With the popularity of personal computers, there are several programs that can be used to determine the future value. Worksheet 6.3 illustrates the use of Microsoft's Excel program and Quicken's software.

Using Quicken software, click on the financial planner.

WORKSHEET 6.3 Using a computer to determine the future value

Using Microsoft's Excel spreadsheet, click on *f**, which is on the top row of the toolbar. A list of functions pops up. Highlight *FV* in the right-hand box and click OK. A box comes up with five rows, as shown below.

Rate	
Nper	
Pmt	
PV	
Type	

Step 1 Enter the interest rate per period.
Step 2 Enter the total number of periods.
Step 3 Enter the payments made each period.
Step 4 Enter the principal or present value.
Step 5 Enter the value representing timing of the payment: 1 for payment at the beginning of the period; 0 for payment at the end of the period.

Using the previous example, key in the numbers:

Rate	.02
Nper	40
Pmt	0
PV	–$2,000
Type	0

Formula result = $4416.079

Using Quicken software, click on the financial planner.

Step 1 Select savings account.
Step 2 Enter information as shown in the boxes:

Opening savings balance	$2,000
Annual yield	8%
Number of quarters	40
Contribution each quarter	0
Ending savings balance	$4,416.08
Inflation	0%

Calculate

Step 3 Click on the calculate button.
Step 4 Ending savings balance is calculated and appears in the box ($4,416.08).

What You Need to Know About Nominal Versus Effective Interest Rates and How to Calculate the Effective Rate

WHEN GIVEN A CHOICE BETWEEN investing in a simple interest account or a compound interest account, you would obviously choose compound interest. With simple interest only the principal is used to calculate interest, whereas compound interest uses the principal plus accumulated interest to earn interest.

The difference between simple interest and compound interest is magnified further when the rate of interest and/or the number of compounding periods are increased. When the interest rate is doubled using compound interest, interest earned is more than doubled.

For example, if $1,000 is invested at 6 percent compounded annually for 10 years, the interest earned is $791. A doubling of the interest rate to 12 percent compounded annually results in interest of $2,106, almost triple the growth.

Carrying this example further, if the $1,000 is invested for 20 years (instead of 10) at 6 percent and 12 percent, the accumulated interest would be $1,397 and $4,474, respectively. Thus, higher interest rates and a greater length of time result in accelerated growth of interest.

In order to make the right decision with regard to investing or borrowing money, you need to make sense of the stated interest rates so that they are comparable. Generally, banks do not quote their rates the same way. Some quote their rates for deposit accounts as compounded annually, while others quote their rates as compounded semiannually, quarterly, monthly, or daily. You cannot compare accounts with different compounding periods unless you convert them to a common compounding period, also known as an *annual percentage rate* (APR) or *effective yield*.

For example, consider one bank's certificate of deposit offered at 7 percent compounded annually versus another offered at a second bank at 6.95 percent compounded monthly. These are *nominal* or *stated rates* and are not comparable.

The more frequent the compounding, the greater the future value and the amount of interest that accrues. Thus, the effective rate is always greater than the nominal rate when the compounding of interest is done more than once a year. Table 7.1 provides a comparison of some nominal and effective rates.

As Table 7.1 shows, the nominal rate of interest is not the true rate if there is frequent compounding within the year. Also important to note is that the effective annual rate increases at a decreasing rate. For instance, the nominal rate of 7 percent increases by 0.12 percent with semiannual compounding, then by a further 0.07 percent with quarterly compounding, and then by only 0.04 percent with monthly compounding.

Investors should choose savings and deposit accounts that offer the highest effective rates. In order to compare different rates, effective rates should be compared with other effective rates.

TABLE 7.1 A comparison of nominal and effective rates compounded annually and semiannually

Nominal rate compounded annually	Semiannually	Effective rates Quarterly	Monthly	Daily
5%	5.06%	5.09%	5.12%	5.13%
6%	6.09%	6.13%	6.16%	6.18%
7%	7.12%	7.19%	7.23%	7.25%
8%	8.16%	8.24%	8.30%	8.33%
9%	9.20%	9.31%	9.38%	9.42%

How to Calculate the Effective Rate

The formula for calculating the effective rate is as follows:

$$\text{Effective rate} = (1 + I)^f - 1$$

where

I = Interest rate per period
f = Compounding frequency

For example, if the nominal rate is 10 percent compounded quarterly, the effective rate is 10.381 percent:

$$\text{Effective rate} = (1 + I)^f - 1$$

$$= (1 + 0.025)^4 - 1$$
$$= (1.10381) - 1$$
$$= 10.381\%$$

Worksheet 7.1 provides the format for calculating the effective rate.

WORKSHEET 7.1 How to calculate the effective rate

Effective rate $= (1 + I)^f - 1$

$$= (1 + \underline{\quad}) \; \frac{\quad}{} -1$$
$$= (\underline{\qquad}) - 1$$
$$= \underline{\qquad}$$

Step 1 Insert values into the formula.
Step 2 Add 1 to the interest per period and multiply to the power f. Subtract 1 to obtain the answer.

FINANCIAL CALCULATOR #8
Present Value and
How to Calculate It

NTEREST RATES AND TIME RELATE present and future values mathematically. Future values focus on the movement of money forward in time. How much will money grow in the future when compounded at a particular interest rate? Present value is the opposite of future value. It is the movement of money back in time to the present. How much is money to be received in the future worth today? In other words, a future amount of money is discounted for a period of time to give an amount in today's dollars.

The example in the future value financial calculator (section 6) showed that $100 invested at 5 percent compounded annually for three years grows to $115.76. The reverse also applies: $115.76 to be received in three years discounted at 5 percent compounded annually has a present value of $100.

The equation for determining the future value can be manipulated algebraically to calculate the present value as follows:

$$FV = P(1 + i)^n$$

where

FV = Future value
P   = Present value or principal
I   = Interest per period
n   = Number of periods that the principal earns interest

Divide both sides of the equation by $(1 + i)^n$ and you arrive at the formula for calculating the present value (P or PV):

$$PV = \frac{FV}{(1 + i)^n}$$

Using Financial Tables to Determine the Present Value

The present value of $1 table shown in Appendix B simplifies the computation of the present value. The table eliminates the need to compute the present value interest factor (1 ÷ 1 + the interest rate to the power n) because the computation is included in the table. Table 8.1 shows how the interest factors are computed in the financial tables for 5 percent.

The present value amounts shown in the fourth column in Table 8.1 are found in the present value of $1 table in Appendix B under the 5 percent column, the first three rows indicating the first, second, and third discount periods. Worksheet 8.1 illustrates how to determine the present value using financial tables.

To illustrate the use of financial tables, consider the following problem. What is the present value of $10,000 to be received in 10 years discounted at 8 percent?

PV = FV(present value of 1 discounted at 8% for 10 years)
PV = $10,000(0.463)
PV = $4,630

Present value calculations can also be made using a financial calculator. As long as you have three of the four variables, you can solve for the fourth. The exact steps for the calculation depend on the type of calculator.

TABLE 8.1 Determining the present value of $1

Discount period	Future value	Formula	Present value
1	$1	$1 \div (1 + 0.05)^1$	0.952
2	1	$1 \div (1 + 0.05)^2$	0.907
3	1	$1 \div (1 + 0.05)^3$	0.864

WORKSHEET 8.1 How to determine the present value using financial tables

PV = FV (present value of 1 discounted at i% per period for n periods.)

PV = _____ (_____)

PV = _____

Step 1 Insert values into the formula.
Step 2 Find the row for the number of discounting periods n in Appendix B.
Step 3 Find the column for the discount rate i.
Step 4 The intersection of the row and column locates the factor.
Step 5 Multiply the factor by the future value. The product is the present value.

Using a Financial Calculator to Determine the Present Value

Worksheet 8.2 outlines the steps to determine the present value using a financial calculator.

The following example illustrates these steps using a financial calculator. What is the present value of $5,000 to be received in five years discounted at 6 percent per annum?

Step 1 Key annual payments into the default mode of your calculator.

Step 2 Key in 5 as the number of discounting periods into *N*.

Step 3 Key the discount rate of 6 percent into *I*.

Step 4 Enter $5,000 into *FV*.

Step 5 Press the *PV* button, which calculates the answer: $3,736.29.

Using a Computer to Determine the Present Value

Microsoft's Excel spreadsheet is used here to illustrate the ease of calculating the present value on a computer, but there are other software programs that can also be used. Worksheet 8.3 on page 37 illustrates the determination of the present value with an example.

WORKSHEET 8.2 How to determine the present value using a financial calculator

Most financial calculators have the following keys:

N = Total number of discounting periods
I = Interest rate per period
PV = Present value
FV = Future value
PMT = Annuity payment or receipt

Step 1 Key the number of discounting periods per year (annual, semiannual, monthly) into the default mode of the calculator.
Step 2 Key the number of discounting periods into the N button.
Step 3 Key the discount/interest rate into the I button.
Step 4 Key the future value into the FV button.
Step 5 Press the PV button to calculate the present value.

The present value of an amount is always less than the future value because the future value is always discounted back to the present. The relationships in the discounting process are:

- The higher the discount rate, the lower the present value.
- The later the future payment or receipt is extended into the future, the smaller the present value becomes.
- If the frequency of discounting is increased; for example, from annually to quarterly, the present value of an amount will decrease.

WORKSHEET 8.3 Using a personal computer to determine the present value

Using Microsoft's Excel spreadsheet, click on *f**, which is on the top row of the toolbar. A list of functions pops up. Highlight *financial* in the left-hand box and *PV* in the right-hand box and click OK. A box comes up with five rows, as shown below.

Rate	
Nper	
Pmt	
FV	
Type	

Step 1 Enter the interest rate per period.

Step 2 Enter the total number of periods.

Step 3 Enter the payments made each period.

Step 4 Enter the future value.

Step 5 Enter the value representing timing of the payment: 1 for payment at beginning of the period; 0 for payment at the end of the period.

What is the present value of $2,000 to be paid in 4 years discounted at 8%?

Rate	.08
Nper	4
Pmt	0
FV	–$2,000
Type	0

Formula result = $1,470.059

FINANCIAL CALCULATOR #9

Annuities and How to Calculate Them

THERE ARE MANY FINANCIAL SITUATIONS that involve a series of payments or receipts, such as loans, installment contracts, leases, pension and retirement plans, and life insurance contracts. (For discussions of the future value and present value of a single principal amount, see sections 6 and 8, respectively.)

An annuity is a series of equal payments or receipts made or received at regular intervals. These payments (receipts) can be made (received) at the beginning or the end of a period. When payments are made at the end of a

FIGURE 9.1 Difference between an ordinary annuity and an annuity due

Ordinary annuity
An annuity of four payments of $1,000 made at the end of each year.

Payment		$1,000	$1,000	$1,000	$1,000
Year	0	1	2	3	4

Annuity due
An annuity due of four payments of $1,000 made at the beginning of the year.

Payment	$1,000	$1,000	$1,000	$1,000	
Year	0	1	2	3	4

period, it is called an *ordinary annuity*. When payments are made at the beginning of a period, it is called an *annuity due*. Figure 9.1 illustrates the difference between the two types of annuities.

As you might well infer from the time value of money, it is important to recognize the difference between an ordinary annuity and an annuity due. With an annuity due, the payments (receipts) are made (received) earlier, and therefore have a greater present value and future value than an ordinary annuity.

Future Value of an Ordinary Annuity and Annuity Due

Future Value of an Ordinary Annuity

The future value of an ordinary annuity involves payments (receipts) of an equal sum of money at the end of each period for a certain number of periods and allows the interest to accumulate over the total period of time. For example, a deposit of $1,000 made at the end of every year for five years earning 6 percent will grow to $5,637.10, as shown in Table 9.1.

TABLE 9.1 Future value of ordinary annuity of $1,000 compounded at 6% for 5 years

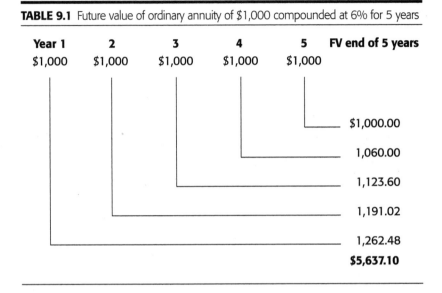

Year 1	2	3	4	5	FV end of 5 years
$1,000	$1,000	$1,000	$1,000	$1,000	
					$1,000.00
					1,060.00
					1,123.60
					1,191.02
					1,262.48
					$5,637.10

In Table 9.1 the future value of an ordinary annuity is found by compounding each deposit and summing the interest earned on the deposits. This annuity can also be expressed in equation form as follows:

$$FV = 1,000(1+0.06)^4 + 1,000(1+0.06)^3 + 1,000(1+0.06)^2$$
$$+ 1,000(1+0.06) + 1,000$$

$$= 1,262.48 + 1,191.02 + 1,123.60 + 1,060.00 + 1,000$$

$$= \$5,637.10$$

This calculation can be cumbersome if you don't have a calculator or if the time period is long. Financial tables can simplify the calculation, as shown in Worksheet 9.1 using the same example. The future value of an ordinary annuity table is shown in Appendix C.

WORKSHEET 9.1 How to determine the future value of an ordinary annuity using financial tables

---

FV = PMT (FVIFA i, n)

Where

PMT = Annuity or regular payment/receipt
FVIFA = Future value interest factor of an annuity
   i = Interest rate per period
   n = Number of periods

FV = _____ (FVIFA _____)
FV = _____ (_____)
FV = _____

Example:

PMT = $1,000
   i = 6%
   n = 5

FV = PMT (FVIFA i, n)
FV = 1,000 (FVIFA 6%, 5)
FV = 1,000 (5.637)
FV = $5,637

Step 1 Fill in the values.
Step 2 Fill in the FVIFA factor from Appendix C at intersection of i row and n column.
Step 3 Multiply the annuity by the interest factor to obtain the future value.

Future Value of an Annuity Due

The difference between an ordinary annuity and an annuity due is the timing of the payments/receipts. For an annuity due, the payments are made at the beginning of the period.

TABLE 9.2 Future value of annuity due of $1,000 compounded at 6% for 5 years

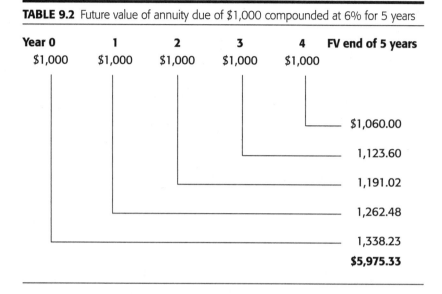

Year 0	1	2	3	4	FV end of 5 years
$1,000	$1,000	$1,000	$1,000	$1,000	
					$1,060.00
					1,123.60
					1,191.02
					1,262.48
					1,338.23
					$5,975.33

Using the same example as the one used for the ordinary annuity, the future value of an annuity due of $1,000 invested for five years at 6 percent is $5,975.33, as calculated in Table 9.2.

With the future value of an annuity due, each deposit earns interest in the period deposited, whereas with an ordinary annuity the last deposit does not earn interest in the period deposited. In other words, the future value of an ordinary annuity has one less interest earning period than the number of deposits.

Although it is possible to calculate the future value of an annuity due by summing the interest calculations, as shown in Table 9.2, it is easier to use the future value of an ordinary annuity table in Appendix C and convert the factor as shown in Worksheet 9.2.

The use of financial calculators and computers can easily simplify the task of calculating the future value of both an ordinary annuity and an annuity due. Worksheets 9.3, on page 43, and 9.4, on page 44, illustrate the use of these tools.

WORKSHEET 9.2 How to determine the future value of an annuity due using financial tables

---

Analysis of Tables 9.1 and 9.2 shows that there is one less interest payment for an ordinary annuity. Thus, if the last deposit or payment is deducted, the amount will equal an annuity due for one less period.

Determine the future value of an annuity due of $1,000 deposited at the beginning of each year for five years compounded at 6%.

FVIFA 6%, 6 = 6.975

6.975 − 1 = 5.975

1,000 × 5.975 = $5,975

Step 1 Look up the factor for an ordinary annuity in Appendix C for one more period.
Step 2 Deduct 1 from the factor, which is the same as reducing the number of deposits by one.
Step 3 Multiply the converted factor by the amount of the deposits.

Using a Financial Calculator to Determine the Future Value of an Annuity (Ordinary and Annuity Due)

Worksheet 9.3 outlines the steps to determine the future value of both an ordinary annuity and an annuity due using a financial calculator. The following example illustrates these steps to determine the future value of an ordinary annuity first, and then an annuity due.

Example 1 What is the future value of an ordinary annuity of $1,000 to be deposited at the end of every year for five years invested at 6 percent per year?

Example 2 What is the future value of an annuity due of $1,000 to be deposited at the beginning of each year for five years invested at 6 percent per year?

WORKSHEET 9.3 How to determine the future value of an annuity (both ordinary and annuity due) using a financial calculator

Most financial calculators have the following keys:

N = Total number of discounting periods
I = Interest rate per period
PV = Present value
FV = Future value
PMT = Annuity payment or receipt

Step 1 Key the number of discounting periods per year (annual, semiannual, monthly) into the mode of your calculator.
Step 2 Set the mode at the end of the period or beginning of the period.
Step 3 Key the number of discounting periods for the investment into the *N* button.
Step 4 Key the discount/interest rate into the *I* button.
Step 5 Key the amount of the annuity into the *PMT* button.
Step 6 Press the *FV* button to calculate the future value.

Example 1 Future Value of an Ordinary Annuity

Step 1 Key the annual mode into your calculator and set the end mode for an ordinary annuity.
Step 2 Key the number of payments as 5 into the *N* button.
Step 3 Key 6% into the *I* button.
Step 4 Key the deposit of $1,000 into the *PMT* button.
Step 5 Press the *FV* button to calculate the future value, which is $5,637.09.

Example 2 Future Value of an Annuity Due

Step 1 Key the annual mode into your calculator and set the beginning mode for an annuity due.
Step 2 Key the number of payments as 5 into the *N* button.
Step 3 Key 6% into the *I* button.
Step 4 Key the deposit of $1,000 into the *PMT* button.
Step 5 Press the FV button to calculate the future value, which is $5,975.32.

WORKSHEET 9.4 How to determine the future value of an annuity (both ordinary and annuity due) using a computer

Using Microsoft's Excel spreadsheet, click on *f**, which is on the top row of the toolbar. A list of functions pops up. Highlight *financial* in the left box and *FV* in the right box. Click OK. A box comes up with five rows, as shown below:

> Rate is the interest per period.
>
> Nper is the total number of periods.
>
> Pmt is the payment amount made.
>
> PV is the present value; in this case, 0.
>
> Type represents the timing of the payment: 1 for payment made at the beginning of the period, 0 for payment made at the end of the period.

Enter this information and the future value is calculated.

Using the same example as used previously, key in the numbers to determine:

Future value of an ordinary annuity	Future value of an annuity due

Rate 6%	Rate 6%
Nper 5	Nper 5
Pmt $1,000	Pmt $1,000
PV 0	PV 0
Type 0	Type 1
Formula result = $5,637.0929	Formula result = $5,975.316

Future value of an ordinary annuity is $5,637.09
Future value of an annuity due is $5,975.32

Using a Computer to Determine the
Future Value of an Annuity (Ordinary and Annuity Due)

Microsoft's Excel spreadsheet is used here to illustrate the ease of calculating the future value of an annuity on a computer. There are any number of other software programs that can also be used. Worksheet 9.4 illustrates the determination of the future value of both an ordinary annuity and an annuity due using the same example used in the financial calculator worksheet.

Not only does the timing of the payments/receipts have an impact on the future value, but the rate of interest also has an enormous impact on the accumulation of the future value.

Table 9.3 illustrates these two factors using the example of an ordinary annuity and an annuity due of $1,000 deposited each year for a 10-year and a 20-year period invested at 6 percent and 12 percent per annum.

TABLE 9.3 Future value of an ordinary annuity and an annuity due invested at 6% and 12% for 10-year and 20-year periods

Investment Rate	6%	12%	Difference
Ordinary annuity of $1,000 invested for 10 years	$13,180.79	$17,548.74	$4,367.95
Annuity due of $1,000 invested for 10 years	$13,971.64	$19,654.58	$5,682.94
Difference	$790.85	$2,105.84	
Investment Rate	**6%**	**12%**	**Difference**
Ordinary annuity of $1,000 invested for 20 years	$36,785.59	$72,052.44	$35,266.85
Annuity due of $1,000 invested for 20 years	$38,992.73	$80,698.74	$41,706.01
Difference	$2,207.14	$8,646.30	

Changing the timing of deposits from the end of the period to the beginning of the period increases the future value (note the differences of $790.85 and $2,105.84 for a 10-year period, and $2,207.14 and $8,646.30 for a 20-year period). The differences are due to the first deposit earning additional interest for the annuity due.

Similarly, when the interest rate per period is doubled from 6 percent to 12 percent, the differences in the future values grow (from $4,367.95 to $5,682.94 for a 10-year period). When the investment period is doubled from 10 years to 20 years, the difference between the two rates accelerates.

The conclusions to be drawn from this table are:

- Save earlier as opposed to later in the year.
- Look for investments with a higher rate of return where you are comfortable with the level of risk.

Present Value of an Ordinary Annuity and Annuity Due

The present value of an annuity is the present value of a series of equal payments to be received (or paid) in the future discounted at a rate of interest. There are many uses for determining the present value of an annuity. In retirement planning, if you project that you will need $50,000 a year for 20 years, you can calculate how much you need to invest now to support those payments.

Present Value of an Ordinary Annuity

As with the future value of an annuity, the timing of the payments will have an impact on the amount of the present value. For an ordinary annuity, payments (deposits) are made at the end of a period, and for an annuity due, payments (deposits) are made at the beginning of a period. As an example, the present value of an ordinary annuity of $1,000 discounted at 6 percent for five years is shown in Table 9.4.

TABLE 9.4 Present value of an ordinary annuity of $1,000 discounted at 6% for 5 years

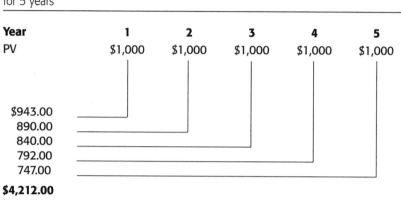

Year	1	2	3	4	5
PV	$1,000	$1,000	$1,000	$1,000	$1,000

$943.00
890.00
840.00
792.00
747.00

$4,212.00

Financial tables can simplify the calculation of the present value of an ordinary annuity. Worksheet 9.5 illustrates the use of financial tables in determining the present value of an ordinary annuity. The present value of an annuity table can be found in Appendix D.

Present Value of an Annuity Due

In Table 9.4, which shows the determination of the present value of an ordinary annuity, each payment/receipt is discounted for the same number of periods.

Table 9.5 shows the computation of the present value of an annuity due where there is one less discount period than in Table 9.4. The first payment/receipt is not discounted. Therefore, the present value of an ordinary annuity tables can be converted to determine the present value of an annuity due. The present value of an annuity due factor is equal to the present value of an ordinary annuity factor multiplied by one plus the interest rate per period. Refer to Worksheet 9.6, which shows the steps for using financial tables to determine the present value of an annuity due.

TABLE 9.5 Present value of an annuity due of $1,000 discounted at 6% for 5 years

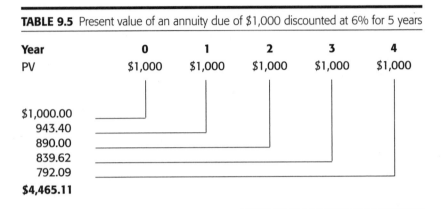

Year	0	1	2	3	4
PV	$1,000	$1,000	$1,000	$1,000	$1,000

$1,000.00
  943.40
  890.00
  839.62
  792.09
$4,465.11

Using a Financial Calculator to Determine the Present Value of an Annuity (Ordinary and Annuity Due)

A financial calculator takes out all the number crunching in the determination of the present value of an annuity. The only difference in determining an annuity due from an ordinary annuity is the setting of the mode of payments (for an annuity due the mode is set to the beginning of the period, and for an ordinary annuity the mode is set to the end of the period). All the other keys are punched in the same way with the same information. Worksheet 9.7 outlines the steps in calculating the present value of an ordinary annuity in example 1 and the present value of an annuity due in example 2.

Using a Computer to Determine the Present Value of an Annuity (Ordinary and Annuity Due)

Worksheet 9.8 illustrates the use of Microsoft Excel's spreadsheet software to determine the present value of both an ordinary annuity and an annuity due using the same examples as in the previous section.

As seen from the totals in Worksheet 9.8, the present value of an annuity due is always greater than the present value of an ordinary annuity because the payments are received sooner and the first payment is not discounted. The following conclusions can be drawn for the present value of an annuity:

WORKSHEET 9.5 How to determine the present value of an ordinary annuity using financial tables

---

PV = PMT (PVIFA i, n)

Where

PMT = Annuity or equal payments/receipts
PVIFA = Present value interest factor of an annuity
i = Interest/discount rate per period
n = Number of periods

PV = _____ (PVIFA ___, ___)
PV = _____ (_____)
PV = _____

Example:
PMT = $1,000
i = 6%
n = 5

PV = PMT (PVIFA i, n)
PV = $1,000 (PVIFA 6%, 5)
PV = $1,000 (4.212)
PV = $4,464.72

Step 1 Fill in the values.
Step 2 Fill in the PVIFA factor from Appendix D at the intersection of the i row and the n column.
Step 3 Multiply the annuity by the interest factor to obain the present value.

- The greater the rate of interest used to discount the annuity payments, the smaller the present value of the annuity.
- The sooner the annuity payments are received, the greater the present value.

WORKSHEET 9.6 How to determine the present value of an annuity due using financial tables

$$PV = PMT \ (PVIFA \ i, n \ ) \times (1 + i \ )$$

Where

PMT = Annuity or equal payments/receipts
PVIFA = Present value interest factor of an annuity
i = Interest/discount rate per period
n = Number of periods

PV = _____ (PVIFA ___, ___) × (1 + ___)
PV = _____ (_____) × (1 + ___)
PV = _____

Example:
PMT = $1,000
i = 6%
n = 5

$$PV = PMT \ (PVIFA \ i, n \ ) \times (1 + i \ )$$
$$PV = \$1,000 \ (PVIFA \ 6\%, 5 \ ) \times (1 + .06 \ )$$
$$PV = \$1,000 \ (4.212) \times (1.06 \ )$$
$$PV = \$4,464.72$$

Step 1 Fill in the values.
Step 2 Fill in the PVIFA factor from Appendix D at the intersection of the i row and the n column. Multiply this factor by 1 plus the interest rate.
Step 3 Multiply the annuity by the interest factor to obain the present value.

WORKSHEET 9.7 How to determine the present value of an annuity (both ordinary and annuity due) using a financial calculator

Most financial calculators have the following keys:

N = Total number of discounting periods
I = Interest rate per period
PV = Present value
FV = Future value
PMT = Annuity payment or receipt

Step 1 Key in the number of discounting periods per year (annual, semiannual, monthly) into the mode of your calculator.
Step 2 Set the mode at the end of the period or beginning of the period for payments.
Step 3 Key the number of payment periods for the investment into the N button.
Step 4 Key the discount/interest rate into the I button.
Step 5 Key the amount of the annuity into the PMT button.
Step 6 Press the PV button to calculate the present value.

Example 1 Present value of an ordinary annuity

Step 1 Key the annual mode into your calculator.
Step 2 Set the end mode for an ordinary annuity.
Step 3 Key the number of payments as 5 into the N button.
Step 4 Key 6% into the I button.
Step 5 Key the deposit of $1,000 into the PMT button.
Step 6 Press the PV button to calculate the present value, which is $4,212.36.

Example 2 Present value of an annuity due

Step 1 Key the annual mode into your calculator.
Step 2 Set the beginning mode for an annuity due.
Step 3 Key the number of payments as 5 into the N button.
Step 4 Key 6% into the I button.
Step 5 Key the deposit of $1,000 into the PMT button.
Step 6 Press the PV button to calculate the present value, which is $4,465.11.

WORKSHEET 9.8 How to determine the present value of an annuity (ordinary and annuity due) using a computer

Using Microsoft's Excel spreadsheet, click on *f**, which is on the top row of the toolbar. A list of functions pops up. Highlight *financial* in the left-hand box and *PV* in the right-hand box and click OK. A box comes up with five rows, as shown below.

Rate
Nper
Pmt
FV
Type

Step 1 Enter interest rate per period.
Step 2 Enter the total number of periods.
Step 3 Enter the payments made each period.
Step 4 Enter the future value.
Step 5 Enter the value representing timing of the payment: 1 for payment at beginning of the period; 0 for payment at the end of the period.

Using the same examples as in the previous section using a financial calculator, key in the numbers:

	Present value of an ordinary annuity	**Present value of an annuity due**
Rate	= .06	= .06
Nper	= 5	= 5
Pmt	= $1,000	= $1,000
FV	= 0	= 0
Type	= 0	= 1
	Result: $4,212	**Result: $4,465**

FINANCIAL CALCULATOR #10

How to Determine the Amounts Needed to Fund Your Objectives

SAVING TO FUND FINANCIAL OBJECTIVES is important, particularly for people who are concerned about the future. Everyone has different goals and priorities, and irrespective of what they are, something should be done to address them before it becomes too late. Worksheet 10.1 on page 56 illustrates the process of determining the amounts needed to fund objectives. The step-by-step process is elaborated on in the discussion that follows.

Step 1: List Your Objectives

Some of the most common objectives are:

- Establishing an emergency fund
- Saving to buy and own a house
- Saving to pay for children's educations
- Saving to start a business
- Saving for retirement

Emergency Fund This is the fund that is used for unexpected events. There is always the possibility of losing a job, getting sick, or having some other unfortunate situation occur, which could cause financial chaos. Having an emergency fund can help in such situations. The question is: How much should be kept in an emergency fund?

The rule of thumb is to have three to six months of living expenses in an emergency fund. The exact amount depends on your circumstances. If you have a stable employment situation and other accounts or sources that you can tap into for your short-term needs, then three months of living expenses would probably be adequate. However, if your income fluctuates, there is a greater risk of losing your job, and you have no relatives or friends who could assist you, then you should keep at least six months of living expenses in this account. There may be circumstances in which you need to keep more than six months of living expenses. If you have a high probability of losing your job and might not be able to find another job within a reasonable period of time, and you have no relatives or friends who could assist you, then you should keep nine months' to one year's worth of living expenses in an emergency fund.

Saving to Buy a House Owning a house is a high priority for most people. Not only are there the tax breaks of being able to deduct the mortgage interest and real estate taxes from personal taxes, but there is also the buildup in equity that comes from paying down a mortgage.

Funding Children's Education Expenses This is not as straightforward an objective as it seems because the current financial aid system works against parents with substantial assets and includes similar penalties for savings invested in children's names. As of this writing, parents are responsible for an amount worth roughly 6 percent of their assets for their children's college costs annually, and children are responsible for an amount worth 35 percent of the savings in their names. People with substantial savings and assets may not qualify for financial aid, and children with assets of $100,000 in their names would also disqualify themselves for aid, assuming private education costs are $35,000. Thus, funding this objective over retirement savings may be a mistake under certain circumstances. Parents should look into all aspects of their financial situations before funding this objective over other objectives.

Saving for Retirement The rule of thumb is that most people will need about 75 to 80 percent of their preretirement income in retirement to maintain their standard of living.

Some people may be able to get by on less and others may need more money to live on. Determining your needs for retirement is important because you can fund most of them through tax-deferred retirement accounts such as a 401(k), a 403(b), SEP-IRAs, Keoghs, Roth IRAs, and IRAs. Contributions to these accounts are generally tax deductible below threshold amounts and the earnings in these accounts accumulate free of taxes until they are withdrawn.

If the amounts saved in these tax-deferred retirement accounts are not sufficient to meet your expected retirement needs, you may want to save additional amounts outside of your tax-deferred retirement accounts.

The future cannot be predicted, but by setting aside amounts for an emergency fund, big ticket purchases (car, home), educational needs, and retirement, you are preparing to cope for any financial changes in the future.

Now list the objectives that are most important to you.

Step 2: Prioritize Your Objectives

There are many factors that will determine your objectives, such as your age or stage in life, your income level, the size of your family, and your perspective on the future. People in their twenties will have decidedly different objectives from people in their forties. Achieving objectives requires regular, disciplined deposits to savings and investment accounts. The longer the investment period, the greater the accumulation of interest, as shown in the time value of money financial calculator (section 4).

Most people do not have the financial resources to fund all of their objectives, and the difficulty comes in deciding which ones to fund. Should you save for retirement or a down payment on a house, or should you use the funds to start a business? Some objectives are short term while others are longer term. It is often easier to concentrate on the short-term objectives and neglect the long-term objectives. Assigning priorities to your objectives can help you determine which ones to fund.

Step 3: Assess the Cost and
Time Frame for Each Objective

By quantifying the cost for each objective and the time frame for when you will need this amount, you make it easier to determine how much to save for each objective. The example in Worksheet 10.1 shows two objectives with costs of $15,000 and $1,000,000 and time frames of six months and 30 years, respectively. A simple way to determine the monthly amount needed to finance each objective is to divide the cost by the number of months until needed, as shown below:

$$\text{Monthly amount for emergency fund} = \frac{\$15,000}{6}$$

$$= \$2,500$$

$$\text{Monthly amount for retirement} = \frac{\$1,000,000}{360}$$

$$= \$2,777.78$$

The astute reader is bound to observe that the amounts computed are not accurate determinations of what to save because they do not take into

---

WORKSHEET 10.1 Steps to determine the amounts needed to fund objectives

Objectives	Priority	Cost	Time needed	Rate of return	Monthly savings required
_____	_____	_____	_____	_____	_____
_____	_____	_____	_____	_____	_____
_____	_____	_____	_____	_____	_____
_____	_____	_____	_____	_____	_____
_____	_____	_____	_____	_____	_____
_____	_____	_____	_____	_____	_____
_____	_____	_____	_____	_____	_____
_____	_____	_____	_____	_____	_____

Examples:

Emergency fund	1	$15,000	6 months	1% per annum	$2,494.80
Retirement	2	$1,000,000	30 years	8% per annum	$670.98

Step 1 List your objectives.
Step 2 Attach priorities.
Step 3 Assess cost and time needed.
Step 4 List rates of return.
Step 5 Compute monthly savings required.

account the time value of money. This is correct, because the deposits made into various investments will earn a rate of return, which will result in having to make smaller monthly deposits.

Step 4: List the Rates of Return for Each Objective

The investment choice for the deposits for each of your objectives depends on several factors, such as the time frame, the level of risk, and the expected rate of return. Generally, with a short-term time horizon of one year or less, *money market securities* offer low rates of return but almost no risk of loss of principal. Money market securities consist of Treasury bills, certificates of deposit, commercial paper, bankers' acceptances, money market funds, and bank and savings accounts. For intermediate-term time horizons (one to five years), notes and bonds offer higher returns, but they also carry greater risk. Common stocks offer the highest returns of most financial investments, but they carry much greater risk of loss of principal. Consequently, you need a long time horizon (greater than five years) to ride out the loss of having to sell stocks at less than their purchase prices.

Current rates of return used in the examples in Worksheet 10.1 are 1 percent per annum for a savings account and 8 percent per annum for an investment in stocks. In the event of inflation, you would have to save more than the cost listed, as inflation erodes future purchasing power. If inflation is estimated to be 2 percent per year, the real rate of return for stocks in this example would be 6 percent (8 percent minus 2 percent).

Step 5: Compute the Monthly Amounts Needed to Fund Objectives

The easiest methods for determining the monthly amounts needed to fund objectives into the future are to use either a financial calculator or a computer. Using financial tables becomes cumbersome if the monthly interest rate is not a whole number. However, there are financial tables printed with fractional interest rates that can be used.

Using a Financial Calculator to Determine the Monthly Amounts Needed to Fund Objectives

Example 1 in Worksheet 10.1
Determine the monthly amount to save for an emergency fund of $15,000 in six months' time.

Step 1	Key in the number of interest periods as monthly.	12 per year
Step 2	Key in the end mode for an ordinary annuity.	end mode
Step 3	Key the number of payments into the *N* button.	6
Step 4	Key the interest rate per annum into the *I* button.	1%
Step 5	Key the future value into the *FV* button.	$15,000
Step 6	Press the *PMT* button to determine the monthly amount.	$2,494.80

Example 2 in Worksheet 10.1
Determine the monthly amount needed to save for a retirement fund of $1,000,000 in 30 years' time.

Step 1	Key in the number of interest periods as monthly.	12 per year
Step 2	Key in the end mode for an ordinary annuity.	end mode
Step 3	Key the number of payments into the *N* button.	360

Step 4 Key the interest rate per annum into
    the *I* button.   8%

Step 5 Key the future value into the *FV* button. $1,000,000

Step 6 Press the *PMT* button to determine the
    monthly amount. $670.98

Using a Computer to Determine the Monthly Amounts Needed to Fund Objectives

Microsoft's Excel spreadsheet is used here to illustrate the computation of the annuity amounts needed to fund the two example objectives in Worksheet 10.1, as shown in Worksheet 10.2. There are a few differences from the Excel examples in section 9. Instead of calculating the future value, in these examples you are looking for the payment amount/annuity amount (PMT) that equals the future value at a particular interest rate per period for a specified number of periods. Instead of clicking FV in the right-hand box, you would highlight PMT. Thereafter, you would enter the variables as described in Worksheet 10.2.

What becomes tricky is the determination of the interest rates per period. In example 1, the interest rate is 1 percent per year, which means that interest per month is 0.01 ÷ 12. The same applies for example 2, where the interest rate per month is 0.08 ÷ 12.

WORKSHEET 10.2 How to determine the monthly amounts needed to finance your objectives using a computer

Using Microsoft's Excel spreadsheet, click on *f**, which is on the top row of the toolbar. A list of functions pops up. Highlight *financial* in the left-hand box and *PMT* in the right-hand box and click OK. A box comes up with five rows, as shown below.

Rate	
Nper	
PV	
FV	
Type	

Formula result =

Step 1 Enter the rate, which is the interest rate per period.
Step 2 Enter the total number of periods.
Step 3 Enter the present value, which is 0.
Step 4 Enter the future value.
Step 5 Enter the value representing timing of the payment: 1 for payment at beginning of the period; 0 for payment at the end of the period.

Using the same examples as in Worksheet 10.1, key in the numbers:

Payment of a future value, example #1:

Rate	0.01 ÷ 12	= .0008333
Nper	6	= 6
PV	0	= 0
FV	$15,000	= $15,000
Type	0	= 0

Formula result = $2,494.80

Payment of a future value, example #2:

Rate	.08 ÷ 12	= .0066667
Nper	360	= 360
PV	0	= 0
FV	$1,000,000	= $1,000,000
Type	0	= 0

Formula result = $670.98

FINANCIAL CALCULATOR #11

How to Reconcile
Your Checking Account*

FAILURE TO RECONCILE YOUR CHECKING ACCOUNT can cost you money over time. If either you or the bank make any errors, they might not be discovered in a timely fashion unless you reconcile your account on a monthly basis. If the bank deducts more for a check than the amount written or does not credit your account for a deposit made, you need to let it know about these errors in a timely manner or it will not do anything about them. Similarly, you could have made a mistake and assumed that your balance was higher than it really was, which could result in an overdrawn check, which in turn would result in additional bank fees.

The starting point in reconciling your checking account is to examine your monthly checking account statement. The bank statement shows the deposits that have been credited and the checks that have cleared the account for the monthly period. Figure 11.1 shows a typical bank statement for John Y.

Step 1: Mark Off Canceled Checks in
Your Check Register

Canceled checks or copies of them are included with your monthly bank statement. In addition to marking off canceled checks, you should also check the amounts that the bank has debited for each check. Figure 11.2 shows an example of a check that was written for $1,200.00 but for which the bank charged the account $1,201.00. The amount charged by the bank is shown in the bottom right-hand corner of the check. The figure in the bottom right-hand corner of each canceled check should be checked against the amount written for

---

*Portions of this section have been previously published by Esmé Faerber in *Managing Your Investments, Savings and Credit*, (McGraw-Hill: New York, 2001).

FIGURE 11.1 Example of a monthly bank statement

Everlasting Bank

Account Title: John Y.   Account #: 000-00000

Previous Balance: $2,140.57
4 Deposits/Credits: 3,082.87
15 Checks/Debits: 2,379.10
Ending Balance: 2,844.34

Date	Check #	Debits	Credits	Balance
2/1				$ 2,140.57
2/2	343	$20.00	$2,906.37	5,026.94
2/5	356	1,201.00		3,825.94
2/6	357	56.14		3,769.80
2/9	359	91.12	25.00	3,703.68
2/12	361	150.00		3,553.68
2/14	362	221.50		3,332.18
2/16	363	87.20		3,244.98
2/20	365	200.00		3,044.98
	366	26.00		3,018.98
2/21	367	15.36	150.00	3,153.62
2/23	368	76.12		3,077.50
	369	150.00		2,927.50
2/24	370	56.06		2,871.44
2/28	373	23.50		2,847.94
		5.10 SC	1.50 IN	2,844.34

DM = Debit Memo   SC = Service Charge   FC = Finance Charge   IN = Interest

that check. This way bank errors can be spotted promptly and then corrected when brought to the bank's attention.

Arrange checks you have written that have cleared the bank in numerical order of check numbers and then mark them off in your check register as shown in Figure 11.3. Checks not marked with a (√) are outstanding and have not cleared Mr. Y's account as of the bank statement date. Similarly,

FIGURE 11.2 A canceled check

you should check off all the ATM withdrawals that are listed on the bank statement against your checkbook register.

Step 2: Determine Your Adjusted Checkbook Balance

Begin with your checkbook balance at the closing date of the monthly statement, add interest income, and then deduct bank charges and fees.

Balance per checkbook at end of month	$4,877.90
Deduct: service charge	(5.10)
Add: interest income	1.50
Adjusted checkbook balance	$4,874.30

Step 3: Compare the Deposits Listed on Your Bank Statement with the Deposits in Your Register

Determine whether there are any deposits that you have recorded in your checkbook that are not on your bank statement. Looking at the checkbook register in Figure 11.3, we see that the deposit of $2,906.37 on 2/28 is in

FIGURE 11.3 Mr. Y's checkbook register

Mr. Y's Checkbook Register

NUMBER	DATE 2002	DESCRIPTION OF TRANSACTION	PAYMENT/DEBIT (−)		√T	FEE IF ANY (−)	DEPOSIT/CREDIT (+)		BALANCE $ 2120	57
356	2-1	Complete Financial Service	$ 1200	00	✓	$	$		$ 1200 920	57
	2-2	Deposit			✓		2906	37	2906 3826	37 94
357	2-3	Bell Telephone	56	14	✓				56 3770	14 80
358	2-4	Electric Company	124	16					124 3646	16 64
359	2-5	EZ Food Market	91	12	✓				91 3555	12 52
	2-9	Deposit—Forever S&L Dividend			✓		25	00	25 3580	00 52
360	2-10	Ace Insurance Company	650	00					650 2930	00 52
361	2-11	Cash	150	00	✓				150 2780	00 52
362	2-12	Leak Free Roofers	221	50	✓				221 2559	50 02
363	2-15	EZ Food Market	87	20	✓				87 2471	20 82
364	2-16	Animal Hospital	35	00					35 2436	00 82
365	2-17	Last County Bank	200	00	✓				200 2236	00 82
366	2-18	Kraft Pharmacy	26	00	✓				26 2210	00 82
367	2-19	First Bookstore	$ 15	36	✓	$	$		$ 15 2195	36 46
	2-20	Deposit—Seave Brokerage Dividend			✓		150	00	150 2345	00 46
368	2-21	Gas Company	76	12	✓				76 2269	12 34
369	2-21	Cash	150	00	✓				150 2119	00 34
370	2-22	EZ Food Market	56	06	✓				56 2063	06 28
371	2-23	Playful Toy Store	23	25					23 2040	25 03
372	2-24	Numero Uno Department Store	45	00					45 1995	00 03
373	2-27	EZ Food Market	23	50	✓				23 1971	50 53
	2-28	Deposit					2906	37	2906 4877	37 90

transit. In other words, the funds have not been credited to John Y's bank account as of the bank statement date. All deposits in transit need to be added to the bank balance.

Similarly, if your bank has received electronic fund transfers into your account that you have not recorded in your checkbook register, you will need to add these to the balance.

Step 4: List All Outstanding Checks

List the outstanding checks from the checkbook register. These are the checks that have not been presented to the bank for payment as of the bank statement date.

Checks outstanding:

#	Amount
358	$ 124.16
360	650.00
364	35.00
371	23.25
372	45.00
	$ 877.41

Step 5: Determine Your Adjusted Bank Balance

Start with the ending balance shown on your bank statement, add all deposits in transit (step 3), and deduct any checks outstanding (step 4). The resulting balance should equal the adjusted balance in your checkbook (step 2). If there are any errors, they need to be adjusted, as shown below with the example in John Y's account.

Balance per bank	$ 2,844.34
Add: deposits in transit	2,906.37
Deduct: outstanding checks	(877.41)
	4,873.30
Add: bank error (check #356 written for	
$1,200.00, bank charged $1,201.00)	1.00
Adjusted bank balance	$ 4,874.30

See Worksheet 11.1 for a summary of this process. If the adjusted bank balance and the adjusted checkbook balance are not the same, you have made an error. Proceed to step 6.

WORKSHEET 11.1 Reconciling your checking account

Your checkbook		Bank statement	
Ending balance $_____		Ending Balance $_____	
Deduct fees/charges shown on bank statement _____		Add deposits in transit _____	
Add interest earned _____		Deduct outstanding checks _____	
Add direct deposits _____			
Adjusted checkbook balance _____		Adjusted bank balance _____	

Step 6: Looking for Errors

1. Confirm that you have included all the outstanding checks and that they are correctly added.
2. Check that you have included all the deposits in transit.
3. Check your bank statement to see that you have included all bank charges and interest earned.
4. Recheck the addition and subtraction in your checkbook register.
5. Recheck the amounts written on the canceled checks with the amounts written in your checkbook register.
6. Recheck the amounts written on the canceled checks with the coded digits in the bottom right-hand corner of the checks.

If you still have not found the error, it is more than likely that you are overlooking something obvious. Leave it for a while and come back to it later.

Using a Computer to Reconcile Your Checking Account

Computers can be used to reconcile a checking account, which eliminates the arithmetic errors that can so easily be made when determining checkbook register balances. There are many different software programs available. Worksheet 11.2 outlines the steps to reconcile your checking account using Quicken software. For other software programs, consult the software guide for the specific steps to reconcile your account.

There is a basic similarity between manually reconciling your account and doing it on a computer. The advantage of using a computer is that reconciling your account is much easier because arithmetic errors are eliminated. The disadvantage is that it is time consuming to enter the transactions from your paper checkbook register into the computer checkbook register.

By reconciling your checking account monthly, you confirm that your checking account balance is what it should be, and you safeguard an important asset—your cash.

WORKSHEET 11.2 Using Quicken software to reconcile a checking account

Step 1   Enter transactions into the Quicken checkbook register.

The Quicken checkbook register looks the same as the one shown in Figure 11.3. Enter all the transactions from your checkbook register into your computer checkbook register.

Step 2   Click on the reconcile box.

When you have finished entering all the transactions from your checkbook register into your computer checkbook register, you are ready to begin the reconciliation process. On the top row above the register, there is the word *reconcile*. Click on the reconcile box and you will get a larger box on the next screen. In number 1, there is an opening balance figure; fill in the ending balance as it is stated on your bank statement. In number 2, fill in any service charges and interest earned also from your bank statement. When you have finished, click on the OK box.

Step 2   Check off checks, withdrawals, and deposits that have cleared the bank.

As you did in your manual reconciliation, you want to check off all the transactions that have cleared the bank. A large box appears with transactions sorted into two categories. One includes all withdrawals and checks written and the other includes all deposits. Click on each transaction that has cleared the bank, as indicated on your bank statement. When you have completed marking these off, you will see a balance differential in the lower right-hand corner below the box. If you have not made any mistakes, the differential will equal 0, indicating that you have successfully reconciled your checkbook register balance to your bank balance.

FINANCIAL CALCULATOR #12

How to Prepare Your Records for Your Tax Accountant*

THERE ARE MANY REASONS WHY you should keep orderly and complete tax records. When you keep inclusive records of your income and deduc-

*Portions of this section have been previously published by Esmé Faerber in *Managing Your Investments, Savings and Credit* (McGraw-Hill: New York, 1992).

tions, you are able to prepare an accurate tax return. If the Internal Revenue Service (IRS) audits your return, the orderly records you've kept can easily verify your deductions with a minimum of effort. (This won't prevail for any nondeductible items or highly questionable deductions you may have taken.) By keeping all-inclusive records of your expenses, you may be able to reduce the amount of income taxes you pay. If you can't prove your deductions because of sloppy record keeping, you may have to pay more income tax than necessary.

Copies of your tax returns should be kept in your home file as part of your tax records, with all records and receipts pertaining to income, deductions, and credits that appear on your tax return. Worksheet 12.1 lists all the tax records you should keep, not only to present to your accountant but also for the reasons listed above. All the 1099 series of forms should be retained to support receipts of different types of income. Other such records, such as brokerage statements and mutual fund statements that can prove the amounts of income shown on your tax return, should be kept in your tax folder.

Your checkbook and credit card statements provide basic records of your deductible expenditures. However, canceled checks alone may not be sufficient evidence for the IRS, so you should keep records of receipts and sales invoices. Dated and signed sales receipts are important if you paid cash.

Many people meet with an accountant at least once a year to prepare their income tax returns. By organizing and summarizing your tax information ahead of the appointment, you can save your accountant considerable time, which should reduce the cost of preparing your tax return.

By organizing and summarizing your information, you can do the "legwork" rather than have your accountant plow through your receipts, canceled checks, and other documentation. Many accountants require photocopies of supporting documentation along with a summary sheet of information or a completed questionnaire requesting similar information. Also, most accountants require a copy of your prior year's tax return if prepared by another accountant. Worksheet 12.2 lists the categories of information required to process a basic 1040 tax form.

Your summary sheet should show your name, name of spouse (if applicable), address, telephone number, Social Security number(s), marital status,

WORKSHEET 12.1 What tax records to keep

Income	Records
Wages and salary	W-2 issued by employer
Independent contractor	1099-Misc issued by the entity you have provided services for
Business income: proprietorship, partnership, estates, trusts, S-corporations, rents, royalties	Business books, K-1 issued by partnership
Interest and dividends	1099-Int and 1099-Div issued by the financial institutions paying the interest and dividends
Capital gains and losses	1099-B issued by broker who sold the assets; 1099-S issued by broker reporting proceeds on the sale of real estate
State and local tax refunds	1099-G issued by state or local government that provided the refund
Payments/distributions from retirement plans and annuities	1099-R or W-2P issued by the trustee of the plan making the payment
Social Security benefits	SSA-1099 issued by the federal government
Unemployment compensation	1099-G issued by government agency paying unemployment compensation
Barter income	1099-B issued when services or properties are exchanged

Expenditures	Records
Medical and dental expenses	Canceled checks and receipts
Taxes	Canceled checks and receipts for real estate taxes, personal property taxes, and state and local taxes
Interest	1098 issued by mortgage company, canceled checks, and receipts for deductible interest
Charitable contributions	Canceled checks and receipts from donees
Miscellaneous deductions	Canceled checks and receipts
Business use of auto, home	Canceled checks, receipts, and documentation
Alimony	Canceled checks, copy of divorce decree or separation agreement

---

WORKSHEET 12.2 Income tax summary

Name: Date of birth: Social Security #:
Name of spouse: Date of birth: Social Security #:
Marital status:
  Children:
  Name: Date of birth: Social Security #:
  Name: Date of birth: Social Security #:

Income

Salary W-2

Gross   Federal withholding   Social Security   State tax   Local tax

Business income

Refund of state tax

Interest income   **Dividend income**

Capital gains

Description   Date of purchase   Date of sale   Proceeds   Cost

Adjustments

IRA/Keogh deposit

Deductions

Mortgage interest expense   Real estate taxes

---

names of dependents (if applicable), their Social Security number(s), and their dates of birth. List all sources of income. If your financial activities have not changed very much since last year, your prior year's tax return is a good source to check to see if you have omitted any sources of income.

List your adjustments, such as deposits to IRA accounts, and alimony and child support payments.

If your deductions exceed the amount of the standard allowable deduction, you may choose to itemize your deductible expenses. By organizing and summarizing your deductible expenses, you will save your accountant time

FIGURE 12.1 Check analysis of deductible expenses

Check #	1990 Date	Payee	Amount	Taxes	Medical	Interest	Contributions	Other
1	215	1/5	F.A.S. Bee, CPA	200 00					200 00
2	216	1/15	State-Personal Prop Tax	39 00	39 00				
3	230	2/10	Dr. B. Well	80 00		80 00			
4	231	2/10	Ds. P.D. Rad	90 00		90 00			
5	256	3/15	Church-Temple Donation	200 00				200 00	
6	270	4/20	Super Quick Motors-Auto	187 00					187 00
7	291	5/08	Fail Safe Bank-Personal Interest	150 00			150 00		
8	296	5/30	Central School-Child Care	500 00					500 00
9	315	6/15	IRS 1040 ES	750 00	750 00				
10	316	6/15	State Estimated Payment	150 00	150 00				
11	325	7/20	State Bank-Safe Deposit Box	40 00					40 00
12	380	8/29	Go Moving Company	2 000 00					2 000 00
13	399	9/15	IRS 1040 ES	750 00	750 00				
14	400	9/15	State Estimated Payment	150 00	150 00				
15	450	10/30	SPCA-Donation	50 00					50 00
16	490	11/16	Best Auto Insurance	500 00					500 00
17									
18			Subtotals	5 836 00	1 839 00	170 00	150 00	200 00	3 477 00
19			From W2						
20			State Tax	1 050 00	1 050 00				
21			City Tax	2 156 00	2 156 00				
22									
23			From 1098						
24			Real Estate Tax	2 100 00	2 100 00				
25			Mortgage Interest	5 001 00			5 001 00		
26									
27			Totals	16 143 00	7 145 00	170 00	5 151 00	200 00	3 477 00
28									

and yourself money. Figure 12.1 shows a worksheet on which checks of deductible expenses are sorted and summarized. If you are not sure which expenses are deductible, check with your accountant. You should give your accountant your W-2 forms, which are then attached to your federal, state, and local tax returns.

Your accountant may ask you to fill out a checklist or questionnaire so that all relevant information is obained. The aim of working closely with your accountant is to prepare an accurate tax return and not overpay your taxes.

PART TWO

MANAGING YOUR PERSONAL WEALTH—DEBT

Determine Your Debt Capacity

S INCE CREDIT CARD COMPANIES SET debt limits on the amount of credit that they will issue to credit card holders, it would be prudent for people to set their own limits on their total debt capacities. Before immersing yourself in debt, you should determine how much debt you can comfortably afford. In other words, you should set your own debt limit, which is the maximum amount that you can comfortably afford to service the interest payments.

One method of determining your debt limit is to draw up a monthly budget with your cash receipts of income and your cash disbursements for expenses. Worksheet 13.1 provides the framework for this approach.

The amount left over when monthly cash disbursements are subtracted from monthly receipts is the amount available for debt payments. If disbursements are greater than receipts, you cannot afford to take on any new debt, as you will not be able to pay the interest and principal payments without drawing down on your assets.

Not everything is as simple or clear-cut as this first approach suggests, which leads to a second approach for determining whether you can afford to take on debt. This approach involves analyzing your budget to determine where potential trade-offs may lie. By forgoing spending in some areas, you can increase the amount available to finance debt payments. Cutting vacation and entertainment expenses, for example, can free up funds for servicing debt, but it becomes progressively harder to cut down on necessary types of expenses.

The rule of thumb of a 20 percent ceiling on the amount of debt payments to monthly disposable income is a useful guideline. This means that if your monthly disposable income is $2,000, your debt payments should not exceed $400. This does not include your mortgage.

WORKSHEET 13.1 Budgetary approach to determining your debt capacity

Monthly cash receipts

Net monthly income	_____
Other income	_____
Total monthly receipts	**A** _____

Monthly cash disbursements

Mortgage/rent	_____
Food	_____
Household expenses	_____
Transportation/auto expenses	_____
Child care expenses	_____
Savings and investments	_____
Other expenses	_____
Total monthly disbursements	**B** _____

Annual expenses

Taxes	_____
Real estate taxes	_____
Other taxes	_____
Insurance	_____
Medical and dental expenses	_____
Other	_____

Total annual expenses   **C** _____

Divide total by 12   _____ ÷ 12

Equals monthly expenses (C ÷ 12)   **D** _____

Total monthly disbursements (B + D)   **E** _____

Cash receipts minus disbursements (A − E)   **F** _____

(If F is positive, this is the amount available for debt payments.)

The greater the level of income, the easier it becomes to support this level of debt. For example, it may be difficult for someone with take-home pay of $1,000 per month to support debt payments of $200 per month, whereas someone with disposable income of $3,000 per month may have an easier time supporting debt payments of $600.

The following are the warning signs of taking on too much debt:

- You are unable to save any money.
- You have to cut back on necessary expenses just to make ends meet.
- You only pay the minimum amounts on your credit card bills.
- You are juggling certain payments in order to pay other obligations, which are all due at the same time.
- You are unable to meet payments in emergency situations.

Fill in Worksheet 13.1, which shows the amount that you can afford for debt, and set your debt limit at a comfortable level.

FINANCIAL CALCULATOR #14
How to Determine the Best Source of Credit

CREDIT IS COSTLY, AND IF YOU CAN GET by without using expensive sources of credit you will be better off financially. If you do have to use credit, use it sparingly. There are many different sources of credit, and you should investigate them carefully as their costs can differ significantly. Commercial banks, credit unions, savings and loan associations, consumer finance companies, and life insurance companies are all sources of credit. Not only will the types of credit and the terms vary from source to source but so too will the costs. Using credit cards as a source for credit purchases can be the most costly if you do not repay the full amount of the credit balance within the grace period offered by the credit card issuer. Rates can range as high as

12 to 30 percent per annum, which puts things into perspective when compared with the puny returns of 1 to 3 percent currently received from savings and money market accounts. This situation points to the importance of comparing the rates charged by the different sources of credit. The yardstick of comparison is the annual percentage rate (APR). Lenders are required by the Federal Truth in Lending Act to use the APR when quoting interest rates on sources of credit.

Worksheet 14.1 outlines the different sources of credit with the different types of loans and typical lending policies. As interest rates fluctuate with market conditions in the economy, you will need to check with each individual source of credit as to the APR for the different types of credit in which you are interested.

The sources of credit that are least expensive are family members and friends. You should always check these sources first before going to institutional lenders, which will generally charge much more for credit. Family members may be willing to lend to you at rates that are only slightly in excess of what they can earn from their savings accounts and money market securities, which are currently quite low at 1 to 3 percent. If such an arrangement is made, the loan agreement, interest rate, maturity date, and/or repayment schedule should be in writing. The downside to borrowing from friends and family is that if there are any deviations from the terms of the agreement it could strain the relationship.

Some generalizations that you should keep in mind in determining the best sources of credit are as follows:

- The most expensive sources of credit are from consumer finance companies. The reason is because they lend to people who cannot obtain financing from other sources, such as banks, savings and loan associations, and credit unions.
- Cash advances through credit card charge accounts are also extremely expensive. Fees are levied in addition to having to pay interest on a daily basis. The interest rate is usually at the high end of the range, and there is no grace period for cash advances like there is for charge purchases.

WORKSHEET 14.1 Determine your best sources of credit

Sources of credit	Types of loans	Lending policies	Cost and terms (APR)
Commercial banks	Single-payment loan	Customers with established credit history	
	Installment loan		_____
	Credit card loan	May require collateral	
	Passbook loan		_____
	Check-credit plan		_____
	Second mortgage		_____
			_____
Credit unions	Credit card loan	Available to members only	
	Installment loan		_____
	Share draft-credit plan		
	Second mortgage		_____
			_____
Savings & loan associations	Installment loan	Need an established credit history	_____
	Savings account loan		
	Education loan	May require collateral	_____
			_____
	Home improvement loan		
	Second mortgage		_____
			_____
Consumer finance companies	Installment loan	Do not need an established credit history	_____
	Second mortgage		_____
Life insurance companies	Loans up to 95% of the insurer's cash value	Need to have a life insurance policy in force	_____

- Before going to a bank for a car loan, check with the car dealer to find out if there are any special financing deals available from the auto manufacturer. During tough economic times, many auto manufacturers provide 0 percent loans to potential buyers as an incentive to increase sales of new cars.
- Credit unions may charge lower rates than banks, but you have to be a credit union member.
- Unsecured loans have higher rates than secured loans.
- Expanding the term of an installment loan results in smaller monthly payments, but the total interest paid will be greater than a shorter-term loan.

Using Worksheet 14.1, fill in the APRs and the terms charged by the different sources of credit to determine your best sources of credit.

Should you decide to make a sizable purchase and know that you will be in a position to pay for it in full within a few weeks, use a credit card and pay off the entire amount within the grace period. Credit card companies normally provide a grace period, which is a period of time between the recording of the transaction and the due date during which interest is not charged if the balance is paid in full. If there is a balance due after the grace period, interest is charged on the daily balance.

The use of credit is costly, and if you can pay cash instead of using credit you will save more in the long run, as shown in Worksheet 14.2. In this worksheet, you can compare the cost of using credit versus paying cash.

When financing costs and fees related to the use of credit are added, the total cost of credit is much greater than the use of cash.

WORKSHEET 14.2 Cost of using credit versus paying cash for a purchase

Cash		**Credit**	
Net cost of item	_____	Down payment	_____
Sales tax	+ _____	Credit-related fees	+ _____
Delivery, service costs	+ _____	Financing costs*	+ _____
Interest revenue forgone			
by purchasing for cash	+ _____		
Total cash cost	_____	**Total credit cost**	_____

*To determine the financing costs, multiply the monthly cost by the number of months payments are to be made.

FINANCIAL CALCULATOR #15

How to Determine the Annual Percentage Rate Costs of Using Credit Loans

W HEN COMPARING THE CREDIT COSTS of different borrowing situations, it is helpful to know how the costs are determined. Since 1969, lenders have been required to disclose the annual percentage rate (APR) and the total dollar amount paid in finance charges. The APR is the true cost of the debt and is determined by dividing the total finance charges by the loan balance. By comparing the APRs of competing sources of credit, you can choose the source with the lowest cost.

How to Determine the APR for Single-Payment Loans

Single-payment loans can charge interest using the simple interest method or the discount interest method.

Simple Interest Method

Using simple interest, the finance charge is calculated by multiplying the stated annual rate by the amount of the loan. For example, if you borrow $2,000 from the Friendly Bank for two years at 10 percent simple interest, the interest expense is $200 per year and the APR is 10 percent, as shown in Worksheet 15.1.

When simple interest is used, the annual percentage rate is equal to the stated rate.

Discount Interest Method

With the discount interest method, the lender deducts the interest payments at the inception of the loan. For example, with a single-payment discount loan of $2,000 at 10 percent for two years from the Friendly Bank, the loan will have the same total interest expense of $400 ($200 per year) as a simple interest loan.

The difference with this method is that the borrower will receive only $1,600, as the finance charge of $400 is deducted from the loan. The true cost or APR of this loan is 12.5 percent. This is shown in Worksheet 15.2, which outlines the steps for determining the APR for a single-payment loan using the discount interest method. The discount interest method results in a higher APR than the simple interest method.

WORKSHEET 15.1 How to determine the APR using simple interest

Total interest expense $\quad\quad = I \times P \times T$

I = Interest rate $\quad\quad\quad = 10\% \times \$2{,}000 \times 2$
P = Amount of the loan $\quad = \$400$
T = Length of time for the loan

Total interest expense $\quad = I \times P \times T$

$\quad\quad\quad\quad\quad\quad\quad\quad = \underline{\quad} \times \underline{\quad} \times \underline{\quad}$

$\quad\quad\quad\quad\quad\quad\quad\quad = \underline{\quad}$

$$APR = \frac{\text{Average annual finance charge}}{\text{Average annual loan balance}}$$

$$= \frac{\$400 \div 2}{\$2{,}000}$$

$$= 10\%$$

$$APR = \frac{\text{Average annual finance charge}}{\text{Average annual loan balance}}$$

$$= \underline{\quad}$$

$$= \underline{\quad} \%$$

Step 1 Fill in the interest rate, amount of the loan, and time to determine the total interest expense.

Step 2 Determine the average annual finance charge and divide this by the average annual loan balance.

WORKSHEET 15.2 How to determine the APR using discount interest

Total interest expense	$= I \times P \times T$
I = Interest rate	$= 10\% \times \$2,000 \times 2$
P = Amount of the loan	$= \$400$
T = Length of time for the loan	

Total interest expense $= I \times P \times T$

$$= \underline{\quad} \times \underline{\quad} \times \underline{\quad}$$

$$= \underline{\quad}$$

Discounted loan balance = loan balance – total interest expense

$$= \$2,000 - \$400$$

$$= \$1,600$$

Discounted loan balance = loan balance – total interest expense

$$= \$\underline{\quad} - \$\underline{\quad}$$

$$= \$\underline{\quad}$$

$$APR = \frac{\text{Average annual finance charge}}{\text{Average annual loan balance}}$$

$$APR = \frac{\$400 \div 2}{\$1,600}$$

$$= 12.5\%$$

$$APR = \frac{\text{Average annual finance charge}}{\text{Average annual loan balance}}$$

$$= \underline{\quad}$$

$$= \underline{\quad}\%$$

Step 1   Fill in the interest rate, amount of the loan, and time to determine the total interest expense.

Step 2   Subtract the total interest from the total amount of the loan.

Step 3   Determine the average annual finance charge and divide this by the average annual loan balance.

How to Determine the APR for Installment Loans

Installment loans are used mainly to buy consumer goods such as cars, furniture, and appliances. The amounts range widely, from under $100 up to $40,000 and more, as do the finance rates, which range from 10 to 30 percent per annum. These rates change with market changes in interest rates.

There are different methods for determining the APRs for installment loans. There is the precomputed interest method (also know as the effective interest rate method), the simple interest method (a variant of the precomputed interest method), the add-on method, and the discount method (rarely used). These methods are used by different financial institutions. Understanding how the interest is calculated can assist you in the choice of the lowest-cost provider of installment loans.

Precomputed Interest or Effective Interest Rate Method

An installment loan requires you to make regular payments of interest and principal. Under this method, the total interest is computed at the outset of the loan. Table 15.1 gives an example of a $1,000, 12 percent, one-year installment loan, with payments on a monthly basis.

The total precomputed interest is $66.20 and the monthly payments are $88.85, due on the last day of the month. Table 15.1 shows how the payments are divided into principal and interest. The interest remains the same even if payments are made before the due date. If payments are made significantly after the due date (usually two weeks after), a late penalty is assessed. The outstanding loan balance declines every month by the amount of the principal reduction, which is the greater part of the monthly payment in this loan schedule.

With the precomputed interest method, the APR is always the same as the stated rate unless there are additional fees that are charged on the installment loan.

TABLE 15.1 Installment loan—precomputed interest method

Monthly payment $88.85; interest rate 12%; term in months: 12

Month	Payment	Interest	Principal reduction	Loan balance
				$1,000.00
January	$88.85	$10.00	$78.85	921.15
February	88.85	9.21	79.64	841.51
March	88.85	8.42	80.43	761.08
April	88.85	7.61	81.24	679.84
May	88.85	6.80	82.05	597.79
June	88.85	5.98	82.87	514.92
July	88.85	5.15	83.70	431.22
August	88.85	4.31	84.54	346.68
September	88.85	3.47	85.38	261.30
October	88.85	2.61	86.24	175.06
November	88.85	1.75	87.10	87.96
December	88.85	0.89	87.96	0.00
Totals	**$1,066.20**	**$66.20**	**$1,000.00**	

The following formula can be used to determine the APR of precomputed interest loans:

$$APR = \frac{2 \times M \times I}{P(n+1)}$$

where

M = number of payment periods in the year
I = total interest charge
P = initial amount of the loan
n = total number of payments

The APR for the precomputed interest loan example is:

$$\text{APR} = \frac{2 \times 12 \times \$66.20}{\$1,000(12 + 1)}$$

$$= \frac{\$1,588.80}{\$13,000}$$

$$\text{APR} = 12.2\%$$

The *simple interest method* is a variant of the precomputed interest method. With the simple interest method, you pay simple interest on the outstanding balance only for the time that the money is used. For example, using the same loan of $1,000 with a 12 percent simple interest calculation and a term of 12 months, the monthly interest expense is determined by when payments are received. Monthly payments of $88.85 will be the same, but the interest expense will be determined by the number of days before the payment is received.

Assume that the first payment is made after 20 days, the second after 36 days, and the third after 21 days. Table 15.2 shows the amortization schedule for the first three months.

TABLE 15.2 Installment loan—simple interest method

Monthly payment $88.85; interest rate 12%; term in months: 12

Month	Days between payment	Interest	Principal reduction	Loan balance
				$1,000.00
January	20	$6.58	$82.27	917.73
February	36	10.86	77.99	839.74
March	21	5.80	83.05	756.69

The interest expense of $6.58 for January is calculated as follows: $1,000 × 20 days × 12 percent ÷ 365. The principal reduction of $82.27 is the monthly payment of $88.85 minus the interest expense of $6.58. For February, the interest expense is $10.86 ($917.73 × 36 days × 12 percent ÷ 365). The February interest expense of $10.86 is greater than the interest expense using the pre-computed interest method because there is a 36-day lapse since the first payment date. In March, the interest expense is less than the precomputed interest method because the interest period is 21 days as opposed to the regular 30- or 31-day cycle used for the precomputed interest method.

The advantage of the simple interest loan is that if you make your payments before the due dates, especially at the beginning of the loan when the principal balance is the highest, your interest charges will be lower than they would be using the precomputed interest method. However, with both of these types of installment loans, you should check to see that there are no restrictions or penalties to making early payments of additional principal.

Add-On Method

The add-on method of computing interest on an installment loan results in a higher APR than the stated rate. Suppose you get an installment loan of $1,000 with a 12 percent add-on rate for one year with payments on a monthly basis. The total interest is calculated as follows:

$$\text{Interest expense} = \$1,000 \times 12\%$$
$$= \$120$$

The total interest is added to the loan amount and then divided by 12 to get the monthly payment of $93.33 [(1,000 + 120) ÷ 12]. With this method, the monthly interest expense is $10 even though the loan balance declines with each payment. Simply stated, the true interest rate is higher than the 12 percent stated rate because the borrower is still paying $10 per month in interest even after the loan balance has declined.

Table 15.3 shows the first four months of the amortization schedule for the add-on method.

There are actuarial tables to determine the APR of the add-on method, but the use of the formula stated previously will approximate the APR:

$$APR = \frac{2 \times M \times I}{P(n + 1)}$$

where

M = number of payment periods in the year
I = total interest charge
P = initial amount of the loan
n = total number of payments

The APR for the 12 percent add-on loan is:

$$APR = \frac{2 \times 12 \times 120}{1,000(12 + 1)}$$

$$APR = 22.2\%$$

TABLE 15.3 Installment loan—add-on method

Monthly payment $93.33; interest rate 12%; term: 12 months

Month	Payment	Interest	Principal reduction	Loan balance
				$1,000.00
January	$93.33	$10	$83.33	916.67
February	93.33	10	83.33	833.34
March	93.33	10	83.33	750.01
April	93.33	10	83.33	666.68

The lender is required by federal law to disclose the APR. If you see that the APR is significantly higher than the stated rate, you know that the loan is an add-on method installment loan. Of the three methods (precomputed, simple interest, and add-on) used to calculate interest charges, the add-on method results in the highest interest charges and the greatest APR.

FINANCIAL CALCULATOR #16

How to Determine the Rate of Interest on Your Credit Cards

B ANKS AND FINANCIAL INSTITUTIONS, retail and oil companies offer credit cards. These companies are obliged to tell consumers the annual percentage rate (APR) charged as well as the method used to calculate the finance charges. In addition, they are obliged to disclose the *periodic rate*, which is the APR divided by the number of billing cycles per year (12 per year). For example, if the APR is 15 percent, then the periodic rate is 1.25 percent per month. However, if you are not in the habit of paying off your credit card balances in full, then the effective rate is much higher than 15 percent.

Credit card issuers are very creative with their enhancements to entice you to choose their cards. For example, most gold cards offer buyer protection packages and extended warranties on goods purchased with the cards. Besides the waiving of the annual fee, there are other factors to consider in choosing a credit card: the range of acceptance, the interest rates charged, the length of the grace period (the time between the billing date and the payment date), and other enhancement features.

If you are in the habit of paying your credit card bills in full every month, then choosing a credit card that has no annual fee and a grace period becomes important. However, if you are not in the habit of paying your credit card balances off in full, the interest rates charged become important. Interest rates charged by credit card issuers can vary significantly. Some issuers charge more than 20 percent. By shopping around, it is possible to find interest rates in the

9 to 15 percent range, possibly even lower. Bear in mind that even a 12 percent per annum rate works out to a monthly rate of 1 percent on the unpaid balance. This is still a substantial rate when you consider that savings accounts are only paying between 1 to 2.5 percent per annum. Be aware that some issuers of low-interest credit cards may not include a grace period.

If you sometimes pay your balances in full and other times run up a balance, you should carry two types of cards: a no-annual-fee card and a second, low–interest rate card. Credit card issuers can use several different methods to determine the average daily balance, which can make the effective interest rate much greater than the stated APR.

Outlined below are four different methods of determining finance charges: the first determines the average daily balance excluding new purchases, the second computes the average daily balance including new purchases, the third is the adjusted balance method, and the fourth is the previous balance method.

To illustrate the calculations, the same example is used for all methods. Assume the following:

APR	= 18%	New purchases on the 20th day of the month = $200
Periodic rate	= 1.5%	Payments on the 15th day of the month = $250
Unpaid balance = $500		

Average Daily Balance Excluding New Purchases

Step 1: Determine the Average Daily Balance

$$\text{Average daily balance} = \frac{(\$500 \times 15 \text{ days}) + (\$250 \times 15 \text{ days})}{30 \text{ days}}$$

$$= \frac{\$7,500 + \$3,750}{30}$$

$$= \$375$$

Step 2: Determine the Finance Charge to Be Added to the Next Month's Balance

$$\text{Interest/finance charge} = \text{Average daily balance} \times \text{Periodic rate}$$
$$= \$375 \times 0.015$$
$$= \$5.63$$

Average Daily Balance Including New Purchases

Step 1: Determine the Average Daily Balance

$$\text{Average daily balance} = \frac{(\$500 \times 15 \text{ days}) + (\$250 \times 5 \text{ days}) + (\$450 \times 10)}{30 \text{ days}}$$
$$= \frac{\$7,500 + \$1,250 + \$4,500}{30}$$
$$= \$441.67$$

Step 2: Determine the Finance Charge to Be Added to the Next Month's Balance

$$\text{Interest/finance charge} = \text{Average daily balance} \times \text{Periodic rate}$$
$$= \$441.67 \times 0.015$$
$$= \$6.63$$

Of these two methods, the finance charge will always be higher when the average daily balance includes new purchases.

The Adjusted Balance Method

This method determines the adjusted balance, which is the previous balance minus any payments made.

Step 1: Determine the Adjusted Balance

$$\text{Adjusted balance} = \text{Previous balance} - \text{payments}$$
$$= \$500 - \$250$$
$$= \$250$$

Step 2: Determine the Interest/Finance Charge

$$\text{Interest/finance charge} = \text{Adjusted balance} \times \text{Periodic rate}$$
$$= \$250 \times 0.015$$
$$= \$3.75$$

The Previous Balance Method

This method gives you no credit for payments made during the period. The previous balance is the same as the adjusted balance even if a substantial payment is made against the balance during the billing period.

Determine the Interest/Finance Charge

$$\text{Interest/finance charge} = \text{Adjusted balance} \times \text{Periodic rate}$$
$$= \$500 \times 0.015$$
$$= \$7.50$$

The previous balance method results in the highest interest/finance charge of all the methods. With the Truth in Lending law, the credit card issuer must tell you which method it uses. Worksheet 16.1 outlines the steps for determining the finance charges for the different methods.

WORKSHEET 16.1 Steps to determine the interest/finance charge on credit cards

$$\text{Average daily balance} = \frac{\text{Weighted average account balance}}{\text{Days in the billing cycle}}$$

$$= \underline{\hspace{4cm}}$$

$$= \underline{\hspace{4cm}}$$

Adjusted balance = Previous balance − payments

$$= \underline{\hspace{3cm}} - \underline{\hspace{3cm}}$$

$$= \underline{\hspace{3cm}}$$

Interest/finance charge = Average daily balance × periodic rate

or = Adjusted balance × periodic rate

or = Previous balance × periodic rate

Step 1 Determine the average daily balance for methods including and excluding new purchases.

Step 2 Determine the adjusted balance.

Step 3 Determine the interest/finance charge for all four methods.

FINANCIAL CALCULATOR #17

How to Manage Your Debt

IF YOU FIND THAT YOU ARE NOT SAVING ANY MONEY because most of your income is tied up in debt, or you are having to juggle your payments to service your debt payments on time, you have a problem. You should address your debt problem before it progresses to the point of your having to declare bankruptcy.

If you have too much debt, you need to reduce it. However, before determining a strategy, you need to examine your total debt—the individual components that make up the total—the costs, and the uses for this debt to determine your alternatives. Filling in Worksheet 17.1 is a starting point. By listing all your sources of debt, the uses for this debt, and the APR costs of each source of credit, you will have a better understanding of your situation and how to address any problems that might occur.

WORKSHEET 17.1 Sources of credit, uses, and costs

Sources of credit	Uses	Costs	Total liability	Interest and principal
Credit cards		APR%		
_____	_____	_____	_____	_____
_____	_____	_____	_____	_____
_____	_____	_____	_____	_____
_____	_____	_____	_____	_____
Bank loans				
_____	_____	_____	_____	_____
_____	_____	_____	_____	_____
_____	_____	_____	_____	_____
Education loans				
_____	_____	_____	_____	_____
_____	_____	_____	_____	_____
_____	_____	_____	_____	_____
Home equity loans				
_____	_____	_____	_____	_____
_____	_____	_____	_____	_____
Mortgage loan				
_____	_____	_____	_____	_____

The worksheet shows not only the monthly payments that you need to make to service your debt, but also the APR costs and uses for this debt. You can see your total indebtedness and evaluate whether you need to rein in your spending. For example, being indebted because of education loans is far preferable to being indebted because of frivolous spending on short-term consumption items such as restaurants and entertainment, and living it up. Investing in education improves your long-term earning power.

Based on the analysis of your debt and the costs, there are a number of alternatives that you could pursue. While you are pursuing these alternatives, you should stop making additional purchases using your credit cards. If your debt is more than you can handle, you should cut up all your credit cards and call the issuers to cancel your accounts.

Pay Down Your Debt from Savings

Paying down your debt from savings may seem like a senseless option in that you are urged to take money out of savings/investment plans to pay down debt. In the long-term, this approach can increase your net worth, however, particularly if the debt that you are paying down consists of high-interest credit cards. Borrowing at 12 to 18 percent per annum means that your investments need to earn in excess of these rates in order to justify not paying down debt from savings/investment accounts. Start paying down your highest APR cost debt first. While you are paying down this debt, do not charge any more purchases.

Roll Higher-Interest Credit Card Debt into a Lower-Rate Loan

If you have a good credit record, you can consolidate your high-interest credit card debt into a lower-rate bank loan, or home equity loan if you are a homeowner. This will reduce the amount of your monthly interest and principal payments. The downside to this strategy is that if you are unable to pay the monthly payments on your home equity loan, you could eventually lose your house.

Apply for Lower-Rate Credit Cards

If you have a good credit record, you can ask your credit card issuers to roll over your accounts into lower-rate credit card accounts. If this is not possible, look for other lower-rate credit card issuers and arrange for your balance to be transferred into these new accounts. Beware of low introductory rate credit cards that revert to high interest rates after a few months.

Contact Your Creditors or Get Credit Assistance

If you are having difficulty making your payments to your creditors on time, you should contact them. Tell them of your difficulties, but stress your intentions to pay them in full at a later date when you get your financial affairs back in order. Ask if they can stretch out your payments and waive interest and penalty fees until you can get on your feet again. If they agree, put it in writing so that it is more difficult for them to change their minds.

If they will not agree, seek credit counseling from a nonprofit credit counseling service. The toll-free number of a national nonprofit credit counseling office is 800-388-2227. This office will refer you to a local office. You will meet with a counselor who will, for a small fee, devise a repayment plan. Counselors will also call or meet with your creditors to get their agreement on the plan. For the plan to work, all of your creditors must agree to it and you may be precluded from taking on any new debt. If the credit counseling office manages your payments to creditors, you will be charged a monthly fee.

Declare Bankruptcy

If you are so swamped with debt that you are unable to take corrective action or if the amounts that you are able to repay are so small that it will take years to pay off your debt, there is a last resort—personal bankruptcy.

If you choose bankruptcy, you need to decide whether to seek legal help. Bankruptcy lawyers may charge a flat fee, which would depend on the nature and difficulty of the case. Legal help is expensive, but if you have a significant amount of assets that you want to retain after filing it may be advisable to seek such help.

You have two options to choose from in the Bankruptcy Code: Chapter 7, which accounts for the bulk of personal bankruptcy filings, or Chapter 13. Under Chapter 7, a court-appointed trustee takes title to your assets and sells them to raise money to repay creditors. Generally, the proceeds will not cover all the debts, which means that lenders must settle for less than the amounts that they were owed. The unpaid amounts are canceled. Certain debts are not exempt and must be fully repaid. You must pay student loans, alimony, child support, unpaid taxes, and certain other debts. You may keep certain assets. Some states are more generous than others with regard to assets you may retain.

Chapter 13 of the Bankruptcy Code allows you, under a court-approved plan, to repay debts in part or in full over an extended period of time. This is also known as the *wage earner's plan* because it protects the filer's wages and essential property from being surrendered. Filers pay their debts over an extended period of time and are protected from being sued by creditors.

Filing for bankruptcy may offer some relief from creditors, but there are some major disadvantages. Personal credit records are tainted for a period of 10 years, and many people (employers, landlords) may view you with disfavor. Finally, bankruptcy is an expensive way to correct the excessive use of credit.

The best way to manage your debt is to use credit with care and only when necessary.

FINANCIAL CALCULATOR #18

How Much of a Mortgage Can You Afford?

WHEN YOU ARE READY TO BUY a house or move into a larger house, the question to consider is: How much can you afford to spend on a house? Two rough guidelines apply to the affordability of a house:

- The house price can equal up to roughly 2¼ to 2½ times your annual income.
- All housing expenditures, which include mortgage payments, real estate taxes, and home owner's insurance, should be less than 28 percent of your gross income. If you have other debt payments, the total amount of your housing expenditures plus debt should fall below 35 to 38 percent of your monthly income. With this monthly payment, you can then determine the amount of the loan that you would qualify for and then back into the price of the house that you can afford.

These quick and easy formulas can be inaccurate for a large percentage of cases because everyone's financial circumstances are different. You need to consider many other factors, such as if you have enough cash for a down payment on a house and closing costs at settlement, and enough income to be able to maintain a house.

If you finance the purchase of a house with a mortgage, lenders require that you put some equity into the purchase, which is a down payment. Minimum down payments can vary from 5 to 20 percent of the purchase price. For example, a $150,000 house may be unaffordable if the lender requires a 20 percent down payment ($30,000), as opposed to a 5 percent down payment ($7,500), from someone whose income will qualify for a $142,500 mortgage but who does not have $30,000 in cash for a down payment.

You will also need to have enough cash to cover mortgage points and clos-ing costs. *Mortgage points* are up-front fees that lenders charge for borrowing. These vary from 0 to 3 percent of the mortgage loan. Hence, two points on a $95,000 mortgage would cost the buyer $1,900 (2% × $95,000). *Closing costs* are the costs of settlement, which can average 3 to 6 percent of the cost of the house. They include the costs for a title search, title insurance, attorney's fees, and recording fees.

Even if you have enough cash to cover the down payment, mortgage points, and closing costs, you need to be able to cover the costs of owning the house. These costs include your monthly mortgage payment, real estate taxes, home insurance premiums, utility costs, maintenance, and repairs. You also need to consider whether you can cover future increases in these costs.

Worksheet 18.1 presents a sequence of steps to determine the amount that you can afford for a house. It uses the general rule of thumb that lenders require that payments for housing not exceed 28 percent of gross income. If there are other outstanding debt payments, the combined housing and debt payments should not exceed 36 percent.

By working out how much you can afford for your mortgage payments, you can then determine the maximum amount of your mortgage as outlined in Worksheet 18.2. From this you can determine the range of house prices that you can afford. The actual purchase price that you can afford depends on the amount of your assets, which are not included in this computation. If there are no other assets, this figure may be on the high end of the acceptable range of purchase prices.

WORKSHEET 18.1 How to determine an affordable amount for a house

	Example	Worksheet
1. Fill in your total monthly income.	$8,000	_____ (1)
2. If you have no other debt payments, multiply your monthly income by 28%; if you do have other debt, multiply your income by 36%.	8,000 × 0.36 = $2,880	_____ (2) × 0.28 or 0.36 = (2)
3. Deduct other monthly debt payments.	– 450	_____ (3)
4. Deduct monthly property taxes and home insurance	– 300	_____ (4)
5. Deduct estimated maintenance and repairs	– 200	_____ (5)
6. Determine the monthly payment for a mortgage.	$1,930	_____ (6) = (2) – [(3) + (4) + 5]
7. Use Excel or a financial calculator to determine the total amount of the mortgage. See Worksheet 18.2: interest rate 7%; 30-year term mortgage.	$290,093.61	_____ (7)
8. Purchase price range of house: Divide mortgage amount in (6) by 0.9 with a 10% down payment, or by 0.8 with a 20% down payment	$290,093.61 ÷ 0.8 = $362,617.01	_____ (8) = (7) ÷ 0.9 or 0.8 _____ (9)

1. Click on the *f** key in the toolbar of Microsoft's Excel spreadsheet program.
2. Highlight *financial* in the left box and *PV* in the right box and click OK.
3. The following box comes up:

Rate
Nper
Pmt
FV
Type
Formula result =

4. Enter your data.

Interest rate per period	7% ÷ 12	_____
Number of payments for the term	360	_____
Monthly payment	$1,930	_____
FV	0	_____
Type	0	_____

The formula result is the amount
of the mortgage loan

$290,093.61 _____

Rate	.07 ÷ 12
Nper	360
Pmt	$1,930
FV	0
Type	0
Formula result = – $290,093.61	

FINANCIAL CALCULATOR #19

How to Calculate Your Monthly Mortgage Payment

A MORTGAGE IS A LONG-TERM LOAN taken out on a home/property or a piece of land. A conventional, fixed-rate mortgage has equal payments over the term of the mortgage. These equal payments are composed of two parts: an amount derived from interest on the loan balance, and an amount that goes toward the reduction of the loan balance.

A 30-year mortgage has 360 monthly payments (30 × 12); a 25-year mortgage has 300 monthly payments; and a 15-year mortgage has 180 payments. The amount of the equal monthly payments is highest for the 15-year mortgage as compared with the longer-term mortgages with the same rate of interest. Conversely, the total interest expense for the 15-year mortgage will be the lowest when compared with the longer-term mortgages. Table 19.1 illustrates these points by showing a comparison of the monthly payments, total interest, and total payments made on a $100,000 mortgage with an interest rate of 8 percent for different maturities.

The flexibility provided by the different maturities of the mortgages is important, especially for home owners whose incomes cannot support the higher payments of the shorter-duration mortgages. Many mortgage lenders require that the amount of the monthly payment not be greater than 28 to 36 percent of the home owner's income.

TABLE 19.1 Comparison of a $100,000, 8% mortgage for different maturities

Maturity	Monthly payment	Total interest	Total payments
15 years	$955.65	$72,017.00	$172,017.00
25 years	771.82	131,546.00	231,546.00
30 years	733.76	164,153.60	264,153.60

TABLE 19.2 The effect of different interest rates on a $100,000, 30-year mortgage

Interest rate	Monthly payment
6%	$599.55
7%	665.30
8%	733.76
9%	804.62
10%	877.57

A change in the interest rate has a great impact on the amount of the monthly payment. Table 19.2 illustrates the effect of different interest rates on the monthly payment for a $100,000, 30-year mortgage.

How to Lower Your Monthly Mortgage Payments

- Look for the lowest interest rate when shopping for a mortgage.
- Choose a shorter-term mortgage, which will increase your monthly payments over a longer-term mortgage with the same interest rate. However, the total interest and total amount paid will be lowest with a shorter-term mortgage.

How to Calculate the Monthly Payment

The monthly payment that is paid to the lender is an even annuity, and the amount lent by the lender is the present value of the annuity. Since payments are made on a monthly basis, divide the yearly interest rate by 12 to determine the monthly rate. The formula to determine the monthly payment is:

Present value = Monthly annuity (Present value of an ordinary annuity factor at i% for n periods)

Substituting the mortgage amount for the present value and the PV of an annuity factor from annuity tables, the monthly annuity can be determined. The tables in this book do not include 180, 300, and 360 periods. However, specifically designed mortgage tables can be purchased in most bookstores. With these tables, the monthly annuity payments can be easily determined.

Worksheet 19.1 outlines the steps to determine the monthly payment on a mortgage loan using Microsoft's Excel spreadsheet software. The use of a financial calculator can also assist in the determination of the monthly payment.

WORKSHEET 19.1 How to determine the monthly mortgage payment using Excel

1. Click on the *f** key in the toolbar of Microsoft's Excel spreadsheet program.
2. Highlight *financial* in the left box and *PMT* in the right box and click OK.
3. The following box comes up:

Rate	
Nper	
PV	
FV	
Type	
Formula result =	

4. Enter your data.

Example	**Your worksheet data**

Determine the monthly payment for
a $200,000, 30-year, 7% mortgage.

Rate	0.07 ÷ 12	_____
Nper	360	_____
PV	$200,000	_____
Type	0	_____

Using Excel, the formula result is $1,330.60.   _____

Rate	.07 ÷ 12
Nper	360
PV	$200,000
FV	0
Type	0
Formula result = $1,330.60	

How to Determine Your Mortgage Balance

MORTGAGES AND INSTALLMENT LOANS encompass the same financial principles and are essentially the same except for the length of their terms. Mortgages have terms of 15 to 30 years, whereas installment loans have shorter maturities. The maturities differ because the amount borrowed to finance the purchase of a house is invariably so large that it requires a long period of time to pay it back. The equal payments are made on a monthly basis, with a portion of the payment going toward principal reduction and the balance going toward covering the interest expense charged by the lender. In the early years of the mortgage a large proportion of the payment goes toward interest expense, as shown in the amortization schedule in Table 20.1. As the loan balance declines, the portion of the payment applied to interest expense declines and the portion applied to the principal reduction increases. Toward the end of the term of the mortgage, most of the payment is applied to reducing the loan balance.

There are many software programs that can print an amortization schedule such as the one in Table 20.1, which shows the first 20 payments on a $200,000, 7 percent, 30-year mortgage. Some financial calculators can also determine mortgage balances. However, if you have neither a computer nor a financial calculator, you can quite easily compute an amortization schedule using pen and paper.

How to Calculate an Amortization Schedule Using Pen and Paper

Using the same example as above, a $200,000, 7 percent, 30-year mortgage with equal monthly payments of $1,330.60, the first step is to determine how much of each payment is applied to interest and how much goes toward reducing the loan balance. Assume that in this example the mortgage for $200,000

TABLE 20.1 Amortization schedule for a $200,000, 7%, 30-year mortgage

Payment number	Payment amount	Principal reduction	Interest	Loan balance
				$200,000.00
1	$1,330.60	$163.93	$1,166.67	199,836.07
2	1,330.60	164.89	1,165.71	199,671.18
3	1,330.60	165.85	1,164.75	199,505.33
4	1,330.60	166.82	1,163.78	199,338.51
5	1,330.60	167.79	1,162.81	199,170.72
6	1,330.60	168.77	1,161.83	199,001.95
7	1,330.60	169.76	1,160.84	198,832.19
8	1,330.60	170.75	1,159.85	198,661.44
9	1,330.60	171.74	1,158.86	198,489.70
10	1,330.60	172.74	1,157.86	198,316.96
11	1,330.60	173.75	1,156.85	198,143.21
12	1,330.60	174.76	1,155.84	197,968.45
13	1,330.60	175.78	1,154.82	197,792.67
14	1,330.60	176.81	1,153.79	197,615.86
15	1,330.60	177.84	1,152.76	197,438.02
16	1,330.60	178.88	1,151.72	197,259.14
17	1,330.60	179.92	1,150.68	197,079.22
18	1,330.60	180.97	1,149.63	196,898.25
19	1,330.60	182.03	1,148.57	196,716.22
20	1,330.60	183.09	1,147.51	196,533.13

is taken out on January 1. The first payment of $1,330.60 is made on January 31. The interest expense is the interest rate per month, which is 0.00583333 (0.07÷12). Multiply the loan balance outstanding at the beginning of the month by this monthly rate to get the interest expense for the month (200,000 × 0.00583333 = 1,166.67). Thus, from the payment of $1,330.60, $1,166.67 is applied to interest and the balance (1,330.60 − 1,166.67) of $163.93 goes toward repaying the loan. The new loan balance becomes the old balance minus the principal reduction, which is 199,836.07 ($200,000.00 − 163.93). Repeating this procedure gives February's figures, and by continuing the procedure the entire amortization schedule can be determined. Table 20.2 shows the first few months of the schedule.

Worksheet 20.1 outlines the steps for you to determine your own amortization schedule.

TABLE 20.2 Determination of an amortization schedule

Date	Payment (a)	Interest (b)	Principal reduction (c)	Loan balance (d)
Jan 1				$200,000.00
Jan 31	$1,330.60	$1,166.67	$163.93	199,836.07
Feb 28	1,330.60	1,165.71	164.89	199,671.18

Interest = rate per month multiplied by the loan balance at the beginning of the month

$$= 0.00583333 \times 200,000$$
$$= \$1,166.67$$

Principal reduction = payment minus interest expense (a) – (b)
$$= 1,330.60 - 1,166.67$$
$$= 163.93$$

New loan balance = old balance minus principal reduction (d) – (c)
$$= 200,000 - 163.93$$
$$= 199,836.07$$

February Interest $= 0.00583333 \times 199,836.07$

$$= 1,165.71$$

Principal reduction $= 1,330.60 - 1,165.71$ (a) – (b)

$$= 164.89$$

New loan balance $= 199,836.07 - 164.89$ (d) – (c)
$$= 199,671.18$$

WORKSHEET 20.1 How to determine your own mortgage amortization schedule

Date	Payment (a)	Interest (b)	Principal reduction (c)	Loan balance (d)
_____				_____
_____	_____	_____	_____	_____
_____	_____	_____	_____	_____
_____	_____	_____	_____	_____
_____	_____	_____	_____	_____
_____	_____	_____	_____	_____
_____	_____	_____	_____	_____
_____	_____	_____	_____	_____
_____	_____	_____	_____	_____
_____	_____	_____	_____	_____
_____	_____	_____	_____	_____
_____	_____	_____	_____	_____
_____	_____	_____	_____	_____
_____	_____	_____	_____	_____

Step 1 Fill in the loan balance at the beginning of the period.

Step 2 Fill in the monthly payments in column (a).

Step 3 Divide the interest rate of the loan by 12 to get the monthly rate.

Step 4 Multiply the monthly rate by the beginning loan balance to determine the interest expense (b).

Step 5 Subtract the interest expense from the monthly payment to determine the principal reduction (c) = (a) – (b).

Step 6 Determine the new loan balance by subtracting the principal reduction from the old balance (d) – (c).

For the next month's figures, go through steps 4–6.

Determine Your Mortgage Balance When Additional Principal Payments Are Made

THERE ARE MANY TRADE-OFFS WHEN CHOOSING a mortgage/loan. Most borrowers want to limit the amount that they pay for a mortgage, but this means that they need to put up a larger down payment or borrow less. Similarly, by extending the term of the mortgage/loan, the monthly payments are smaller but the amount of interest paid over the life of the loan increases. This trend is illustrated in Table 21.1.

The flexibility provided by the different lengths of the mortgages is important, especially for home owners whose incomes cannot support the higher payments of the shorter-duration mortgages. However, home owners can still reduce the amount of total interest paid on longer-duration mortgages by making additional payments of principal. This strategy is illustrated in Table 21.2, where the same principles apply as for an amortization schedule except that the loan balance is reduced by the additional principal payment. The table assumes a $100,000, 7 percent, 30-year mortgage, with a monthly payment of $665.30; with the first payment, an additional $300 is sent to the mortgage company.

To complete the amortization schedule, you need to work through the three steps for each month before moving on to the next month. In other words, you cannot work through an additional three months of interest and then move to the principal reduction. You would need to determine the

TABLE 21.1 Comparison of a 13%, $100,000 mortgage with different maturities

Maturity	Monthly payment	Total interest	Total payments
15 years	$1,265.24	$127,743.59	$227,743.20
25 years	1,127.84	238,350.59	338,350.00
30 years	1,106.20	298,231.83	398,232.00

TABLE 21.2 The construction of an amortization schedule with additional payments

Date	Payment (a)	Additional payment (b)	Interest (c)	Principal reduction (d)	Loan balance (e)
6/01					$100,000.00
6/30	$665.30	$300.00	$583.33	$381.97	99,618.03
7/01	665.30	350.00	581.11	434.19	99,183.84
8/31	665.30	150.00	578.57	236.73	98,947.11
9/30	665.30	0.00	577.19	88.11	98,859.00

Interest = monthly interest rate times loan balance of the previous month:
$$0.07 \div 12 \times (e)$$

$6/30 = 0.00583333 \times 100,000.00 = \$583.33$
$7/31 = 0.00583333 \times 99,618.03 = 581.11$
$8/31 = 0.00583333 \times 99,183.84 = 578.57$
$9/30 = 0.00583333 \times 98,947.11 = 577.19$

Principal reduction = payment + addt'l payment − interest: (a) + (b) − (c) = (d)
$6/30$ $\$665.30 + 300.00 - 583.33 = 381.97$
$7/31$ $665.30 + 350.00 - 581.11 = 434.19$
$8/31$ $665.30 + 150.00 - 578.57 = 236.73$
$9/30$ $665.30 + 0.00 - 577.19 = 88.11$

Loan balance = beginning loan balance − principal reduction: (e) − (d)
$6/30$ $\$100,000.00 - 381.97 = 99,618.03$
$7/31$ $99,618.03 - 434.19 = 99,183.84$
$8/31$ $99,183.84 - 236.73 = 98,947.11$
$9/30$ $98,947.11 - 88.11 = 98,859.00$

interest expense for the next month, and then determine the principal reduction and new loan balance before determining the interest for the next month.

Making extra payments of principal decreases the total interest paid on the loan/mortgage. Worksheet 21.1 provides the outline and steps for the construction of your own mortgage schedule with additional payments.

WORKSHEET 21.1 How to determine an amortization schedule with additional payments of principal

Date	Payment (a)	Additional payment (b)	Interest (c)	Principal reduction (d)	Loan balance (e)
____					____
____	____	____	____	____	____
____	____	____	____	____	____
____	____	____	____	____	____
____	____	____	____	____	____
____	____	____	____	____	____
____	____	____	____	____	____
____	____	____	____	____	____
____	____	____	____	____	____
____	____	____	____	____	____
____	____	____	____	____	____
____	____	____	____	____	____
____	____	____	____	____	____
____	____	____	____	____	____
____	____	____	____	____	____

Step 1 Fill in the loan balance at the beginning of the period.

Step 2 Fill in the monthly payments in column (a).

Step 3 Enter the additional payment (b).

Step 4 Divide the interest rate of the loan by 12 to get the monthly rate.

Step 5 Multiply the monthly rate by the beginning loan balance to determine the interest expense (c).

Step 6 Subtract the interest expense from the sum of the monthly payment to determine the principal reduction (d) = (a) + (b) − (c).

Step 7 Determine the new loan balance by subtracting the principal reduction from the old balance (e) − (d)

For the next month's figures, go through steps 3–7.

Making extra payments on a loan not only saves you interest but also shortens the length of the loan. Beware of institutions that offer to assist you in the additional payments of your mortgage. They are offered under the name of biweekly mortgages and various other names. If you do not have a prepayment penalty clause in your mortgage, you can make additional payments by yourself without the help of these institutions. These institutions charge fees and collect your payments twice a month, but they submit a payment to your mortgage company only at the end of the month. Thus, they have the use of your money to your detriment, and you end up paying them for this.

FINANCIAL CALCULATOR #22

Adjustable Rate Mortgages and How They Work

CONVENTIONAL MORTGAGES HAVE A fixed interest rate over the term of the mortgage, but with an adjustable rate mortgage (ARM) the interest rate fluctuates over the life of the loan. With an ARM, the borrower bears the risk of changing interest rates, whereas with a conventional fixed-rate mortgage, the lender bears the risk of changing interest rates in the economy. When interest rates rise, the lender of a conventional mortgage is stuck holding a lower–interest rate mortgage. On the other hand, if interest rates fall the borrower is stuck holding a higher-rate mortgage, but the borrower has the option of refinancing the mortgage with a lower-rate loan.

With an ARM, the interest rate changes according to an index selected by the lender. The adjustment period varies on a quarterly, semiannual, or annual basis, or for longer periods of time. Some indices are more volatile than others, so you should take care in selecting your ARM by investigating the index tied to the mortgage. For example, if you anticipate a decline in interest rates, you would want an ARM that has an index that is tied to one-year Treasury securities versus a slower-moving index tied to five-year Treasury securities.

ARMs are offered at lower rates than conventional mortgages, usually 1 to 3 percent lower. Some ARMs are offered at very low rates, known as *teaser rates*, to encourage borrowers. However, after a short period of time, generally a year, the rate reverts back to normal rates.

With an ARM, a decline in the interest rate results in a drop in the monthly payment; conversely, an increase in the rate results in an increase in the monthly payment. Consequently, borrowers should always work out the worst-case scenario to make sure that they can cover those larger payments.

There are a number of features of these loans that you should consider before settling on a particular ARM. Worksheet 22.1 provides a checklist of these features to assist you in your choice of an adjustable rate loan. Most ARMs have interest rate caps and/or payment caps. *Interest rate caps* limit the amount of the rate increase or decrease over the term of the mortgage. Commonly, there is a limit from one adjustment period to another (for example,

---

WORKSHEET 22.1 Comparison list for choosing an adjustable rate mortgage (ARM)

Financial institution			
Loan amount			
Points			
Down payment			
Beginning APR			
Beginning monthly payment			
Interest rate cap			
Lifetime rate cap			
Payment cap			
Maximum monthly payment			
Negative amortization yes/no			
Type of index			
Prepayment penalty			
Convertible ARM			

no more than 2 percent a year) and a lifetime interest rate cap (no more than 6 percentage points, for example, over the life of the loan).

Payment caps limit the amount of the payment increases or decreases at adjustment periods and over the life of the loan. If an ARM has a payment cap without an equivalent interest rate cap, when interest rates rise significantly, there is the possibility of the payment not covering the interest expense, which causes *negative amortization*. This means that instead of the loan balance declining with the monthly payment, it will increase. For example, an ARM with a payment cap of $700 per month has an interest rate increase to 10 percent, which results in a monthly payment of $720. The additional $20 of the payment is not covered and will be added to the mortgage balance, thereby increasing the amount to be paid back. Avoid an ARM with a payment cap.

In evaluating the different ARMs, the most important factors are the interest rate caps and the frequency of rate changes, the upper and lower limits on the monthly payments, the type of index to which the mortgage is tied, and whether there is negative amortization. Other factors to consider are a prepayment penalty and a conversion privilege. The former refers to the ability to pay down additional principal without being penalized, and with the latter, the borrower has the option to convert to a fixed-rate mortgage within a certain period of time. Avoid loans with prepayment penalties.

How to Calculate an ARM Schedule

Assume an ARM of $100,000 with an initial rate of 4 percent, an adjustment period of a year, and an annual interest rate cap of 1 percent with a lifetime cap of 5 percentage points, for a term of 30 years.

Step 1: Determine the Monthly Payment

The monthly payment can be determined using Microsoft's Excel program, as shown here, or with a financial calculator.

Rate	.04 ÷ 12
Nper	360
PV	$ –770.36
FV	0
Type	0
Formula result = $477.415	

The monthly payment is $477.42. With software programs, you can print out an amortization schedule. Alternatively, you can easily prepare one by hand, as shown next.

Step 2: Determine the Amortization Schedule to the End of the First Adjustment Period

In Table 22.1, the interest is determined by multiplying the monthly rate (0.04 ÷ 12) by the beginning loan balance. The interest is deducted from the payment to determine the principal reduction, which is then deducted from the beginning loan balance to determine the new loan balance.

TABLE 22.1 Amortization schedule to the end of the first adjustment period

Date	Payment	Interest	Principal reduction	Loan balance
				$100,000.00
1	$477.42	$333.33	$144.09	99,855.91
2	477.42	332.85	144.57	99,711.34
3	477.42	332.37	145.05	99,566.29
4	477.42	331.89	145.53	99,420.76
5	477.42	331.40	146.02	99,274.74
—	—	—	—	—
12	477.42	327.96	149.46	98,238.91

Step 3: If the Interest Rate Changes, Determine the New Monthly Payment

There are two changes involved in the determination of the new monthly payment. There is a rate change (the rate could go up or down by 1 percent from the beginning rate of 4 percent) and the new term for the mortgage is 29 years (348 monthly payments). If the rate goes up to 5 percent and the principal balance is $98,238.91, the new monthly payment will be $535.26, determined as follows using Excel:

Rate   0.05 ÷ 12
Nper   348
PV $98,238.91
FV   0
Type   0
Formula result = $535.264

Step 4: Determine the New Amortization Schedule

The following adjusted data is used to determine the new amortization schedule (Table 22.2).

TABLE 22.2 Amortization schedule for the beginning of the second adjustment period

Date	Payment	Interest	Principal reduction	Loan balance
				$98,238.91
13	$535.26	$409.33	$125.93	98,112.98
14	535.26	408.80	126.46	97,986.52

Interest rate   = 0.05 ÷ 12
Loan balance = $98,238.91
Payment   = $535.26

$$\text{Interest} = 0.05 \div 12 \times \$98,238.91$$
$$= \$409.33$$

$$\text{Principal reduction} = \$535.26 - \$409.33$$
$$= \$125.93$$

$$\text{New loan balance} = \$98,238.91 - \$125.93$$
$$= \$98,112.98$$

These steps are repeated to determine the new monthly data until there is a new rate change. If the rate goes down, the new rate will be used together with the remaining months to term and the current loan balance to determine the new monthly payment.

Worksheet 22.2 outlines the steps for you to determine your own amortization schedule.

WORKSHEET 22.2 Steps to determine your amortization schedule

Step 1 Determine your monthly payment.

_____

Step 2 Determine the amortization schedule through the end of the first adjustment period.

Monthly payment _____   Monthly rate _____
Term of loan   _____   Loan balance _____

Date	Payment	Principal interest	Loan reduction	Loan balance
_____	_____	_____	_____	_____
_____	_____	_____	_____	_____

Step 3 With a rate change, determine your new monthly payment.

Use the number of months remaining for the loan, the new monthly interest rate, and the loan balance at the beginning of the month (end of last month).

New monthly payment _____

Step 4 Determine your new amortization schedule.

Date	Payment	Principal interest	Loan reduction	Loan balance
_____	_____	_____	_____	_____
_____	_____	_____	_____	_____

Steps 3 and 4 are repeated at the next rate change.

Which Type of Mortgage Should You Choose?

A LTHOUGH ONLY TWO MAJOR TYPES of mortgages, fixed and adjustable rate, have been discussed, there are many variants of these. No matter what type of mortgage you consider, take the time to understand how the mortgage works and all the intricacies of that mortgage.

Factors to Consider When Choosing a Mortgage

In weighing the choices between fixed-rate and adjustable rate mortgages, you should consider three factors:

1. Market rates of interest
2. The length of time that you plan to hold your mortgage
3. Your willingness to take on financial risk

The trade-off is a fixed monthly mortgage payment for the term of the loan with a fixed-rate mortgage versus initial lower monthly payments and the possibility of future increased monthly payments in the event of rising interest rates with an adjustable rate mortgage.

Market Rates of Interest

If market rates are low or have been declining over the past few years, you should consider a fixed-rate mortgage. Alternatively, if market rates are high and are expected to decline, you may be swayed toward an adjustable rate mortgage (ARM). With the latter, you need to determine the maximum monthly ARM payment in the worst-case scenario to determine whether the initial benefits of lower ARM payments outweigh the risk of higher payments in the future, should interest rates rise.

Length of Time That You Plan to Hold Your Mortgage

The length of time that you plan on holding the mortgage is crucial to your decision. Savings on an ARM are guaranteed until the end of the first adjustment period, and with the adjustments if interest rates do go up, you may still be able to save over a fixed-rate mortgage for a few years. If you plan to hold the mortgage for a short time, three years or less, the total payments on an ARM may be lower than those on a fixed-rate mortgage. You would need to work through the calculations to determine whether you should choose an ARM over a fixed-rate mortgage. Worksheet 23.1 outlines the steps for these calculations.

If you plan on holding your mortgage for longer than five to seven years, you may be better off with a fixed-rate mortgage. After all, even mortgage bankers do not know what will happen with interest rates into the future. If they did, they would not issue loans where they bear the risk of changes in interest rates. For example, if they knew that interest rates were going to decline in the future, they would issue only fixed-rate mortgages. Similarly, if they thought that interest rates were going to increase, they would issue only ARMs.

Your Willingness to Bear Risk

With an ARM, the borrower bears the risk of higher monthly payments if interest rates rise. You need to assess your own situation as to whether you can afford these higher monthly payments. Will these higher monthly payments make it difficult for you to make ends meet in your budget? Is your income from your job stable? If you cannot easily afford the highest possible monthly payments, you should go for a fixed-rate mortgage.

If there are any savings in Step 7, this amount can be invested. The invested savings will be even greater in the future when the time value of money is taken into account.

WORKSHEET 23.1 Adjustable rate or fixed-rate mortgage

Step 1 Fill in the length of time that you plan on holding your mortgage.

_____ (1)

Step 2 Determine the monthly total savings from an ARM over a fixed-rate mortgage through the end of the first adjustment period.

ARM	**Fixed-rate mortgage**

Monthly payment _____ (a)   Monthly payment _____ (b)

Savings with an ARM (b) – (a) _____ – _____ = _____ (c)

Total savings [number of months × (c)] _____ × _____ = _____ (d)

Step 3 Assume the maximum rate increase until the next adjustment period.

ARM	**Fixed-rate mortgage**

Monthly payment _____ (a)   Monthly payment _____ (b)

Savings with an ARM (b) – (a) _____ – _____ = _____ (c)

Total savings [number of months × (c)] _____ × _____ = _____ (d1)

Step 4 Add total savings from Steps 2 & 3 (d) + (d1) _____ + _____ = _____ (e)

Step 5 Repeat Steps 3 & 4 until you reach the length of time in Step 1.

Step 6 Add the total savings, including any negative numbers (if ARM payments are greater than fixed-rate monthly payments) to determine the total savings.

Step 7 If the total is a positive amount, choose an ARM; if it is negative, go with a fixed-rate mortgage.

Worksheet 23.2 is an example that illustrates the use of Worksheet 23.1. Assume a comparison of an ARM with initial monthly payments of $530.20 versus fixed monthly payments of $604.30. With the maximum increase at the end of the first adjustment period (after one year), the monthly payment for the ARM is $576.00. The next maximum increase after the second 12 months raises the monthly payment to $615.65. The holder plans on holding the mortgage for three years.

WORKSHEET 23.2 Adjustable rate or fixed rate mortgage filled in

Step 1 Fill in the length of time that you plan on holding your mortgage.

   36 months (1)

Step 2 Determine the monthly total savings from an ARM over a fixed-rate mortgage through the end of the first adjustment period.

ARM	**Fixed-rate mortgage**

Monthly payment $530.20 (a)   Monthly payment $604.30 (b)

Savings with an ARM (b) – (a) $604.30 – $530.20 = $74.10 (c)

Total savings [number of months × (c)] 12 × $74.10 = $889.20 (d)

Step 3 Assume the maximum rate increase until the next adjustment period.

ARM	**Fixed-rate mortgage**

Monthly payment $576.00 (a)   Monthly payment $604.30 (b)

Savings with an ARM (b) – (a) $604.30 – $576.00 = $28.30 (c)

Total savings [number of months × (c)] 12 × $28.30 = $339.60 (d1)

Step 4 Add total savings from Steps 2 & 3 (d) + (d1) $889.20 + $339.60 = $1,228.80 (e)

Step 5 Repeat Steps 3 & 4 until you reach the length of time in Step 1.

ARM	**Fixed-rate mortgage**

Monthly payment $615.65 (a)   Monthly payment $604.30 (b)

Savings with an ARM (b) – (a) $604.30 – $615.65 = – $11.35 (c)

Total savings [number of months × (c)] 12 × – $11.35 = – $136.20 (d2)

After 36 months the total savings for the ARM is:
   $889.20 + $339.60 – $136.20 = $1,092.60

When Should You Refinance Your Mortgage?

THERE ARE THREE MAJOR REASONS for refinancing a mortgage:

1. To lower monthly payments because interest rates have come down
2. To switch from one type of mortgage to another; for example, from an ARM to a fixed-rate mortgage or any other type of mortgage
3. To create a source of capital by refinancing for a greater capital amount

When interest rates decline, refinancing your old mortgage with a new, lower-rate mortgage can lower your monthly payments. However, there are costs associated with refinancing. The closing costs to refinance a mortgage typically range from 3 to 5 percent of the loan. In order to lower your monthly payments from refinancing, you have to pay a lump sum amount in closing costs. Thus, there are two factors that should be considered in determining whether you should refinance: the length of time that you plan on staying in your house and the amount of the savings from the lower mortgage payments. Taking into account the closing costs and the lower mortgage payments, you can use Worksheet 24.1 to see if you will reach the break-even point to justify refinancing your mortgage.

If you have an adjustable rate mortgage (ARM) and you decide that you are going to stay in your house for a longer period of time than originally expected, you can refinance to a fixed-rate mortgage. The prospect of fluctuating mortgage payments with an ARM may make you uncomfortable, causing you to refinance to a fixed-rate mortgage to give yourself peace of mind. In such a case, you may not save any money by trading in an ARM for a fixed-rate mortgage, as rates are much higher on the latter, but you will have secured some peace of mind with fixed monthly payments.

WORKSHEET 24.1 How much will you save from refinancing?

	Example	Your worksheet
Refinancing costs		
Application fee	50	_____
Points	2,000	_____
Title search and insurance	1,000	_____
Credit report	100	_____
Survey	250	_____
Appraisal	300	_____
Inspection fees	300	_____
Attorney fees	1,000	_____
Recording fees	75	_____
Other fees	0	_____
Total refinancing costs	$5,075	(a) _____
Monthly savings		
Current monthly payment	$1,069	_____
New monthly payment	– 919	– _____
Savings	150	(b) _____

Number of months to break even: 5,075 ÷ 150 = 34   (a) ÷ (b) _____
Refinance costs divided by monthly savings

There are other types of mortgages, such as graduated payment mortgages and mortgages with balloon payments, that you may want to switch to a conventional fixed-rate mortgage for the same reasons as cited above. With a *graduated payment mortgage*, the monthly payments are lower than they would normally be in the early years of the mortgage and then increase over a period of time to take into account the lower earlier payments of the loan. There are a number of disadvantages with this type of mortgage, in that the total interest paid will be much greater than on a conventional loan and there may also be some negative amortization. Also, if your income does not rise as anticipated, it may be harder to meet the higher mortgage payments after the initial low-payment period. A *balloon mortgage* has a shorter term with equal monthly payments, and then at the end of the mortgage there is a large payment. Even if there are no savings from trading one type of mortgage for another, you may want to refinance to give yourself greater peace of mind.

Because interest on a mortgage is still a tax-deductible item for taxpayers who itemize their deductions, many people refinance their mortgages for higher amounts in order to get the additional cash that they need for various purposes. The money might be used to pay off high-interest consumer debt, which is not tax deductible, to raise funds to start a business, or to buy a new car.

Refinancing a mortgage at a lower rate will reduce your monthly payments, as well as the total interest paid on the mortgage.

In the worksheet example, in order to recoup the costs of refinancing, the borrower would need to stay in the house for at least 34 months to break even and longer to experience the benefits of refinancing.

FINANCIAL CALCULATOR #25

Should You Rent or Buy a House?

T HE QUESTION OF WHETHER TO RENT or buy is a matter of individual choice. It is relatively easy to list the financial factors concerning renting and buying, but the nonfinancial considerations are much more difficult to weigh.

Housing decisions are extremely important from many viewpoints. The purchase of a home is probably the largest single expenditure that individuals make. For renters, rental expenses could account for up to 40 percent of their monthly budgets. However, the housing decision goes beyond expenditures because where you choose to live determines your commuting time to work, access to shopping, your neighborhood friends, your children's friends, the school system, and so on. A tremendous amount of time and thought are invested in making housing decisions.

In addition to financial reasons, some people rent because they may not want to be faced with the responsibilities of home ownership or they may expect to be in a location for only a short period of time.

There are several advantages to renting:

- You have greater mobility when you rent. When your lease expires, you can leave without having to sell the property. If mobility is important to you, do not tie yourself down with a long-term lease without an escape clause.
- You are not tying up your money (other than the amount of the security deposit), which means that you can invest your money or use it for other purposes.
- Renting may result in reduced expenses for maintenance and repairs. Landlords are usually responsible for most, if not all, repairs.

The disadvantages of renting are:

- Your rental payments give you no ownership interest.
- You have no control over rental increases.
- If the property appreciates, you do not share in the appreciation.
- You cannot deduct your rental payments against your federal taxes (interest on a mortgage and real estate taxes are currently tax-deductible expenses).
- Your lease may restrict you from having pets or starting a family.
- You could have loud, messy neighbors or an ineffectual landlord.

Renting is much simpler and less time consuming than buying a house. For example, if you rent a house in a neighborhood that has poor schools or high crime, you can easily move out. If you have bought the house, the problem will be more time consuming to rectify, and probably more costly.

From a home owner's point of view, there are several advantages to home ownership:

- Over long periods of time, most housing units appreciate in value and prices tend to keep pace with inflation. Home ownership could be considered an investment as well as a hedge against inflation.
- Home ownership provides some tax relief in that the interest expense on the mortgage and the real estate taxes are deductible items from taxable income at the federal level. Interest expense on a mortgage is not subject to being added back to the computation of the alternative minimum tax (AMT).
- Over time, home owners increase their equity position in their homes if they had financed their purchase. A portion of each mortgage payment goes toward the repayment of the mortgage. Thus, over time, home owners owe less and their equity stake increases.
- Home owners who have sufficient equity in their homes or who have seen price appreciation of their homes can use the buildup as a source to provide new loans, such as home equity loans.
- Home ownership provides more freedom than renting. There are no landlords and no restrictions concerning pets, children, and so on.
- Home ownership often brings about a greater personal commitment to the neighborhood and community activities.

The disadvantages of home ownership are:

- With home ownership, you bear the financial risk if property values fall. If you have to sell your house when the property market is depressed, you could lose money.
- Home ownership decreases your mobility. It may not be that easy to sell a house and move to another location in a short period of time.

The decision of whether to rent or buy is not always clear-cut or easy. An evaluation of both the financial and nonfinancial aspects helps to resolve the dilemma. Worksheet 25.1 compares the costs of renting versus buying to see which is lower. The calculation in this example is used only to illustrate the process involved and is not meant to show that it is always less costly to

WORKSHEET 25.1 Comparison of the costs of renting versus buying

		Example	Your worksheet
Annual cost of renting			
Rent ($1,000 × 12)		$12,000	_____
Utilities (150 × 12)		1,800	_____
Tenant's insurance		200	_____
Interest foregone on the deposit			
($1,000 × 6% × (1 – 30%*))		42	_____
Total annual cost of renting		**$14,042**	_____
Annual cost of buying			
(with a mortgage of $90,000 at 10%)			
Mortgage payment ($967 × 12)		$11,604	_____
Real estate taxes		2,400	_____
Maintenance & repairs (100 × 12)		1,200	_____
Utilities (200 × 12)		2,400	_____
Insurance		500	_____
Interest foregone on the down payment			
10,000 × 6% × (1 – 30%*)		420	_____
Gross annual cost of buying		**$18,524**	_____
Less tax savings from deductions:			
Interest on mortgage	$8,877		_____
Real estate taxes	2,400		_____
	11,277		_____
× marginal tax rate*	× 0.30	×	_____
Tax savings		(3,383)	_____
Less equity buildup		(2,727)	_____
Net annual cost of buying		**$12,414**	_____

These costs could be adjusted further for any appreciation of the property.

*A 30% marginal tax rate is assumed.

buy. In some areas, rental expenses may be low and interest rates on mortgages may be comparatively high, making mortgage payments very high. Consequently, it may be beneficial to rent until mortgage interest rates come down.

In the worksheet example, the cost of renting ($14,042) is higher than the after-tax cost of buying ($12,414). You need to consider, however, that many of these figures will change over a period of a few years: rent increases, increased home maintenance costs, decreasing mortgage interest expenses, and possible short-term appreciation/depreciation of home prices. Home ownership provides many more financial advantages. However, if you intend to move in the near future, renting may be more advantageous than buying.

FINANCIAL CALCULATOR #26
What You Should Know About Leasing a Car and How a Lease Works

THE POPULARITY OF LEASING CARS has increased, as evidenced by the growing number of automotive advertisements in print and on radio and television containing information about specific leases. However, just because leasing is popular does not mean that it is the right alternative for you. There are a number of things that you should know about leasing before taking the plunge.

Leasing an automobile is a contractual obligation to make monthly payments over a predetermined period of time, usually two, three, or four years. Depending on the type of lease, the car may be returned to the leasing company at termination.

There are two basic types of leases: open end and closed end. An open-end lease involves monthly lease payments made for the period of the lease. At the end of the lease, a final payment based on the resale value is made to buy the car. With a closed-end lease, lease payments are made over the lease period. At the end of the lease, you hand in the keys and walk away from the car. Certain conditions apply, such as returning the car in reasonable condition and not exceeding the maximum mileage set by the lease agreement.

Most of the advertisements in the media are for closed-end leases, in which there is the implication that leasing is cheaper than financing a car. Don't be misled until you do your homework on the specifics of the lease. Leasing companies have to buy the cars that they lease, and after the leasing period these cars have depreciated considerably. Consequently, leasing companies charge to recover both the interest costs that they have paid to buy the cars and the amount of the depreciation of the cars (the fall in resale value) when they are returned to them, in addition to their overhead costs and a certain amount of profit. Thus, you need to know the details of your lease, as outlined in Worksheet 26.1, because they determine the amount of the lease payments.

The first item in the worksheet is the *capitalized cost* of the car, which is the selling price of the car. To lower your lease payments, you need to negotiate the selling price of the car. The lower the capitalized cost, the lower your lease payments. Thus, don't fall into the trap of thinking that you do not need to negotiate when you lease a car.

The *capitalized cost reduction* includes the trade-in value of your old car, or the amount of the down payment. This category also includes dealer rebates and discounts.

The *adjusted capitalized cost* is the capitalized cost minus the cost reduction, which is the amount used to determine the monthly lease payment.

The *residual value* is the estimated value of the car at the end of the lease. The percentage is supplied by the car dealer or lease company. In this case, it is 47 percent, which is then multiplied by the manufacturer's suggested retail price (MSRP). Should you decide to buy the car at the end of the lease, this is the amount that you would pay. There is no reason why you cannot negotiate an amount that is less than the residual value when you are ready to purchase the car at the end of the lease.

Depreciation is the amount charged for the decline in value of the car. The amount for depreciation is divided by the number of months in the lease term to determine the monthly amount for depreciation that is a major part of your lease payment.

WORKSHEET 26.1 How to determine your lease payment

The example uses the following figures, as provided by Clews & Strawbridge, Inc., to lease a new Saab 9-5 with a MSRP of $37,990. The negotiated price is $36,990.

	Example	Your worksheet
Depreciation		
1. Capitalized cost*	$36,990.00	_____
2. Capitalized cost reduction*	5,000.00	_____
3. Adjusted capitalized cost (1 – 2)	31,990.00	_____
4. Residual value*	17,855.40	_____
5. Depreciation (3 – 4)	14,134.60	_____
6. Number of months in lease term	36	_____
7. Depreciation per month (5 ÷ 6)	392.63	_____
Finance expense		
8. Adjusted cap. cost plus residual value (3 + 4)	49,845.40	_____
9. Money factor*	0.0028	_____
10. Monthly finance expense (8 × 9)	139.57	_____
Sales Tax		
11. Monthly sales tax (7 + 10) × 0.09*	47.90	_____
Monthly lease payment (7 + 10 + 11)	580.10	_____

*Figures provided by Clews & Strawbridge, Inc.

The second factor that contributes toward your monthly lease payment is the finance expense. Many lease companies use a *money factor* instead of an interest rate. Multiplying the money factor by 24 will give an approximation of the interest rate charged. In this case, the money factor of 0.0028 equals 6.72 percent.

The last item that contributes toward your monthly lease payment is sales tax. In this case it is 9 percent of the sum of the monthly finance expense and the depreciation charge.

How to Lower Your Monthly Lease Payments

1. Negotiate the price of the car. The lower the price, the lower the capitalized cost and the lower the lease payments.

2. Do your homework to determine the resale value of the cars that you are interested in leasing so that you can negotiate a higher residual value. The higher the residual value, the lower the depreciation and the lower the monthly payments.

3. Convert the money factor into an approximate interest rate and negotiate a lower interest rate.

4. Negotiate the monthly payment to see if you can reduce it.

5. If you are trading in a vehicle, do your homework to see what the resale value is so that you get a fair price, which is used to reduce the capitalized cost.

6. Study the terms of the contract and understand them.

7. Watch for the excessive mileage charge. Negotiate additional miles before you sign the contract. For example, if the lease agreement is for 12,000 miles per year and you generally do 15,000 miles per year, negotiate the extra mileage into the contract. This can save you additional charges at the end of the lease.

8. Do not make larger up-front payments than are required and be on your guard for any add-on payments.

9. Shop around at different dealers for their lease terms. In general, dealers—due to their backing from the car manufacturer—can offer better leasing deals than lease companies.

Advantages and Disadvantages of Leasing

The advantages of leasing a car are:

- The monthly lease payments may be lower than financing or buying a car.
- If you use your car for business, a lease agreement provides detailed records for tax purposes.
- You don't have to put out a large amount of cash at the inception of the lease.

The disadvantages of leasing a car are:

- You are faced with a never-ending obligation of monthly lease payments.
- If you plan on buying the car at the end of the lease, you will end up paying more for the car than if you had originally bought or financed the car.
- If you turn in the car early, a termination fee is charged.

Leasing a car is good for someone who likes to exchange cars every two or three years and who does not mind the everlasting monthly lease payments. Understanding how the lease payment is determined will assist you in negotiating better terms for your lease agreement.

Should You Buy, Lease, or Finance Your Car?

THE LEAST COSTLY METHOD of owning a car is to buy it with cash. If you have the money and there are no special low–interest rate loans available from the automobile manufacturing companies, pay cash. For example, currently many of the automobile manufacturers are offering 0 percent finance deals on many of their cars. If you cannot get a further discount for paying cash, it makes sense to use the 0 percent financing to buy the car. This way you have the use of your money, which can be invested at current rates of interest until it is finally used to pay for the car.

Another reason to pay cash for the purchase of a car is that a car is not an investment. It depreciates in value, and finance costs and lease costs add significantly to the overall cost of the car.

Since automobiles are expensive, many people do not have the cash available to buy their cars. Financing then becomes an option. Even though you may decide at the outset to finance, you should still go through the negotiation process to obtain the best price in order to lower your monthly payments. Car loans are available from several sources: banks, credit unions, dealer financing, and other financial institutions. Ask the dealer if subsidized low–interest rate loans are available from the automobile manufacturer. However, even if the rate of interest is lower than competitive rates, you need to make sure that the loan amount is based on your negotiated price and not the list price. Often manufacturers will offer low-interest rates of 0 percent, 1 percent, and so on, but they will inflate the price to get back part of their subsidy.

Car manufacturers have also offered rebates instead of low-rate subsidized loans (often where the car price is inflated to the list price). In certain cases, it may be better to take the rebates, which will lower the purchase price, and then find your own financing from banks, credit unions, and so on.

When comparing different sources of financing, check the annual percentage rates (APRs), which represent the true cost of the loan. For example, the loan with the lowest monthly payments may not necessarily have the lowest cost because you may be making the payments for a longer period of time, and the finance charges may be greater.

When you take out financing, do not buy life or disability insurance in conjunction with the loan. These premiums are expensive and you do not need them. If you are underinsured, you are better off looking at your needs independently of your purchase.

Worksheet 27.1 outlines the steps to determine whether you should pay cash or finance the purchase of a car. In general, financing is more costly than paying cash, but there are certain situations with special low-rate financing that would make it necessary for you to use this worksheet to see which situation is least costly.

As mentioned earlier in this section, it is almost always cheaper to pay cash than to finance the purchase of a car. However, when special low–interest rate loans are provided by the auto manufacturers, you need to work through the specifics. A shortcut to Worksheet 27.1 is to compare the APR of the special financing with the after-tax rate of return on the use of the money.

In this case, assume the money could be invested at 3 percent for three years. If the marginal tax rate of the investor is 39 percent, then the after-tax rate of return on the money forgone is 1.83 percent $[(1 - 0.39)0.03]$. The rate of return is less than the special low-rate financing of 1.9 percent, so it would be more costly to finance than to pay cash.

Worksheet 27.2 outlines the steps for comparing the interest rates to determine whether to finance or pay cash.

Special low–interest rate financing and manufacturer's rebates cloud the issue for buyers as to which is cheaper in the acquisition of a car. Worksheet 27.3 shows the steps to determine whether you should go for the cash rebate or the special low-rate financing.

In the example in Worksheet 27.3, it is cheaper to accept the cash rebate and pay cash. However, if you do not have the cash, you could take the rebate and arrange for financing from other sources (banks, credit unions). You would need to work through this worksheet to compare the cost of financing with the rebate versus the low-rate financing provided by the dealer.

WORKSHEET 27.1 Financing versus paying cash for the purchase of a car

Example: You can buy a car for $25,000 or finance it with a special low-rate loan of 1.9% for three years.

	Example	Your worksheet
Cash cost to purchase		
Total sales price	$25,000	_____
Interest income lost on the payment of cash		
($25,000 invested at 3% for 3 years)	2,325	_____
Less taxes		
(assume a 30% marginal tax bracket)		
(.30 × 2325)	(697.50)	_____
Cost to buy the car	$26,627.50	_____

		Example	Your worksheet
Cost to finance the car			
Total sales price	$25,000		_____
Down payment		2,000	_____
Interest income lost on down payment			
($2,000 invested at 3% for 3 years)		186	_____
Less taxes (30% marginal rate)			
(.3 × $186)		(55.80)	_____
Sales price minus down payment	$23,000		_____
Monthly payments			
(1.9% for 36 months)	$657.78		
Total payments (36 × 657.78)		23,680.08	_____
Total cost to finance the car		$25,810.28	_____

Cash price $26,627.50   **Cash price** _____

Finance cost $25,810.28   **Finance cost** _____

Cheaper to finance

WORKSHEET 27.2 Comparing interest rates to determine whether to finance or pay cash for a car

Cash   **Finance**

Interest rate forgone on cash payment _____
After-tax rate of return
   (1 − marginal rate) × interest rate _____   APR _____

Compare the cash rate and the finance rate.

If the cash rate is higher, it is cheaper to finance the purchase of the car and
   to invest your cash.

If the finance rate is higher, it is cheaper to pay cash for the purchase of
   the car.

Should you finance your car or lease it? In general, it is cheaper to finance the purchase of a car than to lease. The reason is because a lease payment includes an amount for the depreciation of the car plus an amount for the financing of the car by the dealer plus the sales tax. The finance charge builds in a rate of interest, which is typically quite high. However, there are exceptions, particularly when the auto manufacturers are saddled with a glut of cars. To move them, they will offer special low lease rates. By working through Worksheet 27.4, you will be able to determine whether it is cheaper to lease or finance.

Leasing a car often turns out to be more costly than financing a car, even though the monthly payments on a closed-end lease are less than the monthly payments to finance the car. In a closed-end lease, you have rented the car for the lease period. If you were to buy the car and finance the purchase, you would pay the entire purchase price plus the interest expense. However, if you keep the car in relatively good condition, you can sell the car at the end of the same period, and the net outlay for financing generally will be less than the net outlay for leasing.

WORKSHEET 27.3 How to determine whether to take a cash rebate or special low-rate financing

Example: Should you choose the $6,000 cash rebate or the 2.9% financing?

	Example	Your worksheet
Cost of the car with the rebate		
Vehicle price	$36,000	_____
Less manufacturer's rebate	6,000	_____
Net cash cost	30,000	_____
Interest income forgone on cash		
(3% of $30,000 for 3 years)	2,790	_____
Less taxes on interest income		
(30% marginal tax bracket)	(837)	_____
Total cash cost of purchase	$31,953	_____
Cost with 2.9% financing		
Vehicle price	$36,000	_____
Less down payment	3,000	_____
Amount to be financed	33,000	_____
Interest forgone on down payment		
(3% of $3,000 for 3 years)	279	_____
Less taxes (30% marginal tax bracket)	(83.70)	_____
Monthly payment $958.23 × 36	34,496.28	_____
Total cost using financing	$37,691.58	_____

WORKSHEET 27.4 Should you finance or lease a car?

Example: You can finance a car at 3.9% for 4 years or lease it for $499 per month for 4 years.

	Example	Your worksheet
Costs to finance		
Vehicle price	$32,000	_____
Less down payment	2,000	_____
Amount to be financed	30,000	_____
Down payment	2,000	_____
Finance costs ($676.03 × 48 months)	32,449.44	_____
Interest income forgone on down payment		
(3% of $2,000 for 4 years)	252	_____
less taxes (39% marginal tax bracket)	(98.28)	_____
Less estimated value of car		
at the end of the loan	(14,000)	_____
Total cost to finance	$20,603.16	_____
Cost to Lease		
Total up-front security payment	2,000	_____
Interest income forgone on security payment		
(3% of $2,000 for 4 years)	252	_____
Less taxes (39% marginal tax bracket)	(98.28)	_____
Total payments ($499 × 48)	23,952	_____
End-of-lease payments (mileage, etc.)	1,000	_____
Total cost to lease	$27,105.72	_____

To summarize, it is generally cheapest to buy a car by paying cash; the second-cheapest method is to finance, and leasing comes last. In all transactions, read through the sales contract before signing, and always check the figures.

FINANCIAL CALCULATOR #28
How to Create a Simple Interest Loan Schedule

M ANY AUTOMOBILE MANUFACTURERS choose to use simple interest loans for the financing of their cars. The simple interest loan is a variant of the effective rate or precomputed interest method. Table 28.1 shows the first 12 payments of a precomputed interest loan for the purchase of a new car. This is the same method that is used for the majority of mortgage loans, as illustrated in sections 19 and 20 in this book.

The difference with a simple interest loan is that you pay simple interest on the outstanding balance only for the time that the money is used. The payment per period is determined at the beginning of the loan, in the same manner described in earlier sections. Then the interest is determined for each period based on the number of days until the payment is received. The interest expense for the month is deducted from the monthly payment to determine the principal reduction. This amount is deducted from the loan balance to determine the new loan balance. These steps are then repeated to determine the next month's loan balance.

Table 28.2 illustrates the steps in determining the interest expense, principal reduction, and loan balance for a simple interest loan. For comparison purposes, the same loan details as in Table 28.1 are used in the simple interest illustration.

Assume that the loan payment is due on the first day of each month and the loan is taken out on January 1, 2002. The first payment is due on February 1, 2002. If the payment is received earlier than the due date, the interest expense is less than the amount shown in Table 28.1, and if the payment

TABLE 28.1 Precomputed amortization schedule for the purchase of a car

Loan amount:	$18,426.68
Annual interest rate:	3.9%
Number of years:	3
Periods per year:	12
Total payments:	36
Payment per period:	$543.21

Payment number	Payment amount	Interest	Principal reduction	Loan balance
				$18,426.68
1	$543.21	$59.89	$483.32	17,943.36
2	543.21	58.32	484.89	17,458.47
3	543.21	56.74	486.47	16,972.00
4	543.21	55.16	488.05	16,483.95
5	543.21	53.57	489.64	15,994.31
6	543.21	51.98	491.23	15,503.08
7	543.21	50.39	492.82	15,010.26
8	543.21	48.78	494.43	14,515.83
9	543.21	47.18	496.03	14,019.80
10	543.21	45.56	497.65	13,522.15
11	543.21	43.95	499.26	13,022.89
12	543.21	42.32	500.89	12,522.00

is made after the due date, the interest expense is greater than the amount shown in that table.

Step 1: Determine the Interest Expense

To calculate the interest expense, start by multiplying the annual interest rate by the outstanding loan balance ($18,426.68 × 0.039). The yearly interest expense equals $718.64. To find the daily interest expense, divide this number by 365 days ($718.64 ÷ 365); the result is $1.969. Count the days until the first payment is received and multiply the daily interest by this number of days. For January the interest is $39.38 ($1.969 × 20).

TABLE 28.2 Simple interest installment loan

Loan amount:	$18,426.68
Annual interest rate:	3.9%
Number of years:	3
Periods per year:	12
Total payments:	36
Payment per period:	$543.21

Month	Days between payments	Payment amount	Interest	Principal reduction	Loan balance
1/1/02					$18,426.68
1/20/02	20	$543.21	$39.38*	$503.83**	17,922.85
2/27/02,	38	543.21	72.77	470.44	17,452.41
3/30/02	31	543.21	57.81	485.40	16,967.01
4/24/02	25	543.21	45.32	497.89	16,469.12

*Interest is explainedin step 1 on page 143.
**Principal reduction is explained in step 2 on page 144.

Step 2: Determine the Principal Reduction

To determine the principal reduction, subtract the interest expense from the monthly payment ($543.21 − $39.38). The result is $503.83.

Step 3: Determine the New Loan Balance

The new loan balance as of January 20, 2002, is the old balance minus the principal reduction: $17,922.85 ($18,426.68 − $503.83).

These three steps are repeated to determine the figures for each successive month. The interest expense for the first payment in the simple interest loan is much lower than that in the precomputed method ($39.38 versus $59.89) because it involves only 20 days versus the full month in the precomputed method. Conversely, in the second month the interest expense for the simple interest method is greater than for the precomputed method ($72.77 versus $58.32) because the days between payments for the former is 38 versus the typical 30 days in the precomputed method.

On balance, if you consistently pay your monthly payments earlier than the due date, you will save on the interest expense using the simple interest method. Worksheet 28.1 outlines the steps to create your own simple interest amortization schedule.

WORKSHEET 28.1 How to create a simple interest amortization schedule

Date	Days between payments	Payment amount	Interest	Principal reduction	Loan balance
————		————			————
————	————	————	————	————	————
————	————	————	————	————	————
————	————	————	————	————	————
————	————	————	————	————	————
————	————	————	————	————	————
————	————	————	————	————	————
————	————	————	————	————	————
————	————	————	————	————	————
————	————	————	————	————	————
————	————	————	————	————	————
————	————	————	————	————	————
————	————	————	————	————	————
————	————	————	————	————	————
————	————	————	————	————	————

Step 1 Fill in the date, monthly payment, and loan balance at the inception of the loan.

Step 2 Fill in the days between payments.

Step 3 Calculate the interest expense. Multiply the annual rate by the loan balance and divide by 365. Multiply the result by the number of days between payments to determine the interest expense.

Step 4 Subtract the interest expense from the monthly payment to determine the principal reduction.

Step 5 Subtract the principal reduction from the old loan balance to determine the new loan balance.

PART THREE

MANAGING YOUR PERSONAL WEALTH— INVESTMENTS

Determine Your Investment Objectives

I NVESTMENT OBJECTIVES ARE LIKE A RUDDER on a ship. The choice of which investments to hold is determined by your objectives. In other words, knowing what you want to accomplish from your investments allows you to manage your portfolio more effectively. In addition, your objectives determine the purpose and time period for the investments. For instance, you may be saving for retirement in five years, while your neighbor may be saving for retirement in 30 years. Although the objectives are the same, the time period, level of risk tolerance, and types of investments held will be very different.

The first step in any plan is to determine short-range, medium-range, and long-range objectives. For example, a young family with small children may have the following objectives:

Short Term:
- Set up an emergency savings fund.
- Buy furniture.
- Save for a vacation.
- Buy a new car.

Medium Term:
- Save for a down payment on a house.
- Invest in a business.

Long Term:
- Save for children's college fund.
- Save for retirement.

Once you have determined your objectives, it becomes easier to see what types of investments to buy, the level of risk that you can withstand, and what your expectations are from your investments.

Filling in Worksheet 29.1 is a first step in your investment program. Noting the time frame and the dollar amounts needed to fund your objectives gives you a better sense of how much to invest for each objective. Asking yourself the following questions can help you formulate your objectives.

- What do I intend to use my money/savings for?
- How much money do I need to fund my objectives?
- Am I committed to making sacrifices to fund these objectives?
- What are the consequences if I am not able to fund these objectives?
- What do I need to do to bolster my savings to fund these objectives?

Besides listing your objectives, it is equally important to quantify the amount of money needed to fund them.

By listing your objectives, you can see what you intend to save for and invest in for the future. Included in your short-term objectives should be the capacity to meet financial emergency needs through the establishment of an emergency fund.

Medium- and long-term objectives vary by individual needs. For example, some people want to save as much as possible to grow as large an estate as they can, whereas others may have more specific uses for their future funds.

WORKSHEET 29.1 List your objectives

	Time horizon in years	Dollar amount needed	Investment to fund objective
Short term (two years or less)			
_____	_____	_____	_____
_____	_____	_____	_____
_____	_____	_____	_____
_____	_____	_____	_____
_____	_____	_____	_____
_____	_____	_____	_____
_____	_____	_____	_____
_____	_____	_____	_____
Medium term (two to seven years)			
_____	_____	_____	_____
_____	_____	_____	_____
_____	_____	_____	_____
_____	_____	_____	_____
_____	_____	_____	_____
_____	_____	_____	_____
_____	_____	_____	_____
Long term (seven-plus years)			
_____	_____	_____	_____
_____	_____	_____	_____
_____	_____	_____	_____
_____	_____	_____	_____
_____	_____	_____	_____
_____	_____	_____	_____
_____	_____	_____	_____
_____	_____	_____	_____

FINANCIAL CALCULATOR #30
Determine Your Risk Tolerance

S ETTING OBJECTIVES IS THE FIRST step in an investment plan, as discussed
in section 29. The next step is to determine your risk tolerance, which then
serves as a guide in the selection of the portfolio investments. An examination
of your personal characteristics is the first step in the determination of your risk
tolerance. See Worksheet 30.1 for a survey of your personal characteristics.

An assessment of your personal characteristics determines which of the
following financial stages you are in and the risk level that you can tolerate
with regard to your investments:

- Accumulation of wealth
- Attainment of wealth
- Use of wealth

WORKSHEET 30.1 An examination of your personal characteristics

Marital status: ☐ single   ☐ married   ☐ widowed   ☐ divorced

Family: ☐ no children   ☐ young children   ☐ teenage children   ☐ empty nest

Age: ☐ under 25   ☐ 25–39   ☐ 40–60   ☐ over 60

Education: ☐ high school graduate   ☐ college degree   ☐ graduate degree

Income: ☐ poor growth prospects   ☐ stable/level   ☐ good growth prospects

Income level: ☐ low   ☐ medium   ☐ high

Job/profession: ☐ low job skills   ☐ average level of skills   ☐ good job skills

Prospects for promotion: ☐ poor   ☐ average   ☐ good

Net worth/size of portfolio:
   Assets/net worth: ☐ small asset base   ☐ medium asset base
                  ☐ large asset base

Level of debt: ☐ high   ☐ medium   ☐ low

Generally, these three stages are coordinated with the stages in the life cycle. Most young people starting their working careers are in the first stage, wealth accumulation, and as people progress to the mature stage in life they have attained most of their objectives. In the retirement stage, people generally use the wealth that they have attained to live on. However, there are many exceptions. In all three stages, risk tolerance varies according to the specifics of the person's characteristics, objectives, and time frames. A young, successful trial lawyer, who has a large salary and bonuses, can withstand more risk from the investments chosen than someone who earns a small salary and is dependent on the earnings of the investments. The latter's investment assets will be more conservative and geared more toward generating current income than capital growth. The trial lawyer, however, can withstand more risk in his or her investment portfolio, which is aimed at expanding capital (net worth) rather than generating current income.

These variables determine the types of investments and the level of risk that can be absorbed in the development and management of the portfolio. For example, a nonworking widow who depends entirely on income generated from her investments will not be able to tolerate the high risk of investments in junk bonds, small-company growth stocks, or newly issued public offerings of common stocks. Her portfolio of assets would need to generate income but not at the expense of capital preservation.

Thus, depending on an investor's objectives, characteristics, and risk tolerance, there is a trade-off between assets generating current income and assets seeking capital appreciation. If investors opt for capital appreciation assets, they may sacrifice current income.

With What Level of Risk Do You Feel Comfortable?

On a continuum of risk, you need to determine your comfort zone with regard to your investments (see Figure 30.1).

Classifying some of the types of investments on a continuum of risk, we see that speculative common stocks are considered the most risky (in terms

FIGURE 30.1 Investment continuum of risk

Speculative stocks	Growth stocks	Blue-chip stocks/ Long-term bonds	Intermediate bonds	Short-term bonds	Money market securities

High risk   Low risk

of variability in share price), followed by long-term bonds, with the shorter maturities on the low-risk end. Bear in mind that there are many other types of investments that are riskier than common stocks, such as commodities, futures contracts, and options. Similarly, there is a great variation of quality among common stocks. The common stocks of well-established, blue-chip companies are considered less risky than the bonds of highly leveraged companies with suspect balance sheets.

The questionnaire in Worksheet 30.2 can assist you in the determination of your comfort level with regard to risk tolerance.

Scoring Your Questionnaire
Give yourself the following points for your answers and then total them:

1. (a) 1 point, (b) 2 points, (c) 3 points
2. (a) 1 point, (b) 2 points, (c) 3 points, (d) 4 points
3. (a) 4 points, (b) 3 points, (c) 2 points, (d) 1 point
4. (a) 1 point, (b) 2 points, (c) 3 points, (d) 4 points
5. (a) 4 points, (b) 3 points, (c) 2 points, (d) 1 point
6. (a) 4 points, (b) 3 points, (c) 2 points, (d) 1 point
7. (a) 4 points, (b) 2 points, (c) 1 point
8. (a) 2 points, (b) 1 point
9. (a) 1 point, (b) 2 points, (c) 4 points
10. (a) 1 point, (b) 2 points, (c) 3 points

1. Do you have an emergency fund consisting of at least 3 month's salary?
   (a) No   (b) Yes, but less than 3 months   (c) Yes
   Investment Planning: These investment funds should be invested in liquid assets (money market securities) so as to avoid any loss of principal
   when the money is needed. The first step is to establish an emergency
   fund, after which an investment fund can be established.

2. When will you need the investment funds (over and above your emergency fund) that you have invested?
   (a) Within 1 year   (b) Within 5 years   (c) Between 5 and 10 years
   (d) Longer than 10 years
   Investment Planning: If you need the money within one year, you need
   to invest in liquid investments. Money needed within a five-year time
   frame should be invested in short-term securities. Investments with a time
   frame longer than five years can be invested more aggressively, depending
   on your circumstances and your risk tolerance, such as in long-term bonds
   and stocks.

3. What percentage of your total investment funds is in retirement accounts?
   (a) Below 25%   (b) Between 25 and 50%   (c) Between 51 and 75%
   (d) Above 75%
   Investment Planning: The lower the percentage in retirement funds, the
   more aggressively you can invest.

4. How stable is your income from employment likely to be over the next
   5 years?
   (a) Likely to decrease   (b) Likely to stay the same   (c) Likely to keep
   pace with inflation   (d) Likely to increase above inflation
   Investment Planning: If there is uncertainty concerning future earnings,
   you may have to withdraw funds from your investments, which means
   that a corresponding amount should be invested conservatively. If there is
   a good chance that employment earnings will increase in the future, you
   can invest more aggressively.

5. How many dependents do you have?
   (a) None   (b) 1   (c) 2   (d) More than 2
   Investment Planning: The greater the number of dependents, the greater
   the responsibilities. Generally, this may require being a little more conservative in your investment approach.

(continued overleaf)

6. What percentage of your earnings goes toward paying off debts including a mortgage?
   (a) Less than 10%   (b) Between 10 and 25%   (c) Between 25 and 50%
   (d) Over 50 percent
   Investment Planning: The higher the percentage of your earnings that goes toward paying off debts, the greater the likelihood that you may need to dip into your investment accounts, which may call for a more conservative approach.

7. With regard to your investment assets, where would you feel comfortable on the scale below?

(a)	(b)	(c)

I am willing to invest aggressively for the maximum possible growth even if there is potential for losses due to market fluctuations.	I am comfortable with some level of fluctuations in my funds in order to achieve reasonable levels of growth.	I am uncomfortable when my investment funds go down in value due to market flucuations.

   Investment Planning: Your appetite for risk will determine whether you can invest aggressively, somewhat aggressively, or conservatively.

8. If you can increase your potential returns by taking on more risk, would you feel comfortable?
   (a) Yes   (b) No
   Investment Planning: If yes, you can be a little more aggressive in your investments. If no, you should invest only in those assets that you feel comfortable with.

9. What rate of return do you expect to earn from your investments?
   (a) Keep ahead of inflation while maintaining stability of principal.
   (b) Earn returns that are greater than inflation even if there is some potential for loss of principal
   (c) Earn high returns regardless of increased potential for loss of principal.
   Investment Planning: Your acceptance of risks of loss of principal will determine whether you should invest aggressively, conservatively, or somewhere in between.

10. What do you need from your investment assets?
    (a) Investment income   (b) Mix of investment income and capital growth
    (c) Long-term capital growth
    Investment Planning: If you need investment income, the investment assets should be allocated more toward bonds. Long-term capital growth can be obtained from diversified investments in common stocks.

If your total score is 10–15 points, you cannot tolerate risk well and you would feel more comfortable with conservative investments. A total of 16–20 points indicates a notch above low risk, with an investment style that is still conservative but includes more investments with higher returns. A score of 21–25 indicates a balanced approach to risk, with an equal mix of investments that seek income and capital growth. A score of 26–31 points indicates greater acceptance of risk in a portfolio, with investments geared more toward capital growth and a small percentage of funds devoted to income-producing investments. All scores above 32 indicate an acceptance of high risk with regard to investments.

Figure 30.2 illustrates a risk continuum. Based on your assessment of your ability to handle risk, determine where you would be comfortable on this continuum.

Your tolerance for risk is an overriding factor in the selection of your investment portfolio. As your personal circumstances and objectives change, so too will there be changes in your assessment of risk. Most people strive for increasing the returns from their investments, but this means taking on more risk. Acceptance of a comfortable risk/return strategy is an important step in the assessment of the different types of investment assets, as discussed in the next section.

FIGURE 30.2 Investment continuum of risk

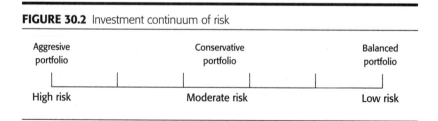

How to Allocate Your Investments

ASSET ALLOCATION IS A PLAN TO INVEST in different types of securities so that the capital invested is protected against adverse factors in the marketplace. This, in essence, is the opposite of putting all your eggs in one basket. Imagine an investor with $200,000 to invest who put it all into Enron stock bought at $70 per share at the beginning of 2001. The value of the portfolio at the end of the year would have been reduced to $1,428 when Enron went into bankruptcy and the stock traded around $0.50 per share.

Developing a portfolio is based on the idea of holding a variety of investments rather than concentrating on a single investment. The purpose is to reduce the risk of loss and even out the returns of the different investments. The latter point can be illustrated with the following hypothetical portfolio.

Assume the investor buys:	Total investment:
1,000 shares of XYZ Co. at $50 per share	$50,000
100 convertible bonds of ABC Co. at $1,000 per bond	100,000
Total	$150,000

A year later, the portfolio is valued as follows:

1,000 shares of XYZ Co. at $70 per share	$70,000
100 convertible bonds of ABC Co. at $800 per bond	80,000
Total	$150,000

The investor has spread the risk of loss by owning two different types of securities, as well as by averaging the returns of the two types of investments. Certainly the investor would have done much better had he or she invested only in XYZ shares, but hindsight always produces the highest returns. The fact that we are not clairvoyant points to the benefits of diversifying across a broad range of investment types. In other words, diversification seeks a balance between the risk-return trade-off.

Diversification is achieved by selecting a portfolio of different types of securities in different industries. For example, investing in the stocks and bonds of General Motors, Ford, and Chrysler hardly achieves any diversification. By carefully selecting the stocks and bonds of different companies in different industries and/or investing in stock and bond mutual funds, some of the risk of loss on any one security (or type of fund) will be evened out.

Asset allocation is the process of determining the right mix for the broad asset classes that conform to your objectives, time horizons, and risk tolerance. The aim of investing in the different classes of assets is to reduce the risk of loss and even out the returns. Generally, these investment classes behave differently.

What is the right mix of stocks, bonds, money market securities, and other investment asset classes? The answer depends on the amount of risk that the investor is willing to tolerate, investment objectives, the time frame for these objectives, personal characteristics, and the size of the portfolio. Generally, stocks are riskier investments than bonds. By increasing the time horizon for stock investments, an investor can compensate for the volatility in the stock market. Maturities on bonds can be matched to the time horizons of the investor's needs. There are short-term bonds with maturities of one to five years, intermediate bonds with maturities of five to 10 years, and long-term bonds with maturities of greater than 10 years (generally 30-year maturities, although there are 100-year maturity bonds). If an investor cannot sleep at night when the amount of his or her investments declines, that investor does not tolerate risk very well and should not have a large percentage of his or her assets invested in stocks. Conversely, an investor who can tolerate risk and who has long time horizons could have a larger percentage of assets allocated to stocks.

Investors who need to live off the interest of their investments will be inclined to allocate more of their portfolio assets to bond investments, which generate regular fixed interest payments. Investors with a long time horizon who do not need the income from their capital to live on can allocate a greater percentage of their assets toward stocks in order to generate growth for the portfolio.

The amount of money available to be invested also has an impact on the asset allocation. If there is a relatively small amount of money, most of it will go toward covering the emergency fund with money market securities, and whatever is left over will be allocated to other investment assets depending on objectives, time frames, risk tolerance, and personal characteristics.

Age is another important factor in the determination of an asset allocation mix. At a young age, an investor's priorities are setting up an emergency fund and probably investing the rest of the funds in growth assets due to the investor's long time horizon. In midlife, the priorities shift toward growth and income, and at retirement the emphasis is more on income generation and some growth.

There is no rigid formula for asset allocation. Rather, it is a good idea to think about the concept as a guideline for investing money. The percentage allocated to the different types of assets can always be changed, depending on circumstances. As individual circumstances change, so too will the investor's objectives. If the emphasis shifts, for example, to greater income generation and preservation of capital from capital growth, the percentage of the investments in the portfolio can be changed accordingly.

A rough rule of thumb for allocating assets is to use age as a yardstick. At age 50, the optimal allocation is 50 percent in bonds and the rest allocated to other asset categories. As age increases above 50, so too will the percentage allocated to bonds. This does not work for all people, as this formula ignores the specific facts pertaining to each individual, such as objectives, amount of money, risk tolerance, and other personal characteristics. Figure 31.1 illustrates some of the determinants for asset allocation models and Figures 31.2 to 31.4 break these models down into greater detail.

The most important aspect of investing is to have an asset allocation plan that reflects the mix of stocks and bonds appropriate for your objectives. Once these have been determined, the individual investments can be purchased. Funds for emergency purposes should be liquid; in other words, they should be easily convertible into cash without the loss of principal. Money market

FIGURE 31.1 Determinants for asset allocation models

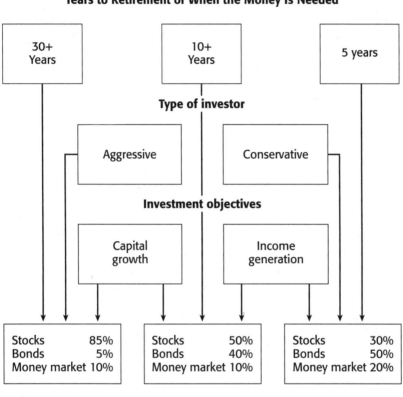

Years to Retirement or When the Money Is Needed

| 30+ Years | 10+ Years | 5 years |

Type of investor

Aggressive   Conservative

Investment objectives

Capital growth   Income generation

Stocks	85%		Stocks	50%		Stocks	30%
Bonds	5%		Bonds	40%		Bonds	50%
Money market	10%		Money market	10%		Money market	20%

securities are an example of liquid investments. Depending on personal circumstances, the rule of thumb is to have an emergency fund equivalent to three to six months of living expenses invested in money market securities.

Asset allocation plans are not etched in stone, and investors should reevaluate their plans on a yearly basis or as personal needs and circumstances change. See Figure 31.5 for the benefits of asset allocation and diversification.

A *conservative portfolio* is one in which the investment goals are to preserve capital and provide for some growth. The weighting is geared toward high-quality bonds, with a small portion toward stocks. (See Figure 31.2.)

FIGURE 31.2 Conservative portfolio

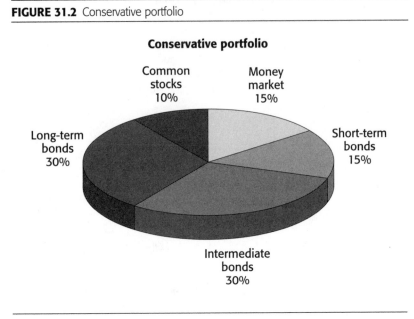

Conservative portfolio

Common stocks 10%

Money market 15%

Short-term bonds 15%

Long-term bonds 30%

Intermediate bonds 30%

A balanced portfolio includes a greater percentage of common stocks, which provide capital growth, but keeps a large percentage of assets in bonds, which provide income. (See Figure 31.3.)

FIGURE 31.3 Balanced portfolio

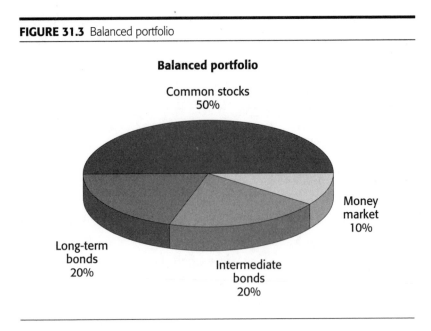

Balanced portfolio

Common stocks 50%

Money market 10%

Long-term bonds 20%

Intermediate bonds 20%

FIGURE 31.4 Aggressive portfolio

Aggressive portfolio

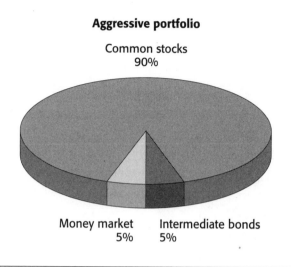

Common stocks
90%

Money market   Intermediate bonds
5%   5%

An aggressive portfolio is weighted to common stocks, which provide capital growth. (See Figure 31.4.)

Figure 31.5 lists the benefits of asset allocation and diversification and Worksheet 31.1 outlines the steps for you to determine your asset allocation.

FIGURE 31.5 Benefits of asset allocation and diversification

1. By investing in different classes of investments, the risk of loss is spread among the different investments rather than being concentrated in one class.
2. A diversified portfolio of investments reduces the total risk. According to Jonathan Clements,* a portfolio assembled over the past 70 years consisting of 23 percent common stock and 77 percent bonds would have the same risk as a portfolio of 100 percent bonds.
3. Diversification can increase overall returns. In the portfolio mentioned above, the overall returns on a diversified portfolio of 23 percent common stock and 77 percent bonds returned were 2 percent higher per year than a 100 percent bond portfolio.

*Jonathan Clements, "Portfolio for the Conservative and the Bold," *The Wall Street Journal*, November 10, 1998, p. C1.

WORKSHEET 31.1 Determining your asset allocation plan

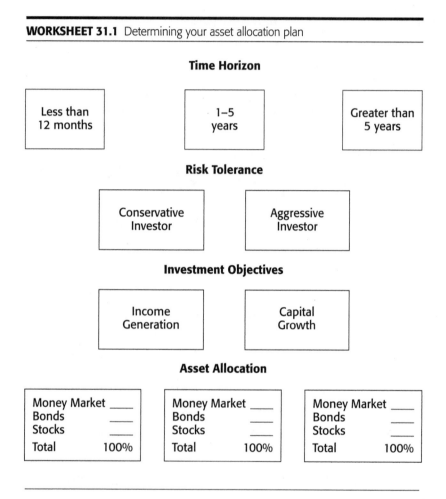

Time Horizon

| Less than 12 months | 1–5 years | Greater than 5 years |

Risk Tolerance

| Conservative Investor | Aggressive Investor |

Investment Objectives

| Income Generation | Capital Growth |

Asset Allocation

Money Market ____	Money Market ____	Money Market ____
Bonds ____	Bonds ____	Bonds ____
Stocks ____	Stocks ____	Stocks ____
Total 100%	Total 100%	Total 100%

After determining your asset allocation plan, you are ready to select the individual securities (stocks, bonds, and money market securities).

Money Market Securities. These include:

• Treasury bills
• Commercial paper
• Certificates of deposit (CDs) (maturities of one year or less)
• Money market mutual funds

Bonds. These include the individual bonds (corporate, U.S. Treasuries, municipal bonds, government agency bonds, foreign bonds) and/or different bond mutual funds.

Stocks. These include individual stocks and/or equity mutual funds.

There are other assets (such as real estate, options, and futures) that can be considered besides stocks, bonds, and money market securities. If you are considering them, you should include them in your asset allocation plan.

FINANCIAL CALCULATOR #32

How to Determine Your Equity Style in the Selection of Individual Stocks

THE QUESTION OFTEN ASKED BY INVESTORS IS, "What types of stocks should I buy?"

Should you rush to buy the small-capitalized stocks that have been responsible for the major moves in the Russell 200 Index? Or should you look for value stocks and technology stocks that have been hit in the downturn of the stock market (Dow Jones Industrial Average and the NASDAQ Composite) in the years 2001–2002? Related to this issue are the sizes of the companies. The rally has included the small-capitalization stocks while the mid-cap and large-cap stocks have been excluded, although small-capitalization stocks were also down in the early months of 2002.

Studies have shown that stocks can be classified into categories that have similar patterns of performance and characteristics. In other words, the returns of the stocks within the categories are similar, whereas the returns of the stocks between the categories are not correlated.* James L. Farrell found four categories for stocks; namely, growth, cyclical, stable, and energy. Other

*James L. Farrell, Jr., "Homogeneous Stock Groupings: Implications for Portfolio Management," *Financial Analysts Journal*, May–June 1975, pp. 50–62.

FIGURE 32.1 Market capitalization of stocks

Small capitalization: less than $1 billion

Medium capitalization: $1–$5 billion

Large capitalization: greater than $5 billion

---

studies have measured stocks by their market capitalization, or size, which was then translated into small-cap, mid-cap, and large-cap stocks. Figure 32.1 lists the categories based on market capitalization of the companies, which is measured by the number of shares outstanding for the company multiplied by the market price of the stock. There are many variations in these amounts, depending on the source. What portfolio managers have found is that they can enhance their performance by moving their money into the different categories of stocks from time to time.

From these categories of stocks two investment styles have emerged; namely, value and growth investing. Figure 32.2 illustrates the common styles of equity investing. This style box originated from Morningstar Mutual Funds for mutual fund investing, but it can also be used to determine individual equity portfolio holdings.

Investors can use this style box to determine the bulk of the equity investments that suit their investment style, as determined by their investment objectives. Value stocks have different financial characteristics and, as we have seen, different performance returns over the past four years compared to growth stocks. Value stocks generally pay some dividends and have low price-earnings (P/E) ratios. (See pages 236–239 for a discussion of P/E ratios.) Growth stocks generally have high P/E ratios and are expected to experience high sales growth for a period of time. A blend would include a mixture of growth and value stocks. The size of the company is measured by market capitalization. Small-cap companies tend to be riskier than mid- or large-cap companies, but as many studies have shown, the returns over long periods of time from the small-caps have exceeded those of the large-caps. This has not occurred over the past four of five years, where large-cap growth stocks have outperformed the small- and mid-

FIGURE 32.2 Types of equity styles

Equity styles

	Value	Blend	Growth
Large-cap stocks			
Mid-cap stocks			
Small-cap stocks			

cap stocks quite handily. However, before then small-cap stocks outperformed the large- and mid-caps. This does not include all the large stocks on the market. In fact, over half the stocks in the S&P 500 Index had declines in share price or ended up with returns of 6.6 percent or less for the calendar year 1998, while only a small number of stocks were responsible for the stellar returns.* This means that stock picking becomes extremely important for individual portfolios, particularly if there is no advantage in replicating an index.

For those investors who had chosen the large nifty 50 stocks in the S&P 500 Index and most of the Dow Jones Industrial Average stocks, the returns were very rewarding, and the implication was that it was easy to make money in the stock market. However, in more broad-based markets the choices are not so overwhelmingly easy to make, and the average annual returns are generally not in the double digits, as has been the case for the past four years.

The style box in Figure 32.2 illustrates the choices in terms of these dimensions. Investors can choose the current winners, which are small-cap growth stocks, in which to invest more money. Alternatively, some investors might not want to pay the high prices for these types of stocks and instead would look

*Anne Tergesen, "Sifting for Clues," *Business Week*, March 29, 1999, pp. 110–111.

for the growth stocks that have been beaten down in the past year. These could be small-cap, mid-cap, or large-cap stocks, or a combination of them. Some investors might want to have a combination of growth and value stocks in the different size stocks. This style box can also be used with international stocks.

Research has shown that value and growth stocks do not perform in the same manner within the same time periods. This was evidenced recently by the spectacular performance of the large-cap growth stocks while the large-, mid-, and small-cap value stocks underperformed the market. Some investors will choose to invest all their funds in the stocks that are performing well and then shift to other investment styles when they perceive that things are about to change. This style of investing would be more conducive to an active management style, as opposed to a passive management style where investors would allocate their stocks among the different categories and then hold them for long periods of time. Active managers are more likely to be market timers, where they will be more inclined to be fully invested in stocks when they perceive the market to be going up. When they think that the market is about to go down, they will exit the market. Passive investors tend to stay fully invested in stocks irrespective of the state of the market.

Whether to be an active or a passive manager, or whether to choose growth stocks over value stocks are decisions that each investor will ultimately have to make. There are differences in investment styles and, therefore, the ultimate selection of stocks, but having a plan and a strategy can make the selection of stocks much easier. The ultimate selection of individual stocks can be made easier if direction is provided through an asset allocation model, which breaks down the different style categories of investments within the class asset. Table 32.1 lists a few examples of the different portfolio models. Investors could invest in a mixture of value and growth stocks, which can be allocated among domestic stocks and international stocks. Following this, investors would then decide on the amounts to allocate to the different stock sizes (large-, mid-, and small-cap). This is illustrated in example 1 in Table 32.1.

Examples 2 and 3 show selections 100 percent weighted toward value and growth stocks, respectively. Diversification within the stock sector of an investor's portfolio offers protection against the downside risk of being fully

TABLE 32.1 Asset allocation of stocks by style

Example 1 Value/growth blend	Example 2 Value	Example 3 Growth
Value stocks	**Value stocks**	**Growth stocks**
Large-cap U.S. stocks 20%	Large-cap U.S. stocks 25%	Large-cap U.S. stocks 25%
Mid-cap U.S. stocks 20%	Mid-cap U.S. stocks 25%	Mid-cap U.S. stocks 25%
International stocks 10%	Small-cap U.S. stocks 20%	Small-cap U.S. stocks 20%
Growth stocks	International large-cap 20%	International large-cap 20%
Large-cap U.S. stocks 20%	International mid-cap 10%	International mid-cap 10%
Mid-cap U.S stocks 20%		
International stocks 10%		
Total portfolio 100%	**Total portfolio 100%**	**Total portfolio 100%**

invested in one sector, such as large-cap value stocks, for example. If in the near future the tide turns against these stocks, investors will be protected by participating in the rising prices of the other sectors should the stock market rally become more broad based.

Many may wonder why they should take the time and effort to classify their stocks into these styles. There are a few convincing arguments. The first is that without the power of clairvoyance we have no way of knowing the future movements of the stock market. Consequently, by diversifying into different sectors of the market, investors can reduce the risk of loss from being too heavily invested in one sector of the market. This is amply illustrated by the sharp decline in technology and growth stocks during the years 2000–2001. Value stocks during that period increased and the small-cap indices outperformed the large- and mid-cap indices. This means, however, that currently small-cap stocks are not as cheap as they were before the rally and may be running out of steam.

Worksheet 32.1 provides the Morningstar grid to help you to determine your investment style and then to choose individual stocks or equity mutual funds.

WORKSHEET 32.1 Determine your equity style and choose your stocks/ mutual funds

Equity styles

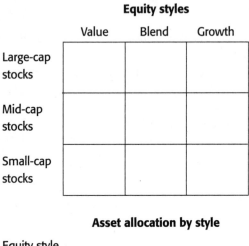

	Value	Blend	Growth
Large-cap stocks			
Mid-cap stocks			
Small-cap stocks			

Asset allocation by style

Equity style   _____
Company size

_____   _____

     _____

     _____

     _____

     _____

     _____

     _____

Step 1 Choose your equity style(s).
Step 2 Determine the size sectors and list the individual stocks.

FINANCIAL CALCULATOR #33
How to Determine Which Types of Bonds to Buy for a Portfolio

INSTEAD OF INVESTING DIRECTLY IN individual bond issues, investors may choose to invest indirectly in bonds through bond mutual funds. The mutual fund pools the money from investors and invests in different bond issues. Investors receive shares in the fund, which are proportionate to the amount of their investments.

The types of bonds an investor chooses are determined by the investor's objectives. Bonds may be categorized in terms of the following:

- Quality. The higher the credit quality of the bond, the lower the risk and the yields. The lower the credit quality of the bond, the higher the risk and potential returns.
- Maturity. This is the length of time of the maturity of the bond. Maturities are generally classified as short term, intermediate term, and long term. The longer the maturity, the greater the risk and the greater the potential returns (assuming a normal yield curve).

Figure 33.1 shows the types of bonds using these two dimensions. This grid is a good planning tool to use to determine which types of bonds (or bond funds) to invest in with regard to these two dimensions.

The lower your risk tolerance, the closer you would move to the left side of the grid, and depending on your time horizon, to the top, middle, or bottom of the grid. If you have a long time horizon, you would choose the middle or bottom rows (intermediate-term and long-term funds), which are also most sensitive to changes in market rates of interest. This grid is a good tool to use to identify the types of bonds or bond funds that conform to both your time horizon and level of risk tolerance.

FIGURE 33.1 Grid to determine which bonds to choose

Maturity	High quality[a]	Medium quality	Low quality[b]
Short term[c]	High quality	Medium quality	Low quality
Intermediate term[d]	High quality	Medium quality	Low quality
Long term[e]	High quality	Medium quality	Low quality

a. High-quality bonds have a low risk of default.
b. Low-quality bonds and junk bonds have a high risk of default.
c. Short-term bonds may be classified as having maturities ranging from one to five years.
d. Intermediate-term bonds have maturities ranging from five to 10 years.
e. Long-term bonds have maturities of greater than 10 years.

Types of Bonds

Treasury notes and bonds are issued by the United States Treasury. There is no credit or default risk on the interest and repayment of principal as these are direct obligations of the federal government.

U.S. government agencies sell long-term debt issues to finance various activities. Although they are not backed by the full credit of the U.S. government, these U.S. agency issues are considered to be of good investment quality. There are many different agencies selling obligations with varying maturities, liquidity, and marketability.

Corporate bonds are debt obligations of corporations and vary considerably in their features and risk.

Municipal bonds are issues sold by states, counties, and cities. The main advantage of municipal bonds is their special tax treatment. The interest received from municipal bonds is exempt from federal income tax and from state and/or local tax if issued in that state and county.

Zero-coupon bonds are hybrid securities that pay no periodic interest but are issued at a deep discount and are redeemed at face value ($1,000) at maturity.

Convertible bonds are debt securities that can be exchanged for the common stock of the issuing company at the option of the bondholder.

There are independent rating services that evaluate the risk of corporate and municipal bonds. See Figure 33.2 for two rating services' ratings, which are similar but not identical.

Bonds with ratings of AAA, AA, A, and BBB from S&P are considered to be investment-grade quality. Bonds with ratings below BBB are considered to be junk bonds and are speculative. The lower ratings of junk bonds mean that the issuers have a greater likelihood of default on their interest and principal repayments. Before buying a bond issue, you should ascertain the rating through your broker, or if buying online, through the Internet Web site.

Use Worksheet 33.1 to determine the types of bonds or bond funds to purchase for your investment portfolio.

FIGURE 33.2 Bond ratings

Moody's	Standard & Poor's	Interpretation of ratings
Aaa	AAA	Highest quality obligations
Aa	AA	High-quality obligations
A	A	Bonds that have a strong capacity to repay principal and interest but may be impaired in the future.
Baa	BBB	Medium grade quality.
Ba	BB	Interest and principal is
	B	neither highly protected nor poorly secured. Lower ratings in this category have some speculative characteristics.
B	CCC	Speculative bonds with
Caa	CC	great uncertainty.
Ca	C	
C	DDD	In default.
	DD	
	D	

WORKSHEET 33.1 Determine the types of bonds to buy for your portfolio

Name and type of bond	Rating	Length of time to maturity	Total investment
_____	____	_____	_____
_____	____	_____	_____
_____	____	_____	_____
_____	____	_____	_____
_____	____	_____	_____
_____	____	_____	_____
_____	____	_____	_____
_____	____	_____	_____

How to Rebalance Your Portfolio

1. Begin with your original asset allocation plan.

For example, assume you had started with the asset allocation plan as illustrated in Figure 34.1.

2. Revisit the asset allocation plan after a period of time.

One year later, with the rapid expansion of the equity portfolio, the original asset allocation mix has changed to the percentages shown in Figure 34.1.

3. If necessary, rebalance the portfolio.

You need to determine whether this new asset allocation mix is consistent with your objectives, personal circumstances, and risk tolerance. With the appreciation of the equity assets, the new equity mix is now 50 percent of the total portfolio value and the bond mix has dropped from 50 percent to 35 percent. This may be unsuitable if you rely more on income-generating assets than growth assets. Rebalancing requires selling off some stocks and buying more bonds with the proceeds in order to realign the asset allocation mix with your needs and goals.

4. The current asset allocation mix and proposed asset allocation mix after rebalancing are shown in Figure 34.2.

Use Worksheet 34.1 on page 178 to rebalance your portfolio.

FIGURE 34.1 Original asset allocation plan and asset allocation mix—one year later

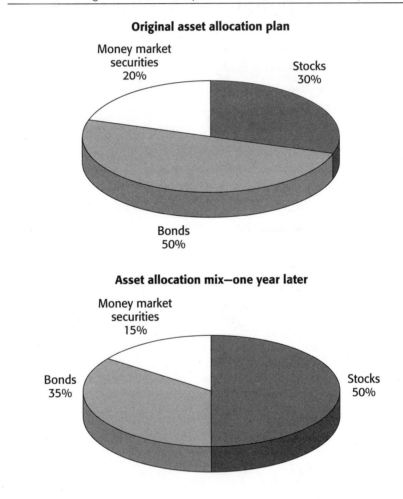

Original asset allocation plan

Money market
securities
20%

Stocks
30%

Bonds
50%

Asset allocation mix—one year later

Money market
securities
15%

Bonds
35%

Stocks
50%

FIGURE 34.2 Current and proposed asset allocation mix

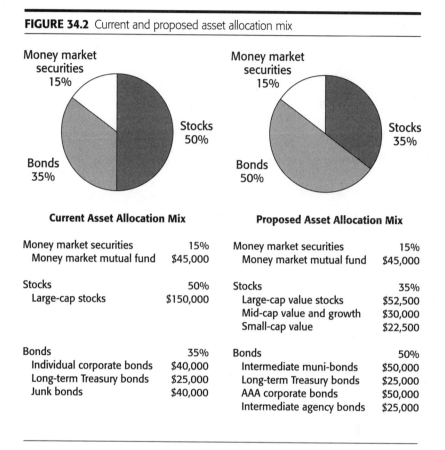

Current Asset Allocation Mix		
Money market securities	15%	
Money market mutual fund		$45,000
Stocks	50%	
Large-cap stocks		$150,000
Bonds	35%	
Individual corporate bonds		$40,000
Long-term Treasury bonds		$25,000
Junk bonds		$40,000

Proposed Asset Allocation Mix		
Money market securities	15%	
Money market mutual fund		$45,000
Stocks	35%	
Large-cap value stocks		$52,500
Mid-cap value and growth		$30,000
Small-cap value		$22,500
Bonds	50%	
Intermediate muni-bonds		$50,000
Long-term Treasury bonds		$25,000
AAA corporate bonds		$50,000
Intermediate agency bonds		$25,000

Step 1 Begin with your original asset allocation plan.

	Dollar amount	Percentage
Money market securities	_____	_____%
Bonds	_____	_____%
Stocks	_____	_____%
Other	_____	_____%
Total	_____	100%

Step 2 After a period of time, fill in your current asset allocation mix.

	Dollar amount	Percentage
Money market securities	_____	_____%
Bonds	_____	_____%
Stocks	_____	_____%
Other	_____	_____%
Total	_____	100%

Step 3 Determine whether it is necessary to rebalance your portfolio. If you decide it is necessary, go to step 4.

Step 4 Create a new asset allocation plan

	Dollar amount	Percentage
Money market securities	_____	_____%
Bonds	_____	_____%
Stocks	_____	_____%
Other	_____	_____%
Total	_____	100%

The Rule of 72 and How to Use It to Determine How Long It Will Take to Double Your Money

THE RULE OF 72 IS AN EASY-TO-USE method for determining how quickly your savings/investment will double. It can also be used in times of high rates of inflation to determine how quickly prices will double.

The formula for the rule of 72 is:

$$\text{Years to double} = 72 \div \text{interest rate}$$

For example, how long it will it take for $10,000 invested at 6 percent to double using the formula?

$$\text{Years to double} = 72 \div 6 = 12 \text{ years}$$

In the late 1970s and early 1980s, inflation in the United States was a problem. With an inflation rate of 9 percent, for example, prices would double every eight years ($72 \div 9$).

Use Worksheet 35.1 to determine the length of time it will take for your investment to double.

The rule of 72 gives an approximation of the years needed for an investment to double. The exact length of time is more accurately determined using financial tables, a financial calculator, or a computer. The rule of 72 is less accurate because it does not take into account the time value of money. However, the rule gives an excellent approximation of the doubling time and is simple and easy to use.

WORKSHEET 35.1 Rule of 72 and how long it will take to double your investment

Years to double $= \dfrac{72}{\text{Interest rate}}$

Fill in the interest rate: $= \dfrac{72}{\rule{1cm}{0.4pt}}$

Years to double = _____

How to Assess and Balance Risk and Return in the Choice of Different Investments

INVESTORS HAVE DIFFERENT REASONS OR *objectives* for investing that are important in determining the choice of investments. Objectives also determine the level of risk tolerance, which then impacts on the choice of the different types of investments. The most common objectives are:

- Capital preservation
- Income generation
- Income and growth
- Growth

Figure 36.1 illustrates a continuum of these objectives as well as the corresponding levels of risk. The level of risk increases as the objectives change from capital preservation at one end to growth at the other.

FIGURE 36.1 Objectives and level of risk

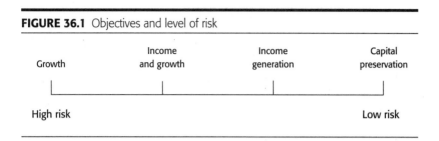

Use Figure 36.1 to determine your objectives and level of risk tolerance. The next step is to determine the levels of risk of the different types of investments, as shown in Figure 36.2.

Classifying some of the types of investments on a continuum of risk, we see that speculative common stocks are considered the most risky (in terms of variability in share price), followed by long-term bonds, with shorter maturities on the low-risk end. There is a great variation of quality among common stocks. The common stocks of the well-established, blue-chip companies are considered less risky than junk bonds.

Speculative common stocks are considered the most risky due to the volatility of their stock prices. Blue-chip, large-capitalized stocks with established dividend records tend to be less volatile and hence less risky than growth stocks and speculative stocks. However, over long periods of time, where the ups and downs of the stock market can be waited out, common stocks as a group have provided higher returns. Common stocks provide the growth in a portfolio and should be included among the investments. The percentage allocated to common stocks depends on your objectives and personal characteristics. For exam-

FIGURE 36.2 Types of investments and their risk levels

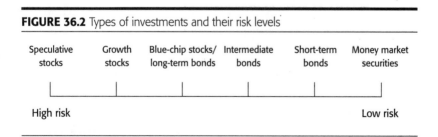

ple, a retired widow who is dependent on the income generated from the investments in her portfolio may have a smaller percentage allocated to common stocks. However, if the portfolio generates more than a sufficient level of income for the widow's current needs, a larger portion of the portfolio could be invested in common stocks to provide more growth in the portfolio for later years.

Bonds are sought by investors primarily for their ability to generate a steady stream of income. However, an often-overlooked fact is that long-term bonds (10- to 30-year maturities) can also be quite risky. Although long-term U.S. Treasury bonds are safe investments in that the U.S. government is not liable to default on the interest and principal payments, they can be quite volatile in price due to changes in interest rates. Corporate and other types of long-term bonds are more volatile than Treasuries due to the increased risk of default.

You need to weigh the advantages of taking on the greater risks of investing in other types of long-term bonds over Treasuries by examining their coupon yields. If the yields are significantly greater than those of long-term Treasuries, you may want to contemplate purchasing these other types of long-term bonds.

Some of the volatility in the price of bonds is reduced by shortening the maturities to intermediate-term bonds. Shortening the length of time to maturity reduces returns, but intermediate-term bonds offer greater flexibility. For instance, if your personal circumstances change so you no longer need current income from investments, intermediate-term securities are generally much more liquid than longer-term bonds and can be more easily changed to more growth-oriented investments.

Low-risk, low-return securities such as certificates of deposit (CDs), Treasury bills, and money market funds should account for the percentage of your portfolio that serves liquidity and emergency fund purposes. Many people make the mistake of keeping too large a percentage of their portfolio in these low-risk, low-return assets for various reasons.

If you are conservative and do not feel comfortable keeping only an amount equal to your liquidity and emergency needs in low-risk investments, you should increase the percentage. Often, however, the returns from these low-yielding money market investments do not even keep pace with inflation, not to mention the effect of taxation on the interest. It is evident that risk cannot be avoided even with the most conservative investments, such as savings accounts and Treasury bills. By understanding and recognizing the different levels of risk for each type of investment, the total risk can be better managed in the construction of the portfolio.

There is a direct correlation between risk and return. The greater the risk in an investment, the greater the potential return to entice investors. In most cases, however, investing in securities with the greatest return and, therefore, the greatest risk can lead to financial ruin if everything does not go according to plan.

Being aware of the risks pertaining to the different types of investments is of little consequence unless you are aware of your own feelings toward risk. How much risk you can tolerate depends on many factors, such as the type of person you are, your investment objectives, the amount of your assets, the size of your portfolio, and the time horizon for your investments.

How nervous are you as an investor? Do you check your stock prices every morning in the financial newspapers? Can you sleep well at night if your stocks have declined below their acquisition prices? If you do watch the prices of your stocks every day, call your broker every time that your stocks fall by a point, and do not sleep well at night when your stocks are down, you do not tolerate risk well. In this case, your portfolio should be weighted toward conservative investments that generate income through capital preservation. The percentage of your portfolio allocated toward stocks may be low to zero, depending on your comfort zone. If you are comfortable with accepting more risk, you would invest a greater percentage of your portfolio in stocks. This would be so even if you are the type of person who monitors your stocks on a daily basis. The difference is whether you can sleep well at night when your stocks go down in value.

Moving along the continuum of greater risk seeking, if you buy stocks and forget about them until you are reminded about them by someone else, your tolerance for risk is much greater, and your portfolio can include a large percentage of stocks.

The risk seeker or speculator will look for investments with the greatest rates of return even though the investments may be extremely volatile and there may be a good chance that some of the principal could be lost.

Bear in mind that there are other factors you need to consider when allocating your investment funds to different types of investments. Understanding your tolerance for risk is just one important step in determining how much of your portfolio should be allocated to common stocks.

There is a wide range of returns associated with each type of investment. Stocks have different classifications, such as growth stocks, income stocks, and speculative stocks. Income stocks generally are lower risk and offer returns mainly in the form of dividends, whereas growth stocks are more risky and generally offer higher returns in the form of capital gains. Similarly, there is a broad range of risks and returns for the different types of bonds; for example, junk bonds versus Treasury bonds of the same maturities. Investors should be aware of the broad range of risks and returns for these different types of investments so that an acceptable level of risk may be found. Figure 36.3 illustrates the risk-return trade-off, in general, for the different types of investments. Bear in mind that with the broad range of risks and returns for each

FIGURE 36.3 General levels of risk and returns for different types of investments

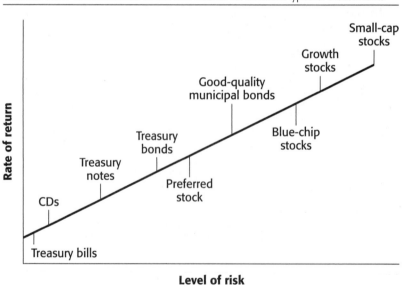

type of investment, you may be exposed to more risk with certain junk bonds, for example, than with certain blue-chip stocks. In general, the risk-return relationship shows that for accepting a higher level of risk in an investment, you should be rewarded with higher returns. Similarly, for lower levels of risk, you can expect lower returns.

Use Worksheet 36.1 to determine your investments by balancing your need for returns with the risk levels.

WORKSHEET 36.1 Choose your investments by balancing your risk-return trade-off

Type of investments	Risk level	Return (percent)	Dollar amount of investment
Short term			
_____	_____	_____	_____
_____	_____	_____	_____
_____	_____	_____	_____
_____	_____	_____	_____
_____	_____	_____	_____
Intermediate term			
_____	_____	_____	_____
_____	_____	_____	_____
_____	_____	_____	_____
_____	_____	_____	_____
_____	_____	_____	_____
Long term			
_____	_____	_____	_____
_____	_____	_____	_____
_____	_____	_____	_____
_____	_____	_____	_____
_____	_____	_____	_____

How to Calculate a Simple Rate of Return for Stocks and Bonds

THE REASON TO INVEST IS TO EARN a return that may be in the form of income (interest and dividends) and/or capital appreciation (when the price of the investment rises between the time of purchase and sale). Some investments, such as savings accounts and certificates of deposit (CDs), offer only income with no capital appreciation; others, common stocks for example, may or may not pay dividends, but also offer the potential for capital appreciation. If the price of the stock goes down, there will be a capital loss. The simple definition of total return includes both income and capital gains and losses.

Why is calculating a return so important? There are two reasons. First, it is a measure of the growth or decline of your investments. Second, it is a yardstick with which to evaluate the performance of your investments against your objectives. The formula for calculating a simple rate of return for stocks or bonds is as follows:

$$\text{Rate of return} = \frac{(\text{Ending Value} - \text{Beginning value}) + \text{Income}}{\text{Gross purchase price}}$$

Spreads and commissions should be included in the calculations. For example, if a stock was purchased at the beginning of the year for $1,000 (including the commission), sold for $1,200 (net proceeds received after deducting the commission) at the end of the year, and earned a dividend of $50, the rate of return is 25 percent:

$$\text{Rate of return} = \frac{(1,200 - 1,000) + 50}{1,000} = 25\%$$

This rate of return is not very accurate, particularly if the investment is held for a long period of time. The reason is because the time value of money is not taken into account. The time value of money is a concept that recognizes that a dollar today is worth more in the future because of its earnings potential. A dollar invested at 3 percent for one year would be worth $1.03 at the end of one year. Similarly, a dollar to be received at the end of one year would be worth less than a dollar at the beginning of the year.

The simple average rate of return of 25 percent discussed above does not take into account the earnings capacity of the interest received. In other words, the $50 of dividends received would be reinvested, which would raise the rate of return above 25 percent.

Using the time value of money to calculate the rate of return gives a more accurate rate of return figure. However, it is more difficult to calculate for stocks. The rate of return on a stock equates the discounted cash flows of the future dividends and the expected sale price of the stock to the current purchase price of the stock. This formula works better for bonds than for common stocks because the cash flows for bonds are much more certain than those for common stocks. The coupon rate for bonds is generally fixed; dividend rates on common stocks may fluctuate. When companies are experiencing losses, they may cut their dividends, as Ford Motor Company did in 2002. On the positive side, if earnings increase, companies may increase their dividend payout ratios. There is even less certainty over the sale price of a stock into the future. Bonds are retired at their par price ($1,000 per bond) at maturity, but when planning to sell a stock in the future, you would be guessing at the sale price.

Whichever formula you use to calculate the rate of return on stocks, you need to be aware that there could be wide fluctuations in return from year to year. This is due primarily to the fluctuations in the price of the stock, since dividend income tends to be relatively stable. Thus, at any point in the future, the price of the stock could be up or down from the acquisition price.

Clearly, many investors dream of tripling their investments overnight by buying stocks. This could happen, but it is not the order of the day. In 1999, many Internet company stocks rose 200 and 300 percent in short periods of time, but unfortunately, they showed that they had the potential to go down by that much and more. The rate of return that investors ought to expect from investing in a diversified stock portfolio should be greater than the returns received on bonds and money market securities. Historically, over long periods of time the stock market has outperformed both long-term and short-term bonds, and although there are no guarantees, this trend will likely prevail in the future. The superior results obtained by stocks are compelling.

Use Worksheet 37.1 to determine the rate of return for your stock or bond investments.

Worksheet 37.2 illustrates the rate of return on a bond for different time periods.

WORKSHEET 37.1 Determine your rate of return for a bond or stock

Ending value _____   Beginning value _____
Interest income/dividends _____   Gross purchase price _____

$$\text{Rate of return} = \frac{(\text{Ending value} - \text{beginning value}) + \text{income}}{\text{Gross purchase price}}$$

$$= \underline{\hspace{2cm}}$$
$$= \underline{\hspace{2cm}} \%$$

Step 1 Fill in the data and enter the figures into the formula.
Step 2 Determine the annualized return if the time period is greater or less than one year.

WORKSHEET 37.2 Calculation of rates of return on a bond for different time periods

---

1. Determine the rate of return for a bond bought at $99 and sold two years later at $101 with a coupon of 7% payable semiannually. (Bonds are quoted in hundreds but trade in thousands.)

Answer:

Cash flows

$990

Rate of return = [(1,010 − 990) + 140] ÷ 990 = 16.16%
Annualized rate of return = 16.16% ÷ 2 years = 8.08%

Reason: The rate of return of 16.16% is for the two-year period, and for an annualized return this figure is divided by two.

2. Determine the rate of return for a bond bought at $98 and sold after six months for $99 with a receipt of one interest payment of $40.

Answer:

Rate of return = [(990 − 980) + 40] ÷ 980 = 5.1%

Annualized rate of return = 5.1% × 2 = 10.2%

Reason: The rate of return for 6 months is 5.1%, which is multiplied by two for an annualized return.

How to Determine a Rate of Return for a Mutual Fund

THE TOTAL RETURN OF A MUTUAL FUND includes the following three components:

1. Dividends and capital gains/capital losses
2. Changes in net asset value
3. Dividends (interest) on reinvested dividends

You can calculate an average total return by taking into account the three sources of return (dividends distributed, capital gains distributed, and the changes in share price) and by using the following formula:

$$\text{Average total return} = \frac{\left(\begin{array}{c}\text{Dividend + capital} \\ \text{gain distributions}\end{array}\right) + \dfrac{(\text{Ending NAV} - \text{Beginning NAV})}{\text{Year}}}{+ \dfrac{(\text{Ending NAV} + \text{Beginning NAV})}{2}}$$

Example:

Assume the following information:

Beginning net asset value (NAV) = $10.00 per share
Ending net asset value (NAV) = $10.30 per share
Dividends = $0.37 per share
Capital gains distributed = $0.70

$$\text{Average total return} = \cfrac{\cfrac{0.37 + 0.70) + (10.30 - 10.00}{1}}{\cfrac{10.30 + 10.00}{2}}$$

$$= 13.5\%$$

This simple yield of 13.5 percent indicates that an investor in this fund would have received double-digit returns, resulting mainly from realized gains and increases in the NAV share price. The more volatile the net asset value of the fund, the greater the likelihood of unstable returns. Thus, when considering whether to invest in a particular fund, don't go by the advertised yield alone, but look at the total return.

Worksheet 38.1 provides the outline to determine a rate of return on your mutual funds.

Step 1 Fill in your mutual fund data.

Beginning NAV (purchase price) _____
Ending NAV (sale price) _____
Dividends _____
Capital gains distributed _____

Step 2 Enter the data into the formula.

$$\text{Average total return} = \frac{\begin{array}{c}(\text{Dividend} + \text{capital} \\ \text{gain distributions}\end{array} + \dfrac{(\text{Ending NAV} - \text{Beginning NAV}}{\text{Year}}}{+\dfrac{(\text{Ending NAV} + \text{Beginning NAV}}{2}}$$

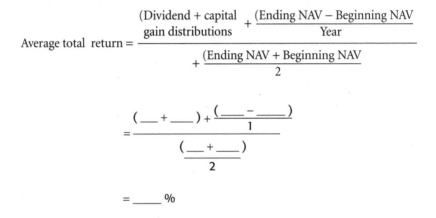

$$= \frac{(\underline{\ }+\underline{\ }) + \dfrac{(\underline{\ }-\underline{\ })}{1}}{\dfrac{(\underline{\ }+\underline{\ })}{2}}$$

$$= \underline{\ \ \ \ }\ \%$$

Step 3 Analyze your return.

Does the major portion of the return come from dividends, capital gains, or an increase in net asset value?

FINANCIAL CALCULATOR #39

How to Determine the Yield on Treasury Bills

TREASURY BILLS ARE THE MOST POPULAR of the short-term individual investments after money market mutual funds.

What Are Treasury Bills?

Treasury bills (T-bills) are short-term, safe-haven investments that are issued by the U.S. Treasury and fully backed by the U.S. government. The risk of default is extremely low. In fact, if the U.S. government defaulted on any of its obligations, all investments in the United States would be suspect. Treasury bills are considered to be the safest of all short-term fixed-income investments.

Treasury bills are negotiable, non–interest-bearing securities that mature in four weeks, three months, or six months. They are available in a minimum denomination of $10,000 and multiples of $1,000 above that. See Table 39.1 for details on the different Treasury bill issues.

The 4-, 13-, and 26-week bills are auctioned every week. The 4-week Treasury bill cannot be bought through the Treasury Direct program, but the other two maturities may be bought directly. The announcements for auctions are generally made two weeks before each auction.

TABLE 39.1 Treasury bills

Term (weeks)	Minimum	Multiples	Auction	Auction time	Issue date
4	$10,000	$1,000	Weekly	Monday	Thursday
13	$10,000	$1,000	Weekly	Monday	Thursday
26	$10,000	$1,000	Weekly	Monday	Thursday

WORKSHEET 39.1 How to determine the yield on Treasury bills

Although there is no stated rate of interest, the yield on Treasury bills can be determined as follows:

$$\text{Yield} = \frac{(\text{Face value} - \text{price paid})}{\text{Price paid}} \times \frac{365}{\text{Days to maturity}}$$

A six-month, $10,000 Treasury bill purchased for $9,908.50 and redeemed at face value has an annual yield of 1.85 percent:

$$\text{Yield} = (10,000 - 9,908.50 \div 9,908.50) \times (365 \div 182)$$

$$= 1.85\%$$

However, to make matters more complex, bids submitted to the Federal Reserve Banks are not quoted on an annual basis, as above, but on a bank discount basis which is computed as follows:

$$\text{Yield} = (\text{Face value} - \text{price paid} \div 100^*) \times (360^{**} \div \text{days to maturity})$$

* Yield is quoted for each $100 of face value.
** Note the use of 360 as opposed to 365 days.

Using the same example as above, the discount is $0.915 for the T-bill selling at $99.085 per $100 face value with a maturity of six months.

The bank discount yield is:

$$= (100 - 99.085 \div 100) \times (360 \div 180)$$
$$= 1.83\%$$

The bank discount yield is always less than the annual yield.

Treasury bills are issued at a discount from their face value. The amount of the discount depends on the prices bid in the Treasury bill auctions. At maturity, the bills are redeemed at full face value. The difference in the amount between the discount value and the face value is treated as interest income. See Worksheet 39.1 for the determination of Treasury bill yields, shown on an annual basis and on a bank discount basis. The distinction between these two methods of determining the yields is important, because if you are submitting a competitive bid you would need to use the yield computed on a bank discount basis. The yield would need to be stated to two decimal places.

Worksheet 39.2 outlines the steps for you to determine the yields on your Treasury bills.

WORKSHEET 39.2 How to determine the yield on your Treasury bills

Step 1 Fill in the following information on your Treasury bill:

Price paid _____ Face Value ($1,000 per T-bill) _____
Days to maturity _____

Step 2 Enter this information into the formula to determine the annual yield.

$$\text{Yield} = \frac{(\text{Face value} - \text{price paid})}{\text{Price paid}} \times \frac{365}{\text{Days to maturity}}$$

$$= \frac{(\underline{\quad} - \underline{\quad})}{(\underline{\quad})} \times \frac{365}{(\underline{\quad})}$$

$$= \underline{\quad\quad}$$

To determine the bank discount yield:

Step 1 Fill in the following information:

Price paid (in hundreds) _____ Days to maturity _____

Step 2 Enter this information into the formula to determine the bank discount yield.

$$\text{Yield} = (\text{Face value} - \text{price paid} \div 100) \times (360 \div \text{days to maturity})$$

$$= \frac{(100 - \underline{\quad})}{100} \times \frac{360}{\text{Days to maturity}}$$

$$= \underline{\quad\quad}$$

Step 3 The bank discount yield is always less than the annual yield.

The bank discount yield is used to place your competitive bid when buying Treasury bills directly from the Treasury.

FINANCIAL CALCULATOR #40
How to Determine the Purchase and Selling Price of Treasury Bills

WHEN YOU BUY TREASURY BILLS that are quoted in the secondary market, you do not see a price quote. Instead, these issues are quoted on a bid and ask spread. Consequently, you need to determine the purchase and selling prices of the issues in which you are interested.

Table 40.1 shows a listing of a Treasury bill quote in a daily newspaper:

- Treasury bills are short-term securities, so all listed T-bills will mature within six months—in this case on August 15, 2002.
- There are 176 days from this date until maturity of this issue. Treasury bills are sold at a discount, which is less than the par or face amount of $1,000, and then redeemed at par at maturity. This difference is attributed to interest. The bid discount of 1.80 percent is the discount (price) that buyers are willing to pay for this bill on that day, and the ask discount of 1.79 percent is the discount at which sellers are willing to sell this security on that day. The spread between the bid and the ask price is $0.05 per T-bill (0.01 percent).
- The ask yield is 1.83 percent, which is the return an investor would get on this issue if bought at the ask price and held to maturity.

TABLE 40.1 Treasury bill quote

Maturity	Days to Mat.	Bid	Ask	Chg	Ask Yld
Aug 15 02	176	1.80	1.79	. . .	1.83

The formulas for calculating the dealer's selling and purchase price are shown in Worksheet 40.1.

From the ask discount, you can determine the price at which dealers will be willing to sell the Treasury bill. In this example, it is $991.25, and at maturity (in 176 days' time) you will receive the face value of the Treasury bill—$1,000. The bid discount indicates what dealers are willing to pay for Treasury bills that you want to sell to them, on the day of this quote. In this case it is $991.20 per bill.

Worksheet 40.2 outlines the steps for determining the purchase and selling price of Treasury bills in which you are interested.

WORKSHEET 40.1 How to calculate the purchase and sale price of Treasury bills

The dealer's selling price can be calculated as follows:

$$= \text{Par value} - \text{Par value} \times \text{Asked discount} \times \frac{\text{Days to maturity}}{360}$$

$$= \$100 - 100 \times 0.0179 \times \frac{176}{360}$$

$$= \$99.125, \text{ or } \$991.25 \text{ per T-bill}$$

The dealer's purchase price can be calculated as follows:

$$= \text{Par value} - \text{Par value} \times \text{Bid discount} \times \frac{\text{Days to maturity}}{360}$$

$$= \$100 - 100 \times (0.018) \times \frac{176}{360}$$

$$= \$99.12 \text{ or } \$991.20 \text{ per T-bill}$$

WORKSHEET 40.2 How to determine the purchase and sale price of your Treasury bills

Step 1 Fill in the following information on your Treasury bill.

Days to maturity _____   Bid discount _____
Ask discount _____

Step 2 If you are buying Treasury bills, use the ask discount.

The purchase price is calculated as follows:

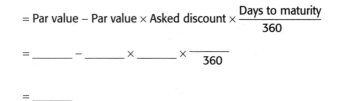

$$= \text{Par value} - \text{Par value} \times \text{Asked discount} \times \frac{\text{Days to maturity}}{360}$$

$$= \underline{\hspace{2cm}} - \underline{\hspace{2cm}} \times \underline{\hspace{2cm}} \times \frac{\underline{\hspace{1cm}}}{360}$$

$$= \underline{\hspace{2cm}}$$

Step 3 If you are selling Treasury bills, use the bid discount.

The selling price can be calculated as follows:

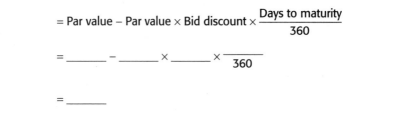

$$= \text{Par value} - \text{Par value} \times \text{Bid discount} \times \frac{\text{Days to maturity}}{360}$$

$$= \underline{\hspace{2cm}} - \underline{\hspace{2cm}} \times \underline{\hspace{2cm}} \times \frac{\underline{\hspace{1cm}}}{360}$$

$$= \underline{\hspace{2cm}}$$

FINANCIAL CALCULATOR #41

How to Buy and Sell Treasury Securities Directly from the Federal Reserve

NEW ISSUES OF TREASURY SECURITIES can be bought directly from any of the Federal Reserve Banks in the primary market with no commissions or fees charged. New Treasury issues can also be bought indirectly through banks and brokerage firms, which charge commissions for their services. Existing Treasury securities that trade in the secondary markets are bought and sold through banks and brokerage firms.

Direct Purchase

An investor can buy directly from the Treasury by opening an account and then submitting a tender form. See Figures 41.1 and 41.2 for a copy of a new account request form and a copy of a tender form for Treasury securities, respectively. See Worksheet 41.1 on page 204 for an explanation of the process for purchasing securities directly through the Federal Reserve Banks.

See Worksheet 41.2 on page 205 to determine whether to submit a competitive or a noncompetitive bid.

Worksheet 41.3 on page 206 summarizes the steps for buying Treasury securities directly through the Federal Reserve Bank or branches.

FIGURE 41.1 New account request

PD F 5182 E
Department of the Treasury
Bureau of the Public Debt
(Revised June 2001)

www.treasurydirect.gov
1-800-722-2678

OMB NO. 1535-0069

NEW ACCOUNT REQUEST

SEE INSTRUCTIONS - TYPE OR PRINT IN INK ONLY - NO ALTERATIONS OR CORRECTIONS

1. *TreasuryDirect* ACCOUNT INFORMATION

ACCOUNT NAME

ADDRESS

City   State   ZIP Code

FOR DEPARTMENT USE

DOCUMENT AUTHORITY

APPROVED BY

DATE APPROVED

EXT REG ☐

FOREIGN ☐

BACKUP ☐

REVIEW ☐

2. TAXPAYER IDENTIFICATION NUMBER

1st Named
Owner   Social Security Number   OR   Employer Identification Number

CLASS ☐

3. TELEPHONE NUMBERS

Work   Home

4. PAYMENT INFORMATION

ROUTING NUMBER

FINANCIAL INSTITUTION
(Limited to 30 characters/spaces)

NAME ON ACCOUNT
(Limited to 22 characters/spaces)

ACCOUNT NUMBER   ☐ Checking   ☐ Savings
(Check One)

5. AUTHORIZATION

I submit this request pursuant to the provisions of Department of the Treasury Circulars, Public Debt Series Nos. 2-86 (31 CFR Part 357), and 1-93 (31 CFR Part 356).

Under penalties of perjury, I certify that:
1. The number shown on this form is my correct taxpayer identification number (or I am waiting for a number to be issued to me) **and**
2. I am not subject to backup withholding because: **(a)** I am exempt from backup withholding, or **(b)** I have not been notified by the Internal Revenue Service (IRS) that I am subject to backup withholding as a result of a failure to report all interest or dividends, or **(c)** the IRS has notified me that I am no longer subject to backup withholding.

I further certify that all other information provided on this form is true, correct and complete.

Signature   Date

SEE INSTRUCTIONS FOR PRIVACY ACT AND PAPERWORK REDUCTION ACT NOTICE.

(OVER)

FIGURE 41.2 Treasury bill, note, and bond tender form

PD F 5381 E
Department of the Treasury
Bureau of the Public Debt
(Revised August 2001)
www.treasurydirect.gov
1-800-722-2678

OMB No. 1535-0069

TREASURY BILL, NOTE & BOND TENDER

For Tender Instructions, See PD F 5382

TYPE OR PRINT IN INK ONLY – TENDERS WILL NOT BE ACCEPTED WITH ALTERATIONS OR CORRECTIONS

1. BID INFORMATION *(Must Be Completed)*

Par Amount:

$ _____
(Sold in units of $1,000)

Bid Type: *(Fill in One)*
○ Noncompetitive
○ Competitive at _____ . _____ %
(Bill bids must end in 0 or 5.)

DEPARTMENT USE
TENDER NO.

RECEIVED BY/DATE

2. TreasuryDirect ACCOUNT NUMBER
(If NOT furnished, a new account will be opened.)

_____

3. TAXPAYER ID NUMBER *(Must Be Completed)*

_____ OR ____-____

Social Security Number (First-Named Owner)   Employer ID Number

ENTERED BY

APPROVED BY

4. TERM SELECTION *(Fill in One)*
(Must Be Completed)

Bill   Circle the Number of Reinvestments

○ 13 - Week........ **0**

○ 26 - Week........ **0**

Note/Bond

○ 2 - Year Note

○ 5 - Year Note

○ 10 - Year Note

○ 30 - Year Bond

○ Inflation-Indexed _____
                    Term

5. ACCOUNT NAME Please Type or Print *(Must Be Completed)*

6. ADDRESS *(For new account or if changed.)* ○ New Address?

_____
City   State   ZIP Code

ISSUE DATE

CUSIP 912795-

CUSIP 912827-

CUSIP 912810-

FOREIGN ☐

BACKUP ☐

7. TELEPHONE NUMBERS *(For new account or if changed.)* ○ New Phone Number?

Work _____   Home _____

8. PAYMENT INFORMATION *(For new account only.)* Changes? Submit PD F 5178.

Routing Number _____

Financial Institution Name _____

Account Number _____

Name on Account _____

Account Type: *(Fill in One)* ○ Checking   ○ Savings

9. PURCHASE METHOD
(Must Be Completed)

○ *Pay Direct** (Existing *TreasuryDirect* Account Only)

○ Checks: _____
Make checks payable to *TreasuryDirect*.
Personal checks accepted ONLY for notes & bonds.

○ Other _____

Total Payment Attached: _____ **$0.00**

CHECKS ARE DEPOSITED IMMEDIATELY

REVIEW ☐

CHECK #

10. AUTHORIZATION *(Must Be Completed – Original Signature Required)*

Tender Submission: I submit this tender pursuant to the provisions of Department of the Treasury Circulars, Public Debt Series Nos. 2-86 (31 CFR Part 357) and 1-93 (31 CFR Part 356), and the applicable offering announcement. As the first-named owner and under penalties of perjury, I certify that: 1) The number shown on this form is my correct taxpayer identification number (or I am waiting for a number to be issued to me), and 2) I am not subject to backup withholding because: (a) I am exempt from backup withholding, or (b) I have not been notified by the Internal Revenue Service (IRS) that I am subject to backup withholding as a result of a failure to report all interest or dividends, or (c) the IRS has notified me that I am no longer subject to backup withholding. I further certify that all other information provided on this form is true, correct, and complete.

Pay Direct: (If using this purchase method.) I authorize a debit to my account at the financial institution I designated in *TreasuryDirect* to pay for this security. I understand that the purchase price will be charged to my account on or after the settlement date. I also understand that if this transaction cannot be successfully completed, my tender can be rejected and the transaction canceled. If there is a dispute, a copy of this authorization may be provided to my financial institution.

Signature(s) _____   Date _____

SEE BACK FOR PRIVACY ACT AND PAPERWORK REDUCTION ACT NOTICE

Step 1 The first step is to fill out the new account request form (Figure 41.1) to establish an account with the Department of the Treasury. The routing number requested on the form is the nine-digit identification number of your financial institution. It can be found on the bottom line of a check before the account number or on a deposit slip before the account number. This step can be done on the Internet.

Step 2 Submit this form to the Federal Reserve Bank/branch. A confirmation of the establishment of the account and an account number will be issued. Purchases of Treasury securities are recorded in this account, which is maintained at no charge up to $100,000 of securities. Over this amount, the Federal Reserve charges $25 to maintain the account.

Step 3 Fill in the tender form to buy Treasury securities directly from the Federal Reserve Bank. See Figure 41.2 for a copy of a tender form.

Step 4 The Federal Reserve Bank auctions new issues of Treasury securities on a weekly basis and investors may submit their bids either on a competitive or noncompetitive basis.

Step 5 Treasury bills purchased directly through the Federal Reserve are held in the TreasuryDirect book-entry system, which is designed primarily for investors who hold their securities to maturity. Should an investor decide to sell Treasury securities before maturity, he or she would have to fill out a Transfer Request Form (PD 5179), which transfers the account to the commercial book-entry system, at which point the Treasury securities could be sold. The commercial book-entry system records those Treasuries bought through financial institutions and government securities dealers. Information on Treasury bills can be obtained from the government's website at (www.publicdebt.treas.gov).

Competitive bids

- Submit a bid on a bank discount basis, to two decimal places. For example, if an investor wanted to buy $100,000 of six-month Treasury bills and pay $99,125, the competitive bid submitted to the Federal Reserve Bank would be 1.79 percent.
- The Federal Reserve accepts those bids with the lowest discount rates (the highest prices) from all the bids received. For the accepted bids there is a range of yields, from the lowest to the highest known as the "stopout yield," which the Federal Reserve will pay. Investors with accepted bids at the "stopout yield" or close to it receive greater returns than those with accepted bids at the lowest accepted yield.
- The yields that investors bid depend upon the money market rates that are currently being offered by competing short-term instruments as well as expectations of what current short-term rates for T-bills will be. By studying these rates, an investor has a better chance of submitting a bid that will be accepted. However, with a competitive bid, investors face the risk of not having their bids accepted, if their bids are above the stopout yields.

Noncompetitive bids

- Less expert investors who may not want to work out their bids or for those who want to be assured of their bids being accepted can submit noncompetitive bids. With noncompetitive bids, investors are able to buy Treasury securities at the average accepted competitive bid in the auction. Generally, all noncompetitive bids of up to $1 million per investor per auction are accepted, which means that investors are assured of their purchases.
- Tender forms to submit bids may be sent by mail, delivered in person to the Federal Reserve Banks and branches before the close of the auction, or submitted on the Internet. Competitive bids must be received by the time designated in the offering circular. Noncompetitive bids that are mailed must be postmarked by no later than midnight the day before the auction and received on or before the issue date of the securities.

(continued overleaf)

- Payment must accompany the tender form. Check the type of payment: cash, check, securities, or other. The amount of the payment should be no less than the amount of the tender for a noncompetitive bid and no less than the bid amount for a competitive bid. If the payment amount is not correct, the tender will be rejected and returned.
- On acceptance of the bid, the investor receives a confirmation receipt from the Federal Reserve and a payment, which is the difference between the tender amount submitted and the discounted price of the T-bills. Investors can stipulate on the tender form whether they want the Federal Reserve to reinvest the T-bills when they mature. If the reinvestment option is not chosen, the Federal Reserve credits the investor's account for the face value of the Treasury bills at maturity.
- The advantage of buying T-bills directly and holding them to maturity is that the investor avoids paying commissions or fees.

WORKSHEET 41.3 Steps for buying Treasury securities directly through the Federal Reserve Bank.

Step 1 Fill in the following data on the Treasury Security tender form:

Par amount _____ Competitive _____ or Noncompetitive bid _____
TreasuryDirect account number _____ (If you do not have one, fill in
   the new account form.)
Social Security # _____
Type of Treasury security _____ Maturity date _____
Routing number (9 digits) _____ Account # _____
Type of account _____ Name of your financial institution _____
Purchase method _____

Step 2 Determine whether you will submit a competitive or a noncompetitive bid.

Competitive bid

Fill in the bid/ask yield to two decimal places. _____

Noncompetitive Bid

Limited to $1 million per auction for Treasury bills
Limited to $5 million in a note and bond auction

(continued)

WORKSHEET 41.3 Steps for buying Treasury securities directly through the Federal Reserve Bank (*continued*)

Step 3 Submit your bid.

This can be done by mail, in person, by touch-tone phone, or through the Internet. Be aware of the time deadline for the auction.

Step 4 File account statements from the Federal Reserve in a safe place.

Step 5 Make a note of the dates of the interest payments.

Interest payment date _____ Amount _____

Maturity date _____

These payments are made directly to the bank account that you wrote on your form. Check to see that these transfers have come in on the due dates.

Step 6 At maturity, TreasuryDirect allows you to reinvest the principal.

If you decide to reinvest the principal, you may do so by mail, by phone, or through the Internet.

Reinvest principal? Yes ____ No ____

FINANCIAL CALCULATOR #42

How to Convert Municipal Bond Yields to Before-Tax Yields

MUNICIPAL BONDS ARE DEBT SECURITIES issued by state and local governments, their agencies, and enterprises with a public purpose. The most important feature of municipal bonds is that the interest income is exempt from federal income taxes and state taxes if the holder lives in the state issuing the municipal bond. The federal tax exemption benefits not only individuals who buy municipal bonds but also the states and localities issuing them, since they can pay lower coupon yields than regular taxable bonds.

Most investors look to lower their tax bills, but municipal bonds may not be the right investment for everyone. Buying tax-exempt issues purely to lower tax liability may mean that some investors in some cases may not be earning as much as they could on an after-tax basis if they had bought taxable bonds. This may be especially true for investors in low tax brackets, who could earn more from taxable bonds even after paying the taxes.

In order to compare municipal bonds with taxable bonds, you need to convert the tax-exempt yield of a municipal bond to the equivalent yield of a taxable bond. See Table 42.1 for some examples of what taxable bonds would have to yield in order to equal the yields of municipal bonds.

The equivalent yield of a taxable bond at the investor's tax bracket is the yield an investor would have to earn on a taxable bond to equal the yield on a municipal bond. For example, an investor in the 15 percent tax bracket purchasing a taxable bond with a yield of 7.65 percent would earn the equivalent from a 6.5 percent tax-exempt municipal bond. Put another way, the investor in the 15 percent tax bracket would purchase a municipal bond yielding 6.5 percent only if taxable bonds of similar maturities were yielding less than 7.65 percent. If this investor could earn more than 7.65 percent on tax-

TABLE 42.1 Comparison of taxable bond yields to those of municipals at different tax brackets

	Municipal bond yield			
	5.0%	5.5%	6.0%	6.5%
Federal income tax bracket		**Taxable bond yield**		
10%	5.50%	6.11%	6.67%	7.22%
15%	5.88%	6.47%	7.06%	7.65%
27%	6.85%	7.53%	8.22%	8.90%
30%	7.14%	7.86%	8.57%	9.29%
35%	7.69%	8.46%	9.23%	10.00%
38.6%	8.14%	8.96%	9.77%	10.59%

able bonds, municipal bonds would not be considered. However, for investors in higher tax brackets, the taxable equivalent yield is much greater. In the 35 percent tax bracket, the taxable equivalent yield on a 6.5 percent municipal bond is 10.00 percent. Thus, as tax brackets (rates) increase, the taxable equivalent yields increase, and municipal bonds become more attractive. For a taxpayer in the highest marginal tax bracket of 38.6 percent, a 5 percent municipal coupon is the equivalent of an 8.14 percent taxable bond coupon.

This presents earnings opportunities for investors in the highest tax brackets when comparing these yields with 10-year Treasury bonds, which are currently yielding under 5 percent. With the current declines in the stock markets around the world, the high yields of municipal bonds, due to their tax-exempt status, make them very appealing to high-income taxpayers.

Before buying tax-free municipal bonds, you should decide whether the yield at your tax bracket is high enough to warrant the purchase.

Brokerage firms publish tables of taxable equivalent yields, like Table 42.1, but it is a simple calculation to convert municipal bond yields to taxable yield equivalents. See Worksheet 42.1 for the formula to convert municipal bond yields to before-tax yields or taxable equivalent yields.

Some states have higher rates of taxation than other states, which brings the next question to mind: Should you buy an in-state or out-of-state bond?

WORKSHEET 42.1 How to convert municipal bond yields to taxable equivalent yields

$$\text{Taxable equivalent yield} = \frac{\text{Municipal bond yield}}{1 - \text{Investor's marginal tax rate}}$$

A 6 percent municipal bond bought by an investor in the 27 percent marginal tax bracket will have a before-tax return of 8.22 percent.

$$\text{Taxable equivalent yield} = \frac{6\%}{1 - 0.27}$$

$$= 8.22\%$$

Most states give favorable tax treatment to in-state municipals by exempting the income from state taxes. This also applies at the local tax level if the issue is a local issue. This exemption from state and local taxes increases the taxable equivalent yield when comparing an in-state municipal bond with a taxable bond. To answer the question of whether to buy an in-state or out-of-state bond requires another simple calculation.

Suppose that you are considering an out-of-state municipal bond with a yield of 6.5 percent and an in-state bond with a yield of 5.75 percent, and the state and local taxes combined are 6 percent.

$$\text{The after-tax out-of-state yield} = (1 - \text{tax rate}) \times \text{the out-of-state yield}$$
$$= (1 - 0.06) \times 0.065$$
$$= 6.11\%$$

The after-tax yield on the out-of-state bond is 6.11 percent, which is higher than the in-state bond yield, and so the out-of-state bond would be more attractive in this case. High-tax states like New York and California have such a high demand for their in-state issues that their yields are often lower than out-of-state municipal bond issues. Bear in mind for comparison purposes that Treasury issues and certain government agency issues are also exempt from state and local taxes. These, however, are not exempt from federal taxes. Investors who are subject to the alternative minimum tax should consult their tax advisors or accountants to determine their equivalent yields.

Worksheet 42.2 outlines the steps to determine your before-tax or taxable equivalent yields.

Tax laws change continually and the marginal tax rates are set to be reduced over the early years of the twenty-first century. Investors should keep abreast of these changes as to the effects on their investments. Municipal bonds are probably the last great tax shelter left in the code. However, they do not benefit all investors. Generally, investors in the higher tax brackets benefit the most from municipal bonds, while those in the lower tax brackets may not find them particularly advantageous to own.

WORKSHEET 42.2 How to convert municipal bond yields to before-tax yields

Step 1 Fill in the following information:

Municipal bond yield _____ Your marginal tax rate _____

Step 2 Plug this data into the formula:

$$\text{Before tax yield} = \frac{\text{Municipal bond yield}}{1 - \text{Investor's marginal tax rate}}$$

$$= \_\_\_\_$$

Step 3 Compare the before-tax yields of municipals with those of Treasuries and agency and corporate bonds to assist in the purchase decision. If the before-tax yield/taxable equivalent yield of the municipal bond yield is greater than the other bond yields, then it is advantageous to go with the municipal bond issue, assuming the risk level is similar.

Taxable equivalent yield of municipal _____ Treasury/other bond yield _____

Duration and How It Can Help You in the Choice of Bonds for Your Portfolio

DURATION IS DEFINED AS THE AVERAGE time that it takes for a bondholder to receive the total interest and principal. It is the point in time in the life of the bond where the bond's return remains the same despite the movement of market rates of interest. For example, the duration on a $1,000 face value bond with a coupon of 6 percent, maturing in three years with a market price of $973.44 and a current market rate of interest of 7 percent, is calcu-lated using the following formula:

$$\text{Duration} = \frac{(1+y)}{y} - \frac{(1+y) + n(c-y)}{c[(1+y)^n - 1] + y}$$

Where

c = coupon rate
y = yield to maturity
n = number of years to maturity

Substituting the figures from the example above:

$$\text{Duration} = \frac{(1 + 0.07)}{0.07} - \frac{(1 + 0.07) + 3(0.06 - 0.07)}{0.06[1 + 0.07)^3 - 1] + 0.07}$$

$$= 2.83 \text{ years}$$

Another method of determining the duration of a bond is to use the time value of money concept. Using the same example as above, a bond with a coupon of 6 percent maturing in three years with a market price of $973.44 and a current market rate of interest of 7 percent, duration is determined as shown in Table 43.1.

Duration is a time-weighted average of the summation of the present val-ues of the coupon and interest payments multiplied by the time periods of the payments, then divided by the market price of the bond. The present value is the opposite of the future or compound value in the time value of money concept. A dollar today is worth more in the future because of its earnings potential. Similarly, a dollar in the future can be discounted to today's value and is worth less now than in the future.

The duration means that the bondholder will collect the average of the coupon and the principal payments of the bond in 2.83 years.

The impact of interest rate risk can be lessened using the concept of dura-tion. Bonds with different maturities and different coupons have different

TABLE 43.1 Duration using the time value of money formula

Time period of payment		Payment amount (Coupon & principal)		Present value interest factor of 7%		Present value of time-weighted payments
1	×	$60	×	0.9346	=	$56.08
2	×	60	×	0.8734	=	104.80
3	×	1,060	×	0.8163	=	2,595.83
						$2,756.71

$$\text{Duration} = \frac{\text{Summation of present value of time-weighted payments}}{\text{Market price of the bond}}$$

$$= \frac{\$2,756.71}{\$973.44}$$

$$= 2.83 \text{ years/periods}$$

durations. Bonds with higher durations experience greater price volatility as market rates of interest change, and bonds with lower durations have lower price volatility. Different bonds with the same durations experience similar price fluctuations due to changes in market rates of interest.

These points are illustrated in Table 43.2, which shows the prices of 6 percent coupon bonds with different maturities when market rates of interest change.

When market rates of interest decline below the coupon rate (6 percent) to 5 percent, the price of the bond increases above par value. Correspondingly, as the maturities increase from two years to 20 years, so do the prices of the bond. The opposite is true when market rates of interest rise to 7 percent (above the coupon rate of 6 percent) as shown in Table 43.2. Bond prices fall below par and decline further as maturities extend into the future.

The following generalizations for bonds help to better explain duration:

1. The longer the maturity of a bond, the greater the price volatility.
2. There is an inverse relationship between bond prices and market

TABLE 43.2 Impact of market fluctuations in interest rates on a par value bond with a coupon rate of 6% with different maturities

Maturity	Market rate of interest 5%	Market rate of interest 7%
2 years	$1,018.56	$981.88
5 years	1,042.27	959.01
10 years	1,077.21	929.72
20 years	1,124.63	894.04

rates of interest: When market rates of interest rise, bond prices fall, and when market rates of interest fall, bond prices rise.

As pointed out, a bondholder with a coupon of 6 percent with a maturity of 30 years faces greater price volatility than a bondholder with a similar coupon bond with a shorter maturity. A lower-coupon bond (for example, 4 percent) with the same maturity experiences even greater price volatility with changes in market rates of interest. A bondholder with the lower-coupon bond receives lower cash flows ($40 per year through maturity versus $60 per year), which when reinvested produces lower future values. The longer the maturity of the bond, the longer the bondholder has to wait to receive the face or par value of the bond. Hence, the present value of the par value of the bond is discounted to a lesser amount than the present value of the par value of a bond maturing earlier.

Duration accounts for this reinvestment rate risk, the coupon rate, and the term to maturity of a bond as follows:

- The lower the coupon, the higher the duration.
- The higher the coupon, the lower the duration.
- The longer the term to maturity, the higher the duration.
- The shorter the term to maturity, the lower the duration.
- The smaller the duration, the smaller the price volatility of the bond.
- The greater the duration, the greater the price volatility of the bond.

Duration explains why a zero-coupon bond has the same duration as its term to maturity. With a zero-coupon bond, there are no coupon payments and only the principal is received at maturity. Thus, except for zero-coupon bonds, the durations for all bonds are less than their terms to maturities.

Duration is a tool that can be used to manage interest rate risk and the maturity of the bonds with the timing of the investor's need for the funds. By matching the duration of bonds with the timing of the need for the funds, investors can lessen their risk of loss on their bonds.

For instance, assume that you need $17,100 in seven years' time and you have $10,000 to invest. You could buy 10 bonds at par, which have a coupon of 8 percent and mature in seven years' time. The cash flow per bond is:

$80 per year for seven years and $1,000 at maturity in seven years

The future value of an annuity of $80 reinvested at 8 percent =	$ 713.84
The par value of the bond at maturity	1,000.00
Total proceeds from bond at maturity	1,713.84
Multiplied by 10 bonds	× 10
Total proceeds in seven years' time	$17,138.40

This is fine if interest rates stay at 8 percent. If interest rates fall, you will have to reinvest your interest proceeds ($80 per year per bond) at lower interest rates, and you will have less than the $17,100 that you need.

Consequently, if you buy a bond with a duration of seven instead of matching the term to maturity of your bond, you will have the amount of money that you need. This is because if interest rates rise and you have a longer maturity bond, the interest is reinvested at higher interest rates, and you would sell your bond at a discount in seven years' time. Similarly, if interest rates fall, your interest will be reinvested at lower interest rates, but you will be able to sell your bond at a premium.

Worksheet 43.1 shows how you can use the concept of duration in the choice of your bonds.

WORKSHEET 43.1 How to use duration in the choice of your bonds

Step 1 Determine the length of time until you will need your funds. _____

Step 2 Determine the duration for each of the bonds you are considering purchasing.

$$\text{Duration} = \frac{(1 + y)}{y} - \frac{(1 + y) + n(c - y)}{c[(1 + y)^n - 1] + y}$$

Where

c = coupon rate _____
y = yield to maturity (reinvestment rate) _____
n = number of years to maturity _____

$$= \frac{(1 + \underline{\quad})}{\underline{\quad}} - \frac{(1 + \underline{\quad}) + \underline{\quad}(\underline{\quad} - \underline{\quad})}{\underline{\quad}[(1 + \underline{\quad}) - - 1] + \underline{\quad}}$$

$$= \underline{\quad}$$

Step 3 Match the duration to the length of time until you need the funds.

Length of time for funds _____ = Duration _____

How to Value Bonds

B OND PRICES FLUCTUATE DUE TO the relationship between their coupon and market rates of interest, their creditworthiness, and the length of time to maturity. After bonds are issued, they rarely trade at their par values ($1,000) in the secondary markets because interest rates are always changing. Some bonds sell at premiums and others sell at discounts.

There is a mathematical formula for determining the price of a bond, but bear in mind that this is conceptual. The market price of a bond depends on the stream of the bond's coupon payments and the principal repayment in the future. Using the time value of money, this stream of future payments is discounted at market rates of interest to its present value in today's dollars.

For example, a bond that pays coupon interest of $100 per year and matures in three years' time with market rates of interest projected at an average of 6 percent per year will have a price of $1,106.92, according to the calculation shown in Worksheet 44.1. Thus, the price of the bond is linked to the coupon yield, market rates of interest, discount rate, and the length of time to maturity.

Comparing the price of a U.S. Treasury note with that of a corporate bond with the same coupon rate and maturity, the prices of the two bonds will differ. Generally, the Treasury note will trade at a higher price than that of the corporate bond because there is a greater risk of default with the corporate bond, and thus the price will be calculated with a higher discount rate (or yield to maturity). The reason is because investors require a greater yield on the corporate bond for assuming the greater risk of default. This confirms why an AAA-rated corporate bond trades at a higher price than a BBB-rated corporate bond if the coupon and maturity are the same. The difference in yield between the AAA- and BBB-rated bonds is referred to as the excess yield, which issuers must pay for the extra grade of credit risk.

Bond prices fluctuate depending on investors' assessment of risk. The greater the risk, the greater the discount rate or required rate of return (and

WORKSHEET 44.1 Determining the value of a sample bond

Step1 List the data for the bond:

Coupon interest per year: $100
Market rate of interest: 6%
Maturity: 3 years

Step 2 Determine the present value or price of the bond using Microsoft Excel. The price of the bond is $1,106.92.

Rate	6%
Nper	3
Pmt	$100
FV	$1,000
Formula result = $1,106.92	

the lower the market price). Therefore, a bond with a greater degree of risk will be discounted at a greater rate of return. Worksheet 44.2 outlines the steps for determining the value of a bond.

For bonds that pay their coupon interest on a semiannual basis, you need to make the following changes. Since the coupon payment is made twice a year, you need to divide the coupon amount by two. For example, a 6 percent coupon payable semiannually results in a coupon amount of $30 per six-month period. Consequently, the rate needs to be adjusted to a six-month period and the Nper or time to maturity is measured in six-month periods. Three years results in six 6-month periods, so six would be entered in the Nper row.

WORKSHEET 44.2 How to determine the value of a bond

Step 1 List the data of the bond you are interested in buying:

Coupon interest _____   Years to maturity   _____
Bond rating   _____   Market rate of interest _____
Risk premium   _____
Discount rate = Risk premium + market rate of interest

_____ + _____ = _____

Step 2 Using Microsoft Excel, determine the price of the bond:

Click on function in the row of tools.
In the left dialog box, highlight *financial*.
In the right dialog box, highlight *PV*.

Step 3 Enter the data in the dialog box as shown in Worksheet 44.1:

Rate _____ Enter the discount rate or market rate of interest
Nper _____ Time to maturity
Pmt _____ Coupon interest payments
FV _____ Future value of the bond, which is the par value ($1,000)
Type _____ Enter 1 if the interest payments are made at the beginning
of the period or 0 if the payments are made at the end
of the period.

Step 4 The formula result is the price of the bond.

How to Value Common Stock

I T IS NOT AS EASY TO VALUE COMMON STOCK as it is to value bonds. Theoretically, the value of any securities, stocks, bonds, and preferred stock is
equal to the discounted future cash flows of dividends/interest and the sale
price of the securities or maturity value of the bonds. Bondholders can count
on fixed payments of interest, but for common stockholders both the receipt
of the dividend and the amount of the dividend are not assured. Similarly,
there is uncertainty as to the future date of the sale of the common stock
and the price of the common stock. Bonds have a stated maturity date, at
which time bondholders receive the par value ($1,000 per bond) of the bond.
There are exceptions, where bonds can be called in at their call price (which
is mostly above par, as it includes a call premium).

The payment of dividends to common stockholders is largely based on
two factors:

1. The profitability of the company
2. The decision by the board of directors to declare and pay dividends
   rather than retain the profits in the company

Profitable companies may decide not to pay dividends, as in the case of
large companies such as Microsoft, Cisco, and Oracle. These companies
have accumulated large amounts of cash, so they are able to sustain the dividend payouts but choose not to pay dividends. Instead these companies have
chosen to retain their profits and reinvest in their future earnings. Consequently, companies fuel their own growth by retaining profits and reinvest-
ing them in future business projects. Generally, when a company's earnings
increase, this is reflected in a higher price for the common stock.

Thus, shareholders value stocks on earnings potential (growth) and direct returns in the form of dividends. The dividend growth model is one method for valuing a stock. This model makes a number of assumptions:

- Common stock does not have a maturity date.
- Dividends may fluctuate over time depending on profitability and the board of directors' decision to either pay dividends or retain the profits for internal reinvestment purposes.
- Companies can grow in different ways, which may or may not affect the valuation of the company.

To get around these difficulties in the valuation of a stock, the dividend growth model makes the following assumptions:

- Future dividends will be paid and will grow at a constant rate.
- The company will have constant growth rate.

The equation shown in Worksheet 45.1 is used to value a common stock based on future dividends that are expected to grow at a constant rate, divided by the investor's expected rate of return minus the growth rate.

See Worksheet 45.2 to determine the value of your common stocks. A good place to start in the determination of the required rate of return is the Treasury bill rate. Add a percentage for the risk premium of the stock to this rate. Small-cap growth stocks in the technology group would fetch higher risk premiums than an established mid-cap regional bank stock, which is in a more stable type of business.

See section 46 for a method to determine the growth rate of a stock.

Using the valuation equation in Worksheet 45.2, you can determine your expected rate of return for any stock by making the same assumption that dividends increase at a constant growth rate. The expected rate of return is the dividend yield of a stock plus its growth rate. See Worksheet 45.3 for how to use the formula to determine the expected rate of return of a stock.

WORKSHEET 45.1 Dividend-growth model to determine the value of a common stock

$$\text{Stock value} = \frac{\text{Future dividend}}{\text{Expected rate of return} - \text{Growth rate}}$$

Future dividend = Existing dividend (1 + Growth rate)
Expected rate of return of the investor includes a risk element for the stock.
Growth rate: see section 46 for one method to determine the growth rate.

Example

Company X has just paid a dividend of $1.20 per share and is expected to grow at 9 percent for the foreseeable future. The investor's required rate of return for such a stock is 12 percent. Using this information, the value of the common stock is determined as follows.

Step 1 Determine the future dividend.

Future dividend = Existing dividend (1 + Growth rate)
$$= 1.20 \ (1 + 0.09)$$
$$= \$1.31$$

Step 2 Determine the value of the common stock.

$$\text{Value} = \frac{\text{Future dividend}}{\text{Required rate of return} - \text{Growth rate}}$$

$$= \frac{1.31}{0.12 - 0.09}$$

$$= \$43.67$$

In order to achieve the required rate of return of 12 percent, the investor would pay no more than $43.67 for each share of this stock.

WORKSHEET 45.2 How to value your common stock

Step 1 Fill in the data:

Dividend   _____

Growth rate of the stock   _____

Required rate of return   _____

Step 2 Determine the future dividend:

Future dividend = Existing dividend (1 + Growth rate)

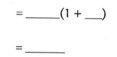

= _____(1 + ___)

= _____

Step 3 Insert values into the formula to determine the value of the common stock.

$$\text{Value} = \frac{\textbf{Future dividend}}{\textbf{Required rate of return} - \textbf{Growth rate}}$$

$$= \frac{(\underline{\hspace{1cm}})}{\underline{\hspace{0.5cm}} - \underline{\hspace{0.5cm}}}$$

= ____

WORKSHEET 45.3 Determining the expected rate of return of a common stock

$$\text{Expected rate of return} = \frac{\text{Future dividend}}{\text{Market price of the stock}} + \text{Growth rate}$$

Example

If Johnson & Johnson Inc. pays a dividend of $0.72, and has a market price of $57.24 per share, and is expected to grow at 10 percent for the foreseeable future, the expected rate of return is:

$$\text{Expected rate of return} = \frac{\text{Future dividend}}{\text{Market price of the stock}} + \text{Growth rate}$$

$$= \frac{\text{Existing dividend} + (1 + \text{Growth rate})}{\text{Market price of the stock}} + \text{Growth rate}$$

$$= \frac{0.72\ (1 + 0.10)}{57.24} + 0.10$$

$$= 11.4\%$$

This expected rate of return on Johnson & Johnson is based on a 1 percent dividend yield and a 10 percent growth rate. However, there is a stronger relationship between a company's future growth and earnings than between growth and dividends in the valuation of a common stock. In reality, a company's earnings and the amount that is retained to fuel the internal growth of the company have a greater influence on the value of common stock.

Worksheet 45.4 outlines the steps to determine the expected rate of return on your stock.

WORKSHEET 45.4 How to determine the expected rate of return on your stock

Step 1 Fill in the data for your stock:

Dividend   _____

Purchase price of the stock   _____

Growth rate   _____

Step 2 Determine the expected rate of return:

Expected rate of return = $\dfrac{\text{Future dividend}}{\text{Purchase price of the stock}}$ + Growth rate

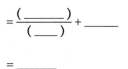

$$= _____$$

Step 3 Evaluate whether this return is sufficient.

How to Determine the Growth Rate of a Stock

T O UNDERSTAND WHAT DRIVES THE MARKET price of a stock, it is important to examine a company's dividends, earnings, and growth rate.

In general, when the earnings of a company increase over a period of time, it has a positive impact on the market price of the stock. The equation showing the valuation of common stock (see section 45) highlights the importance of dividends and the constant growth rate of a company. However, a company's sustained earnings are a major determinant when it comes to whether the company can afford to pay out dividends, maintain its dividend payments, or increase dividend payouts. If the company decides to retain earnings instead of paying them out and reinvest the profits in its business, it can accelerate its earnings growth. Consequently, by measuring the increase in a company's earnings over a period of time, the growth rate can be determined.

Earnings are just one measure of a company's growth rate. Other measures are the growth of a company's assets or sales. These, however, do not have as direct a relationship to the price of the stock as does growth in earnings. Worksheet 46.1 illustrates how the growth rate of a stock can be determined.

Worksheet 46.2 provides the outline for you to determine the growth rate and expected rate of return for your common stock.

WORKSHEET 46.1 How to determine the growth rate of a stock and expected rate of return

Step 1 List the earnings per share (EPS) and dividends per share (DPS) for your stock for the past five years.

This can be found on the company's website, by clicking on *financial statements* or in the company's annual report. The following EPS and dividends per share for Merck, Inc. were found on Merck's website, www.merck.com.

	1997	1998	1999	2000	2001
Earnings per share	$1.87	$2.15	$2.45	$2.90	$3.14
Dividends per share	0.84	0.94	1.10	1.21	1.37

Price per share in 2001: $59.80

Step 2 Determine the growth rate.

The growth rate is determined by solving for the rate of growth of the earnings per share. EPS was $1.87 in 1997 and this grew to $3.14 in four years. Solve for the rate using a financial calculator or Microsoft's Excel spreadsheet as follows:

Click on *f**; two boxes appear on the screen.

Highlight *financial* in the left box and *rate* in the right box.

Enter the data in the box to the right.

Merck's growth rate is 13.834%.

Nper	4
Pmt	0
PV	$ –1.87
FV	$3.14
Type	0
Formula result = 0.13834	

Step 3 Determine the expected rate of return.

$$\text{Expected rate of return} = \frac{\text{Future dividend}}{\text{Price of stock}} + \text{Growth rate}$$

Future dividend = Current dividend (1 + Growth rate)

$$= 1.37(1 + 0.1383)$$

$$= \$1.56$$

$$\text{Expected rate of return} = \frac{1.56}{59.80} + 0.1383$$

$$= 0.0261 + 0.1383$$

$$= 16.44\%$$

The expected return is 16.44% if Merck is bought at the current price of $59.80 per share.

WORKSHEET 46.2 How to determine the growth rate and expected rate of return for your stocks

Step 1 List the earnings per share (EPS) and dividends per share (DPS) for your stock for different periods.

Year _____ _____ _____ _____ _____

EPS					
DPS					

Market price per share _____

Step 1 Determine the growth rate of the stock using a financial calculator or a computer.

Number of periods _____
Present value _____
Future value _____

Solve for the rate _____

Step 3 Determine the expected rate of return for the stock.

Current dividend _____ Growth rate _____
Purchase price of stock _____

Future dividend = Current dividend (1 + Growth rate)

$$= \text{_____} \ (1 + \text{_____})$$
$$= \text{_____}$$

$$\text{Expected rate of return} = \frac{\text{Future dividend}}{\text{Price of stock}} + \text{Growth rate}$$

$$= \frac{(\text{_____})}{(\text{_____})} + \text{_____}$$

$$= \text{_____}$$

Step 4 Evaluate the growth rate and expected return for this stock.

FINANCIAL CALCULATOR #47

How to Analyze and Evaluate
Your Common Stocks

A LTHOUGH THE DIVIDEND GROWTH model for valuing common stock is theoretically sound, there are other approaches to analyzing and evaluating the value of a common stock. One such approach is to examine a company's potential sales and earnings growth, profitability returns, cash flows, and other fundamental factors that affect the value of the company's stock. After such an analysis of the company's financial statements, you will be able to assess the past and present strengths and weaknesses of the company. With this information you can make a better assessment of the company's future trends.

The following ratios can be calculated from the company's financial statements.

Current Ratio

The current ratio is a liquidity measure that indicates the ease or difficulty with which a company can pay off its current liabilities as they become due.

$$\text{Current ratio} = \frac{\text{Current assets}}{\text{Current liabilities}}$$

A current ratio of less than 1 indicates that there are fewer current assets than current liabilities. This means that if the company does not have other sources of raising cash (short term or long term), it may have difficulty covering its short-term liabilities as they become due. Generally speaking, it is desirable for companies to have their current assets exceed their current liabilities, so that if their current assets decline they will still be able to pay off their current liabilities. A low current ratio may indicate weakness, in that the company may not be able to borrow additional funds, or sell off assets, to raise enough cash to meet its current liabilities.

There are exceptions to the foregoing assessment of a low current ratio. The current ratio for Exxon, one of the strongest companies in the oil industry, has dipped below 1 from time to time, but it has the capacity to borrow on a short-term basis to pay off its current obligations. In fact, the notes to Exxon's 1998 financial statements showed that Exxon had unused lines of short-term financing with its banks as well as access to the commercial paper market. Potential investors should always read the footnotes, which contain additional information that can provide more insight into the figures on the financial statements.

It is not a good idea to look at one ratio for one period in isolation. By examining the current ratio of a company for a few years and identifying a trend, it is easier to see whether the current ratio has deteriorated, stayed the same, or improved over time.

What may be the norm for one industry may not hold for another. Utility companies, for example, tend to have current ratios of less than 1, but the quality of their accounts receivable is so good that virtually all of the accounts will be converted into cash. (Most people pay their utility bills, because if they don't they find themselves without power.) Creditors of and investors in utility companies are therefore not as concerned with a low current ratio.

Quick Ratio (Acid Test Ratio)

The major weakness of the current ratio is that it does not distinguish the difference in liquidity among the different types of current assets. In general, inventory is the least liquid, in that it normally takes more time for it to be sold and converted into cash. A more refined measure of a company's ability to pay off its current liabilities as they turn over into cash is the quick ratio. The reason is because inventory is omitted from the calculation.

$$\text{Quick ratio} = \frac{\text{Current assets} - \text{Inventory}}{\text{Current liabilities}}$$

The quick ratio will always be less than the current ratio unless the company has no inventory. The quick ratio indicates the degree of coverage of the current liabilities from cash and other liquid assets. A low quick ratio indicates that the company may have difficulty paying off its current liabilities as they become due. However, this may not always be true for a company, because there are many other factors that influence a company's ability to pay off current debts. These are:

- The company's ability to raise additional funds, long term or short term.
- The willingness of creditors to roll over their debt.
- The rate at which current assets such as accounts receivable and inventory turn over into cash.

The following two ratios indicate the rate at which two of the current assets turn over into cash. They are the accounts receivable turnover and inventory turnover.

Accounts Receivable Turnover

$$\text{Accounts receivable turnover} = \frac{\text{Annual credit sales}}{\text{Accounts receivable}}$$

The larger the accounts receivable turnover, the faster the company turns its credit sales into cash. For example, an account receivable turnover of 8 indicates that sales turn over into cash every 45 days ($365 \div 8$), or one-and-a-half months ($12 \div 8$). A receivables turnover that is too high indicates that the company may be too stringent in giving credit, which lowers sales and profit.

This ratio may also be misleading for companies with seasonal sales or highly fluctuating sales in that it uses year-end receivable figures. It is a good idea to compare this ratio and all other ratios over a five-year period, and if possible compare them to those of the industry. For example, if the norm for the industry is 30 days, you would not want to see a significantly higher deviation in the company's collection period.

Inventory Turnover

$$\text{Inventory turnover} = \frac{\text{Sales}}{\text{Average inventory}}$$

The inventory turnover ratio shows the speed with which inventory is sold. The higher the inventory turnover, the more rapidly the company is able to turn over its inventory into accounts receivable and cash. For example, an inventory turnover of 5 indicates that it takes the average inventory 73 days to turn over (365 days ÷ 5). If the inventory turnover for the same company increases to 7, the inventory turns over in roughly 52 days (365 ÷ 7).

With both the accounts receivable turnover and inventory turnover, you do not want to see extremely low values, which indicate that the company's cash is tied up for long periods. Similarly, extremely high turnover figures indicate poor inventory management, which could lead to stock-outs, and hence customer dissatisfaction.

Profitability

The profits of a company are important to investors because these earnings are either retained or paid out in dividends to shareholders, both of which affect the stock price. Many different measures of profitability indicate how much the company is earning relative to the base used, such as sales, assets, and shareholders' equity. The different profitability ratios are relative measures of the success of the company.

Using sales as a base, the income statement is the starting point. The sales for a selected period can be compared with the sales figures for previous years to see whether there has been growth or a decline. For example, sales may have increased from the previous year, yet the company may report a net loss for the year. This indicates that expenses have risen significantly. An investor would then examine the income statement to see whether the additional expenses were nonrecurring (a one-time write-off) or due to increased operating costs incurred in the normal course of business. If the latter, the investor should question management's ability to contain these costs. Identifying a trend of these expenses over a period of time is useful in the evaluation process.

There are several profitability ratios that use sales as a base: gross profit, operating profit, and net profit.

Gross Profit

Gross profit reflects not only a company's markup on its cost of goods sold but also management's ability to control these costs in relation to sales. The gross profit ratio is computed as follows:

$$\text{Gross profit ratio} = \frac{\text{Sales} - \text{Cost of goods sold}}{\text{Net sales}}$$

The gross profit figure is found in the income statement. The gross profit is sales minus cost of goods sold.

Operating Profit

$$\text{Operating profit} = \frac{\text{EBIT}}{\text{Sales}}$$

The operating profit ratio is the income from operations (also known as the earnings before interest and taxes, or EBIT) divided by sales. This includes the cost of goods sold and the selling, general, and administrative expenses. This ratio shows the profitability of the company in its normal course of operations and provides a measure of the operating efficiency of the company.

The operating profit or loss often provides the truest indicator of a company's earning capacity, as it excludes the nonoperating income and expenses.

Net Profit

The net profit margin includes the nonoperating income and expenses such as taxes, interest expense, and extraordinary items. The net profit ratio is calculated as follows:

$$\text{Net profit} = \frac{\text{Net income}}{\text{Net sales}}$$

To the lay investor, it may not seem that important to calculate all these profit ratios. Instead, there may be an emphasis on the net profit margin only. This could be misleading because if tax rates or interest expenses increase, or if there are some large, extraordinary items in the year, there will be a significant change in the net profit even though operating profits have not changed.

Other measures of profitability, which are more specific to common shareholders in that they measure the returns on the invested funds of the shareholders, are the returns on equity and common equity.

Return on Equity

The return on equity ratio indicates how well management is performing for the stockholders and is calculated as follows:

$$\text{Return on equity} = \frac{\text{Net income}}{\text{Shareholders' equity}}$$

If the company increases its use of debt instead of using equity financing, it can increase its return on equity. The reason is because the earnings are spread over a smaller equity base. This is the use of financial leverage (leverage ratios are discussed later in this section).

For common stock investors, a highly leveraged company means there is great risk, which will require a greater rate of return to justify the risk. This increase in the required rate of return may have a negative impact on the share price.

Thus, the use of leverage can increase the value of the stock when the level of debt used is not perceived as adding a great amount of risk to the company.

When considering the leverage of a company, compare it to the typical leverage for that industry. Investors should look at the debt and coverage ratios of a company to see the extent of its borrowing and its ability to service the debt.

Return on Common Equity

When a company has preferred stock, the common shareholders may be more concerned with the return attributable to the common equity rather than to the total equity. To determine this return, adjustments are made for the preferred dividends and preferred stock outstanding.

$$\text{Return on common equity} = \frac{\text{Net income} - \text{Preferred dividends}}{\text{Equity} - \text{Preferred stock}}$$

Leverage Ratios

While leverage is a major concern for bondholders who use leverage ratios to determine the level of debt and the servicing of the contractual payments of interest and principal, it is also an important issue for common stockholders.

Debt Ratio

The debt ratio indicates how much of the financing of the total assets comes from debt. The ratio is calculated as follows:

$$\text{Debt ratio} = \frac{\text{Total current and noncurrent liabilities}}{\text{Total assets}}$$

A company with a large debt ratio becomes increasingly vulnerable if there is a downturn in sales and/or the economy, particularly in the latter case, if it is a cyclical company.

When examining the financial statements of a company, you should always check the footnotes to see if there is any debt that has not been included on the balance sheet. If a company does not consolidate the financial subsidiaries into its financial statements, any debt that the parent company is responsible for will be reported in the footnotes to the financial statements.

Coverage Ratios

The coverage ratios measure a company's ability to cover the interest payments associated with its debt.

The *times interest earned ratio* indicates the company's coverage of its interest payments. It is calculated as follows:

$$\text{Times interest earned ratio} = \frac{\text{Earnings before interest and taxes}}{\text{Annual interest expense}}$$

If a company has low coverage of its interest payments, a slight downturn in sales or an increase in costs could have disastrous consequences in that the company may not be able to meet its interest payments.

The Price-Earnings (P/E) Ratio

The most commonly used guide to interpret the relationship between stock prices and earnings is the price-earnings (P/E) ratio. It is calculated as follows:

$$\text{Price-earnings ratio} = \frac{\text{Market price of the stock}}{\text{Earnings per share}}$$

The P/E ratio shows the number of times that a stock's price is trading relative to its earnings. The P/E ratios for listed common stocks are published daily in financial newspapers. For example, the P/E ratio for Exxon Corporation as of March 18, 2002, was 20, and the closing price of the stock on that day was $43.61 per share. This means that shareholders were willing to pay 20 times Exxon's earnings for its stock. Looked at another way, it would take 20 years of these earnings to equal the invested amount of $43.61 per share.

By rearranging the formula, the earnings per share can be determined for Exxon:

$$\text{Earnings per share} = \frac{\text{Market price of the stock}}{\text{P/E ratio}}$$

$$= \frac{\$43.61}{20}$$

$$= \$2.18$$

Investors who obtain company information from service organizations, such as Standard & Poor's and Value Line, may find discrepancies between the P/E ratios reported in the newspapers and those reported by information services companies. The reason is because the financial newspapers quote the P/E ratio based on annual earnings of the previous year, whereas the information services companies may quote the P/E ratio based on earnings of the current quarter and projected future quarters.

Theoretically, if the earnings per share increase, the stock price should rise so that the P/E ratio stays much the same. In reality, this does not often happen. P/E ratios may be volatile and fluctuate considerably.

As a rule of thumb, the P/E ratios of drug companies on average trade around the low 20s, while the P/E ratios of many small, emerging growth companies, such as the biotech companies, may be greater than the 50s. P/E ratios of companies whose stock prices have been driven down due to pessimism may be very low. Boeing Corporation, for example, is trading at 14 times earnings, while computer companies are trading at higher P/E multiples. Dell Computer is trading around 56 times earnings.

Thus, P/E ratios by themselves are not relied on very greatly to select stocks. For example, why would an investor pay 200 times earnings for the stock of a company that may or may not succeed when there are solid companies with steady, flat earnings trading at low P/E multiples?

What the P/E ratio of a company will do is show how expensive the stock is relative to its earnings. High P/E ratios (above 20, as a rule of thumb) are characteristic of growth companies—although with the average market multiple currently around 28, a P/E ratio of 20 almost seems like a value stock. Investors may be optimistic about a company's potential growth, and hence the stock price is driven up in anticipation. This results in a high stock price relative to the company's current earnings. Some investors may be willing to pay a high price for a company's potential earnings; other investors may consider such stocks to be overpriced.

What becomes apparent is that high P/E ratios indicate high risk. If the anticipated growth of these high P/E ratio stocks is not achieved, their stock prices will be punished and will fall very quickly. On the other hand, if they do live up to their promise, investors will benefit substantially.

Low–P/E ratio stocks (under 10) are characteristic of either mature companies with low growth potential or companies that are undervalued or in financial difficulty.

By comparing the P/E ratios of companies with the averages in the industries and the markets, investors can get a feeling for the relative value of the stock. For example, the average P/E ratios for companies on the U.S. stock markets are currently around 28 times earnings. During bull markets these ratios go up, and during bear markets the average declines (to as low as 6 times earnings, which happened in 1974).

P/E ratios fluctuate considerably, differing among companies due to many factors, such as growth rates, popularity, earnings, and other financial characteristics.

Earnings Per Share (EPS)

Besides the market price of the stock, the other figure used to determine the P/E ratio is the earnings per share (EPS). The earnings per share indicate the amount of earnings allocated to each share of common stock outstanding. EPS figures can be used to compare the growth (or lack of growth) in earnings from year to year and to project future growth in earnings. EPS per share is calculated as follows:

$$\text{Earnings per share} = \frac{\text{Net income minus preferred dividends}}{\text{Number of common shares outstanding}}$$

The number of shares outstanding equals the number of shares issued minus the number of shares that the company has bought back, called treasury stock. In many cases, companies will report two sets of EPS figures; the regular earnings per share, and the fully diluted earnings per share. For the beginning investor, this can be confusing.

When companies have convertible bonds, convertible preferred stock, rights, options, and/or warrants, their EPS figures may be diluted due to the increased number of common shares outstanding, if and when these securities are converted into common stock. Companies are then required to disclose their fully diluted EPS figures as well.

It is the trend of EPS figures over a period of time that is important for investors. If earnings per share are increasing steadily due to growth in sales, this should translate into increasing stock prices. However, earnings per share can also increase through companies buying back their own shares. This reduces the number of shares outstanding, and if earnings stay the same, there will be an increase in earnings per share. Conceivably, earnings per share could increase when sales and earnings decrease if a significant amount of stock is bought back. The astute investor examines the financial statements to determine whether the increase in earnings per share is due to growth in sales and earnings or due to stock buybacks. If the increase is due to the latter, the result could be a loss of confidence in the stock, which could lead to a decline in the stock price.

Companies with poor fundamentals may try this tactic of buying their shares back to improve their earnings per share and ultimately their stock prices, but over the long term this strategy may not work.

Decreasing earnings per share over a period of time generally has a negative impact on stock prices. However, the reasons for the decrease are important. A decrease in EPS due to an increase in the number of shares outstanding from conversions of convertible bonds or preferred stock issues is not as negative a factor as decreasing sales. If a decrease in EPS is due to decreasing sales, further investigation is required to determine if this is a temporary or permanent situation.

Consequently, when comparing current EPS figures with those of previous periods, it is important to examine the reasons for the changes in order to get a better feeling for the potential changes in the stock price.

Dividends and Dividend Yields

Investors buy stocks for their potential capital gains and/or their dividend payments. Companies either share their profits with their shareholders by paying dividends or retain their earnings and reinvest them in different projects in order to boost their share prices. A company's dividend policy is generally made public. For example, some growth companies and other companies choose not to pay dividends, while some of the established blue-chip companies, utility companies, and real estate investment trusts (REITs) are well known for their dividend payments.

The dividend amount that listed companies pay can be found in the stock listings in newspapers. Generally, companies try to maintain these stated dividend payments even if they suffer declines in earnings. Similarly, increases in earnings do not always translate into increases in dividends. Certainly there are many examples where companies experience earnings increases that result in increases in dividend payments, but this is not always the case. There is an imprecise relationship between dividends and earnings. There are times when increases in earnings exceed increases in dividends and other times when increases in dividends exceed increases in earnings. Thus, growth in dividends cannot be interpreted as a sign of a company's financial strength.

Dividends are important from the standpoint that they represent tangible returns. The cash flow from dividends may be reinvested by shareholders. In contrast, investors in growth stocks that pay little or no dividends are betting on capital appreciation rather than current returns.

To determine the dividend yield, which shows the percentage return that dividends represent relative to the market price of the common stock, the following calculation is used:

$$\text{Dividend yield} = \frac{\text{Annual dividend}}{\text{Market price of the stock}}$$

A strategy of buying high-dividend–yielding stocks may offer some protection against a fall in stock market prices due to rising interest rates. Dividend yields of many utility companies, REITS, and energy companies may be as high as 5 to 7 percent. High dividend yields are characteristic of a few blue-chip and large companies, and utility companies.

It is risky, however, to choose stocks purely because of their high dividend yields. Dividends can always be reduced, which in general puts downward pressure on the price of the stock.

When choosing high-dividend–yield stocks, you should look at the earnings to see that they are sufficient to support the dividend payments. According to Geraldine Weiss, editor of the newsletter *Investment Quality Trends*, earnings should be equal to at least 150 percent of the dividend payout *

$$\text{Dividend payout ratio} = \frac{\text{Dividend per share}}{\text{Earnings per share}}$$

* Earl C., Jr. Gottschalk. "Nervous About Growth Stocks? Try some High-Dividend Ones," *The Wall Street Journal*, May 2, 1994, p. C1.

Book Value

Some investors look for stocks whose market prices are trading below their book values. This may or may not be a sound strategy because there are many factors that overstate or understate the book value of a stock, which makes it a less meaningful measure.

$$\text{Book value} = \frac{\text{Shareholders' equity}}{\text{Number of shares outstanding}}$$

Investors looking for value stocks would place more emphasis on finding stocks whose book values are greater than their market values.

Price-to-Sales Ratio

The price-to-sales ratio indicates how much an investor pays for every dollar of sales for a company.

$$\text{Price-to-sales ratio} = \frac{\text{Market price per share}}{\text{Sales per share}}$$

This ratio measures the valuation of a company on the basis of sales rather than earnings. The price-to-sales ratio should be compared with those of other companies in the industry to determine whether the company is trading at a compelling valuation to its sales base.

Price-Earnings to Growth Ratio

The price-earnings to growth ratio indicates how much an investor pays for the growth of the company.

$$\text{Price-earnings to growth ratio} = \frac{\text{Price-earnings ratio}}{\text{Growth rate}}$$

The lower the ratio, the greater the potential increase in stock price, assuming that the company can grow at its projected rate.

What About a Company's Cash?

Earnings are an important determinant of a company's value and stock price, but the company's cash position is another important place to assess value. The statement of changes in cash position is a good starting point to assess cash flow. This statement can be found in the annual report of a company.

The statement of changes in cash has three sections:

- Cash from operating activities
- Cash from investing activities
- Cash from financing activities

The first section, cash from operating activities, shows the inflows and outflows of cash from operations for the period. Noncash expenses such as depreciation, deferred income tax charges, and annuity and accrued liability provisions are added back to the net income to provide cash flow.

A more refined measure is free cash flow, which is the cash flow minus capital spending. Companies that do not generate strong cash flows have less flexibility, and this is most often reflected in their stock prices.

Worksheet 47.1 provides a framework to evaluate your company's common stock. After completing this worksheet, you will have a better feeling for the strengths and weaknesses of the company.

WORKSHEET 47.1 Framework to evaluate common stock

	Year	Year	Year	Year	Year	Year	Year
Company name	___	___	___	___	___	___	___
Current ratio $= \dfrac{\text{Current assets}}{\text{Current liabilities}}$	___	___	___	___	___	___	___
Quick ratio $= \dfrac{\text{Current assets} - \text{Inventory}}{\text{Current liabilities}}$	___	___	___	___	___	___	___
Acc. rec. turnover $= \dfrac{\text{Annual credit sales}}{\text{Acc. rec.}}$	___	___	___	___	___	___	___
Inv. turnover $= \dfrac{\text{Sales}}{\text{Average inventory}}$	___	___	___	___	___	___	___
Gross profit ratio $= \dfrac{\text{Sales} - \text{Cost of goods sold}}{\text{Sales}}$	___	___	___	___	___	___	___
Operating profit $= \dfrac{\text{EBIT}}{\text{Sales}}$	___	___	___	___	___	___	___
Net profit $= \dfrac{\text{Net income}}{\text{Sales}}$	___	___	___	___	___	___	___
Return on equity $= \dfrac{\text{Net income}}{\text{Shareholders' equity}}$	___	___	___	___	___	___	___
Return on common equity $= \dfrac{\text{Net income} - \text{Preferred dividends}}{\text{Equity} - \text{Preferred stock}}$	___	___	___	___	___	___	___

WORKSHEET 47.1 Framework to evaluate common stock (*continued*)

	Year	Year	Year	Year	Year	Year	Year	Year
Debt ratio = $\dfrac{\text{Total liabilities}}{\text{Total assets}}$	—	—	—	—	—	—	—	—
Coverage ratio = $\dfrac{\text{EBIT}}{\text{Annual interest expense}}$	—	—	—	—	—	—	—	—
P/E ratio = $\dfrac{\text{Market price of the stock}}{\text{Earnings per share}}$	—	—	—	—	—	—	—	—
EPS = $\dfrac{\text{Net income} - \text{Preferred dividends}}{\text{No. of shares outstanding}}$	—	—	—	—	—	—	—	—
Dividend yield = $\dfrac{\text{Annual dividend}}{\text{Price of stock}}$	—	—	—	—	—	—	—	—
Dividend payout ratio = $\dfrac{\text{Dividend per share}}{\text{EPS}}$	—	—	—	—	—	—	—	—
Book value = $\dfrac{\text{Shareholders' equity}}{\text{No. of shares outstanding}}$	—	—	—	—	—	—	—	—
Price-to-sales ratio = $\dfrac{\text{Price per share}}{\text{Sales per share}}$	—	—	—	—	—	—	—	—
P/E to growth ratio = $\dfrac{\text{P/E ratio}}{\text{Growth rate}}$	—	—	—	—	—	—	—	—
Cash flow	—	—	—	—	—	—	—	—
Free cash flow	—	—	—	—	—	—	—	—

FINANCIAL CALCULATOR #48

How to Choose a Mutual Fund*

THERE ARE MORE THAN 8,000 MUTUAL FUNDS on the market, and they are all vying for an investor's savings. Many of the messages in their advertisements lead you to believe that they have attained superior performance. Even if funds do well during good times, however, you need to examine how these funds have performed during a down market. Several business magazines track the overall performance records (during up and down markets) of many of the mutual funds, which is a better yardstick than the advertising messages of the mutual funds themselves. From these publications, potential investors can see how well funds have performed in up markets as well as how the funds have protected their capital during periods of declining prices.

New funds do not have track records. Therefore, a yardstick on performance during a period of declining prices may not be available.

You can evaluate a mutual fund on the basis of performance; namely, yield and total return, and the total expense ratio of the fund. But before doing that you should begin with the objectives of the fund.

Mutual funds are required to send a prospectus to a potential investor before accepting investment funds. Although prospectuses are written in a manner that ranks them high on the list of best cures for insomnia, they still provide investors with information about the fund that they may not be able to get anywhere else. Obtain a prospectus for each of the funds that you are considering so that you can compare them in terms of the following criteria.

---

*Portions of this section have been previously published by Esmé Faerber in *All About Stocks* (New York: McGraw-Hill, 2000).

1. Objectives: Are They Compatible with Your Level of Risk?

The objectives and policies of the fund generally appear near the front of the prospectus. The objectives describe the type of securities the fund invests in as well as the risk factors associated with the securities. For instance, if the prospectus states that the fund will buy growth securities, the investor should not be surprised to find that most of the stocks will have high price-earnings ratios and may include risky small-cap stocks.

The investment policies outline the latitude of the fund manager to invest in other types of securities. This could include trading futures contracts, writing options to hedge bets on the direction of interest rates or the market, or investing in derivative securities to boost the yield of the fund. Many so-called conservative funds, which supposedly only hold blue-chip stocks, have on occasion resorted to small-company and offshore stocks to boost returns. The greater the latitude in investing in these other types of securities, the greater the risk if events backfire.

Determine whether the objectives of each of the funds are compatible with your level of risk tolerance.

2. The Performance of the Fund

Most funds can boast they have attained the number one position in some area of performance at some point in time during their existence. Similarly, good past performance may not be indicative of good future performance. Some funds that have performed well in the past have had poor performance thereafter. In fact, some funds that did well in the past no longer exist.

Organizations such as Morningstar rate a mutual fund's performance relative to other funds with the same investment objectives, but this too can be misleading for investors trying to choose a fund. (Morningstar's Internet address is www.morningstar.com.) First, the funds may not be comparable, even though they have similar objectives. One may have riskier assets than another, for instance. Second, past performance may not be a reliable indicator of future performance.

In choosing a fund, investors are best off looking at what the fund invests in (as well as can be determined), and then trying to determine the volatility in terms of up and down markets.

3. The Total Return for the Fund

Yield is one aspect of performance. Yield is defined as the interest and/or dividends paid to shareholders as a percentage of the net asset value price. Money market funds quote yields over a seven-day period. This is an average dividend yield for seven days, and it can be annualized. Long-term bond funds also quote an annualized average yield, but it is generally over 30 days.

In 1988, the Securities and Exchange Commission (SEC) ruled that funds with average maturities longer than those of money market mutual funds must quote the SEC standardized yield. The SEC standardized yield includes the interest or dividends accrued by the fund over 30 days as well as an adjustment to the prices of the bonds for the amount of the amortization of any discount or premium that was paid for the bond assets. The SEC standardized yield makes the comparison of different mutual funds more meaningful. Make sure that you are not comparing the yield of one fund to that of another fund that is calculated differently.

The SEC standardized yield should be used for comparison purposes only and not as a means to predict future yields. This yield is a measure of the fund's dividend distribution over a 30-day period and is only one aspect of the fund's total return. Mutual funds pass on any gains or losses to shareholders, which can increase or decrease the fund's total return.

Another factor that affects total return is the fluctuations in net asset value. When the share price increases by 6 percent, it effectively increases the total return by an additional 6 percent. Similarly, when the net asset value price of the fund declines, total return will decrease. This explains why funds with a positive yield can have a negative total return. During the bear market of 2001, funds distributed dividends and capital gains, but the total returns for the funds were negative due to the decline in net asset values (prices of the funds).

The interest on reinvested dividends is another factor that may also be in the total return. When the interest or dividends paid out by the fund are reinvested to buy more shares, the yield earned on these reinvested shares boosts the overall return on the invested capital.

Therefore, when comparing the total returns quoted by different funds, you need to make sure you are comparing the same type of total return.

The total return of a mutual fund includes the following three components in its makeup:

1. Dividends and capital gains or losses
2. Changes in net asset value
3. Dividends (interest) on reinvested dividends

When comparing the total returns quoted by funds, you should determine whether all of these components are included in the computation. However, there are funds that choose not to advertise a total cumulative return. Some high-yield junk bond funds have at times chosen not to emphasize total returns, since deep declines in junk bond prices caused them to be negative. Instead they touted their high yields. Thus, basing your choice of fund on yield alone can be misguided, since yields may be easier to manipulate. Investors should, therefore, look at both the yield and the total return of the fund to get a more balanced picture.

4. The Expenses of the Fund

Expenses are a key factor in differentiating the performances of different funds. By painstakingly looking for funds with the highest yields, investors are looking at only half the picture. A fund with a high yield may also be one that charges higher expenses, which could put that fund behind some of the lower-cost funds with lower yields. Fees reduce the total return earned by funds.

The mutual fund industry has been criticized for the proliferation of fees and charges. Granted, these are all disclosed by the mutual funds, but besides the conspicuous charges, investors need to know where to look to find the less obvious fees. Load charges are obvious expenses.

A no-load mutual fund is one where the investor pays no commission or fee to buy or sell the shares of the fund. With an investment of $10,000 in a no-load fund, every cent of the $10,000 goes to buying shares in the fund. You can no longer easily identify no-load funds in the newspapers. However, you can easily find out whether the fund that you are interested in is a no-load fund by calling the mutual fund family, looking at its website, or examining the prospectus.

A load fund charges a sales commission for buying shares in the fund. These fees can be quite substantial, ranging to as much as 8.5 percent of the purchase price of the shares. The amount of the sales (load) charge per share can be determined by deducting the net asset value price from the offer price. Some funds give quantity discounts on their loads to investors who buy shares in large blocks. For example, the sales load might be 5 percent for amounts under $100,000, 4.25 percent for investments between $100,000 to $200,000, and 3.5 percent for amounts in excess of $200,000. When buying load funds, you need to check whether a load is charged on reinvested dividends as well.

Some funds also charge a back-load or exit fee when you sell shares in the fund. This can be a straight percentage, or the percentage charged may decline the longer the shares are held.

The ultimate effect of load charges is to reduce the total return. The impact of the load charge is felt more keenly if the fund is held for a short period of time. For instance, if a fund has a return of 6 percent and there is a 4 percent load to buy into the fund, the total return to the investor for the year is sharply reduced. If there is a back-load fee to exit the fund, this could be even more expensive for the investor. If the share price has increased, the load percentage will be calculated on a larger amount.

Don't be fooled by some funds that tout themselves as no-load funds but assess fees by another name that come right out of the investor's investment dollars like a load. These fees are not called loads, but they work exactly like loads. Their uses are to defray some of the costs of opening accounts or buying stocks for the fund's portfolio. They vary from 1 to 3 percent among the different fund groups.

From the investor's point of view, it should not matter how lofty the purpose is for these fees. They reduce your investment. If you invest $10,000 and there is a 3 percent fee, only $9,700 of your investment will go toward buying shares.

You also need to watch out for redemption fees: sell $10,000 worth of shares with a 3 percent redemption fee and you only receive $9,700.

Why then would so many investors invest in load funds when these commissions eat away so much of their returns? One can only speculate on possible answers:

- Investors may not want to make decisions themselves as to which funds to invest in, so they leave the decisions to their brokers and financial planners.
- Brokers and financial planners earn their livings from selling investments from which they are paid commissions. These include only load funds.
- No-load funds do not pay commissions to brokers and financial planners and are, consequently, not promoted or sold by brokers and planners.

Brokers and financial planners often tout that load funds outperform no-load funds, but there is no evidence to support this opinion. According to CDA/Weisenberger, there was no difference between the performance of the average no-load fund and load fund over a five-year period (1988–1992).* In fact, when adjusting for sales commissions, investors would have been better off with no-load funds.

---

*Jonathan Clements, "The 25 Facts Every Fund Investor Should Know," *The Wall Street Journal*, March 5, 1993, p. C1.

12 (b)-1 fees are less obvious than loads. These are charged by many funds to recover expenses for marketing and distribution. These fees are assessed annually and can be quite steep when added together with load fees. Many no-load funds tout the absence of sales commissions but tack on 12 (b)-1 fees, which are like a hidden load. A 1 percent 12 (b)-1 fee may not sound like very much, but it is $100 less per annum in your pocket on a $10,000 mutual fund investment.

In addition to the above-mentioned charges, funds have management fees that are paid to the managers who administer the fund's portfolio of investments. These can range from 0.5 percent to 2 percent of assets. High management fees also take a toll on the investor's total return.

Thus, all fees bear watching since they reduce yields and total returns. Critics of the mutual fund industry have cultivated a sense of awareness regarding the proliferation of these charges. Indeed, investors should not be deceived by funds that claim to be what they are not. Lowering front-end loads or eliminating them altogether doesn't mean a fund can't add fees somewhere else. Funds have to disclose their fees, which means that investors can find them in the fund's prospectus. Management fees, 12 (b)-1 fees, redemption fees (back-end loads), and any other fees charged are disclosed somewhere in the fund's prospectus. Financial newspapers also list the types of charges of the different funds in their periodic mutual fund performance reviews.

Worksheet 48.1 lists guidelines to assist you in the choice of a mutual fund.

WORKSHEET 48.1 Guidelines in the choice of a mutual fund

Step 1 List the objectives of each fund in which you are interested.

Names of the mutual funds _____   _____   _____
Objectives _____
_____

Risk level of fund: Conservative ☐   Moderate ☐   Aggressive ☐
Risk level of fund: Conservative ☐   Moderate ☐   Aggressive ☐
Risk level of fund: Conservative ☐   Moderate ☐   Aggressive ☐

(continued)

Step 2 Examine the past performance of each fund.

Names of the funds   _____   _____   _____
Rankings of the funds   _____   _____   _____

Step 3 List the returns of the funds in which you are interested.

Names of the funds   _____   _____   _____
Yield   _____   _____   _____
30-day yield   _____   _____   _____
Annual yield   _____   _____   _____
Dividends & gains   _____   _____   _____
Net asset value (NAV)
    changes   _____   _____   _____
Reinvested dividends   _____   _____   _____

Rank funds on the basis of total return.

     _____   _____   _____

Step 4 Compare the expenses and fees of the funds in which you are interested.

Names of the funds   _____   _____   _____
Load/no-load   _____   _____   _____
Back-end load   _____   _____   _____
Redemption fees   _____   _____   _____
12 (b)-1 fees   _____   _____   _____
Ratio of operating
    expenses to average
    net assets   _____   _____   _____

Rank the funds on the basis of their fees, with the lowest expense ratio receiving the highest ranking.

     _____   _____   _____

Step 5 Choose the fund that has the lowest expense ratio if there is no difference in the performance of the funds.

_____

_____

How to Determine the Tax Consequences of Buying and Selling Shares in a Mutual Fund

Tax reporting on mutual funds can be complicated. Even if you buy and hold shares in a mutual fund, there are tax consequences. Dividends paid to investors may be automatically reinvested in the fund to buy more shares. At the end of the year, the mutual fund sends Form 1099 to each mutual fund holder showing the amount of dividends and capital gains received for the year. Individual shareholders pay taxes on these dividends and capital gains. Therefore, these dividends and capital gains need to be added into the cost basis when the investor sells shares in the fund.

For example, suppose you had invested $10,000 in a fund two years ago and had received a total of $2,000 in dividends and capital gains in the fund to date. You now sell all the shares in the fund and receive $14,000. The cost basis is $12,000 (not $10,000), and the gain on the sale of the shares is $2,000 ($14,000 – $12,000), as shown in Worksheet 49.1.

When you sell only a portion of your total shares, the calculation is different and may be tricky. It is further complicated if you have actively bought and sold shares. In fact, many mutual funds encourage shareholders to operate their funds like a checking account by providing check-writing services. However, every time you write a check against a bond or stock fund, there is a capital gain or loss tax consequence. This does not include money market funds due to their stable price of one dollar per share. Active trading can cause a nightmare for you at tax time and produce extra revenue for your accountant for the additional time spent calculating the gains and losses.

The most important thing to do for an actively traded mutual fund (or any mutual fund for that matter) is to keep good records. For each fund, keep a separate folder and store all the monthly statements showing purchases and sales of shares, and dividends and capital gains distributions.

WORKSHEET 49.1 How to determine the capital gain from the sale of all shares in a mutual fund

Date	Transaction	Dollar amount	Share price	Number of shares	Total number of shares
1/1/02	Invest	$10,000	$10	1,000	1,000
12/31/02	Dividends	2,000	8	250	1,250

Total adjusted cost $12,000

Step 1 Determine the adjusted cost.
Add all the dollar amounts invested in the fund, including dividends and capital gains transactions.

Step 2 Determine the capital gain/loss from the sale of all shares.
Subtract the adjusted cost of the shares from the proceeds of the sale.

12/01/03 (sold 1,250 shares @ $11.20 per share)	$14,000
minus (cost basis 1,250 shares)	12,000
Capital gain	$2,000

By keeping records of all transactions, you will be able to determine the cost basis of shares sold. This can be done using either an average cost method, on a FIFO basis, or using the specific identification method. FIFO stands for first in, first out, which means that the cost of the first shares purchased in the fund are used first when shares are sold. Worksheet 49.2 illustrates the FIFO method of calculating a capital gain or loss on the partial sale of shares in a mutual fund. The example shows that the earliest shares purchased are the first to be used in the sale of shares. After all the shares of the invested fund are sold, the basis of the dividends and capital gains shares are used to determine any gain or loss.

Several funds provide the gains and losses on an average cost basis. The average cost basis can get quite complex with additional sales and purchases of shares. Hence, some funds don't allow their shareholders to write checks against their accounts. However, once you make a partial sale in a fund, some

WORKSHEET 49.2 Calculation of gain/losses on the partial sale of shares

Date	Transaction	Dollar amount	Share price	Number of shares	Total number of shares
06/14	Invest	$10,000	$10.00	1,000	1,000
11/26	Invest	4,500	9.00	500	1,500
11/30	Redeem (sell)	12,000	10.00	1,200	300
12/31	Dividends	1,000	10.00	100	400

To calculate gain/loss on a FIFO basis:

Sold 1,200 shares at $10.00 per share; sale price $12,000

Cost basis

06/14	1,000 shares at	$10.00	$10,000
11/26	200 shares at	9.00	1,800
	Total cost		$11,800
	Gain		$200

Cost basis of the growth and income fund after sale

Date	Transaction	Dollar amount	Share price	Number of shares	Total number of shares
06/14	Invested	$2,700	$9.00	300	300
11/26	Dividends	1,000	10.00	100	400

fund companies will no longer provide the average cost basis for that fund.

The specific identification method allows shareholders to identify the specific shares that they wish to sell. Investors can minimize their gains by choosing to sell shares with the highest cost basis first. However, in order to obtain Internal Revenue Service acceptance of this method, the investor must first identify the shares to be sold and notify the mutual fund company in writing and then receive written confirmation from the mutual fund company.

Worksheet 49.3 outlines the steps for determining the capital gains/losses on your mutual funds using the FIFO method, which is the usual method used unless you have written confirmation of a different method from your mutual fund company.

To minimize potential tax hassles, you are better off not writing checks on your stock funds for your short-term cash needs, which creates gains or losses. You are better served investing the money needed for short-term purposes in a money market fund, which alleviates tax complications.

Whether you trade actively or not, the solution to tax computations is to keep good records. If you can't determine the cost basis of your shares, an accountant will be able to do so, provided you keep records. If you don't have all the records of your purchases and sales, you may not be able to prove your cost basis to the Internal Revenue Service if it is disputed.

WORKSHEET 49.3 Steps to determine your capital gain/loss in the sale of shares

Step 1 List all the transactions in your fund.

Date	Transaction	Dollar amount	Share price	Number of shares	Total number of shares
____	_____	_____	_____	_____	_____
____	_____	_____	_____	_____	_____
____	_____	_____	_____	_____	_____
____	_____	_____	_____	_____	_____
____	_____	_____	_____	_____	_____

Step 2 Determine the proceeds from the sale.

Date	Transaction	Number of shares	Share price	Total proceeds
____	_____	_____	_____	_____

Step 3 Determine the cost basis for the shares sold.

Date	Transaction	Number of shares	×	Share price	=	Cost
____	_____	_____		_____		_____
____	_____	_____		_____		_____
____	_____	_____		_____		_____

Total cost _____

Step 4 Subtract total cost from total proceeds to equal total gain/loss.

Total proceeds from sale _____
– Total cost _____
Total gain/(loss) _____

Step 5 List the shares left in your fund.

Date	Transaction	Dollar amount	Share price	Number of shares	Total number of shares
____	_____	_____	_____	_____	_____
____	_____	_____	_____	_____	_____

How to Determine the Average Cost in Dollar Cost Averaging*

DOLLAR COST AVERAGING IS A METHOD of investing the same amount of money at regular intervals over a long period of time. This strategy can be used for stocks, bonds, and mutual funds. Most people build their portfolios over time, and by investing amounts at different times they avoid the risk of putting all their money into stocks at one point in time. By consistently investing the same amount in a security at regular intervals over a period of time, the average cost of the security will be lower than the high price of the security for the period, and higher than the low price of the security for the period. Table 50.1 shows the dollar cost averaging method when $1,000 is invested every month to purchase the stock of Company X. The example assumes fractional shares may be purchased, and commissions are ignored.

In January, $1,000 is invested at $7 per share, resulting in 142.86 shares being purchased. The price of the stock goes up in February to $8 per share, which means that the same investment amount ($1,000) will buy fewer shares (125.00) than in January. Conversely, when the price of the stock goes down to $6.75 in September, more shares are purchased (148.15) with the same investment dollars ($1,000).

Over the 12-month period, $12,000 was invested to purchase a total of 1,467.36 shares. The average cost per share is $8.18. In this example, an investor would lose money if the price falls below $8.18 and would make money if the stock price is above the average cost per share when selling. This average cost per share is $0.09 less than the average price per share during the 12-month period. Part of the reason for this is that during the months when the price per share is low, more shares are purchased for the same dollar amount. Thus, with fluctuating stock prices, the average cost per share will always be lower than the average price per share.

*Portions of this section have been previously published by Esmé Faerber in *All About Stocks* (New York: McGraw-Hill, 2000).

TABLE 50.1 Dollar cost averaging

Date	Investment amount	Price per share	Number of shares purchased
January	$1,000	$7.00	142.86
February	1,000	8.00	125.00
March	1,000	7.50	133.33
April	1,000	9.00	111.11
May	1,000	9.50	105.26
June	1,000	9.00	111.11
July	1,000	8.00	125.00
August	1,000	7.75	129.03
September	1,000	6.75	148.15
October	1,000	8.75	114.29
November	1,000	9.00	111.11
December	1,000	9.00	111.11
Total	$12,000	$99.25	1,467.36

$$\text{Average price per share} = \frac{\text{Total price per share}}{\text{Number of investment periods}}$$

$$= \frac{99.25}{12}$$

$$= \$8.27$$

$$\text{Average cost per share} = \frac{\text{Total investment}}{\text{Number of shares purchased}}$$

$$= \frac{12,000}{1,467.36}$$

$$= \$8.18$$

This does not mean that investors will always make a profit by using dollar cost averaging. If the price of the stock keeps going down, the average cost per share will be lower than the average price per share, but the investor will still lose money if the shares are sold at a declining price. If stock prices are volatile (going up and down), investors can do very well as long as there are systematic and even investments over the period, alleviating the need to time the market.

The disadvantages of dollar cost averaging are as follows:

- Transaction costs are higher using dollar cost averaging to purchase shares on a systematic basis.
- The use of the dollar cost averaging method to buy stocks requires large amounts of money for the regular payments in order to receive the lower commissions of buying shares in round lots over 100 shares. By investing small amounts, investors buy shares in odd lots (fewer than 100 shares), which means that transaction costs are higher. The total transaction costs will also be higher if the shares were purchased in one or two transactions rather than twelve. Dollar cost averaging works well with no-load mutual funds where there are no transaction fees.
- With a rising stock price, the use of dollar cost averaging will result in a higher average cost per share than if the total amount was invested at the beginning of the period.
- When shares are sold, the calculation for the tax basis of the shares is complicated for most investors. Keeping records of all transactions is necessary, and the use of a tax professional to compute the gains or losses for tax purposes may be required. The success of dollar cost averaging requires sticking to the plan and investing, particularly when the stock price falls. However, from time to time, investors should evaluate the stock with regard to its overall performance. A stock that is going downhill with no bright prospects should be viewed as a sunk cost, and an investor should abandon it rather than sink more money into a bad investment. Thus, dollar cost averaging does not alleviate the decision of which stocks to buy and sell.

Worksheet 50.1 lists the steps for determining your average cost in the dollar cost averaging of your investment.

WORKSHEET 50.1 How to determine your average cost in dollar cost averaging

Step 1 List your transactions and total the columns.

Date	Investment amount	Price per share	Number of shares purchased
_____	_____	_____	_____
_____	_____	_____	_____
_____	_____	_____	_____
_____	_____	_____	_____
_____	_____	_____	_____
_____	_____	_____	_____

Step 2 Determine the total average price per share.

$$\text{Average price per share} = \frac{\text{Total price per share}}{\text{Number of investment periods}}$$

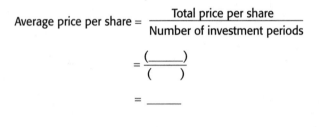

$$= \frac{(\underline{\quad\quad})}{(\quad)}$$

$$= \underline{\quad\quad}$$

Step 3 Jot down your expectations for future changes in rates of interest.

$$\text{Average cost per share} = \frac{\text{Total investment}}{\text{Number of shares purchased}}$$

$$= \frac{(\underline{\quad\quad})}{(\quad)}$$

$$= \underline{\quad\quad}$$

Step 4 Compare the average cost per share with the market price of the shares when selling, if:

Average cost per share is greater than the market price per share, you have a loss.
Average cost per share equals the market price per share, you have neither a gain nor a loss.
Average cost per share is less than the market price per share, you have a gain.

PART FOUR

PLANNING FOR YOUR FUTURE

How to Determine Your Future Financial Needs and How to Fund Them

T HE FIRST STEP IN DETERMINING YOUR FUTURE financial needs is to figure out how much money you will need when you decide to retire. The figure that you come up with should include your assumptions about your lifestyle in retirement. Do you expect to live with the same comforts and enjoy the same spending level, or are you willing to do some belt tightening? For example, if you don't have any extravagant expenses currently, but when you retire you plan to travel to different resorts around the world on a regular basis, you may need to increase your anticipated yearly income to include these expenditures in retirement. Alternatively, you may determine that the majority of your current expenses, such as education costs and other costs for children, and mortgage expenses, will not be a factor in retirement, and hence you will need less to retire on. This may be so, but you may also need to bank on increased health care costs. Thus, whatever your assumptions, you need to make allowances for your projected lifestyle in retirement.

A common rule of thumb is that 80 percent of current living expenses should be sufficient in retirement. Thus, in your planning you need to determine whether you need 100 percent of your current income in retirement or whether it could be less or should be more. Another factor that you need to consider in this determination is inflation. If inflation rears its ugly head, you may not have sufficient future purchasing power to maintain the lifestyle to which you are accustomed. Consequently, you may have to assume an inflation rate for the period between now and retirement to maintain your current purchasing power.

Worksheet 51.1 outlines the steps for determining the amount of your future retirement needs and how you plan on funding that amount.

WORKSHEET 51.1 Planning for retirement

Step 1 Anticipate the amount of money you will need at retirement.

Current income _____ Number of years to retirement _____

Projected inflation rate _____ % assumption of future income _____

Future value of 1 at inflation rate for the number of years to retirement* _____

Current Income × FV of 1 at inflation rate for # of years to retirement ×

Assumption % = Future Amount

_____ × _____ × _____ = _____ (1)

Step 2 Determine where the funds will come from for projected retirement needs.

Income source amount × FV of rate of return × Expected rate of return =
Future assets in retirement

Investments	_____ ×	_____ ×	_____ =	_____
IRAs	_____ ×	_____ ×	_____ =	_____
401(k)s	_____ ×	_____ ×	_____ =	_____
Pensions	_____ ×	_____ ×	_____ =	_____
Keoghs	_____ ×	_____ ×	_____ =	_____
Home equity	_____ ×	_____ ×	_____ =	_____
Other sources	_____ ×	_____ ×	_____ =	_____
Social Security			=	_____
Total				_____ . (2)

Step 3 Compare the projected amount needed in retirement with the total projected sources of income.

If (1) − (2) = a positive amount, you need to save more in your different source accounts.

If (1) = (2) you will have met your projected retirement needs.

If (1) − (2) = a negative amount, you will have exceeded your retirement needs.

*This factor can be obtained from Appendix A in the future value of 1 table. You can also use a financial calculator or computer to determine the future value of the income at the projected inflation rate.

Step 1: Determine Your Anticipated Yearly Amount in Retirement

Step 1 in the worksheet shows how to determine the amount of money that you will need on a yearly basis in retirement. Begin with your yearly current income and determine the number of years until retirement. If you anticipate an increase in inflation through the years to retirement, you will need to take this into account because inflation erodes future purchasing power.

The following example illustrates the process of determining the future yearly income in retirement.

Current yearly income: $120,000   Years to Retirement: 25
Projected inflation rate: 3%   Assumption on lifestyle %: 80%

Current income × Future value factor of 1 at 3% for 25 years × 0.80
= Future retirement amount
$120,000 × 2.094 × 0.80 = $201,024

In this example, with current income of $120,000, assuming an inflation rate of 3 percent for the next 25 years and an 80 percent estimate of current needs, the future yearly income needed in retirement is $201,024.

Step 2: Determine Where the Money Will Come from to Finance Your Projected Future Retirement Income Needs

Investments

Add your investment and savings account balances. Next, assume a rate of return that these investments will earn per year over the period until your retirement. If you expect your investments to return 5 percent after taxes on average for each year in the 25 years to retirement, you can find the future value of 1 factor at 5 percent for 25 years in Appendix A. This figure is multiplied by the total investment amount to equal the future value of these investments at retirement. You then need to anticipate a rate of return in retirement, which may or may not be a higher rate of return than your current projected rate. Assuming that your retirement nest egg will earn a rate of 7 percent per year, you can then determine what your total future investments will earn per year in retirement, as illustrated below:

$$\text{Investments} \times \text{FV of 5 percent for 25 years} \times 0.07$$
$$= \text{Future annual income from investments}$$
$$\$150,000 \times 3.386 \times 0.07 = \$35,553$$

The total investments of $150,000 invested at 5 percent for 25 years will produce a nest egg of $507,900; multiplied by 7 percent, it will produce yearly earnings of $35,553.

Individual Retirement Accounts (IRAs)

With IRAs you make tax-deductible contributions up to the allowable yearly limit, and the principal and earnings on the principal are tax deferred until money is withdrawn from the account. Withdrawals from IRA accounts may be made penalty free after age 59½. Thus, your money is tied up until you reach this age, though there are some exceptions. The rate of return on an IRA may be higher than that on a regular investment account due to the tax deferral of earnings on the former. The types of investment assets held in the account determine the rate of return.

You may need to use two different calculations with an IRA if you already have an account balance and you continue to make yearly contributions until retirement.

Assume that you have a total of $20,000 in your IRA account and you plan on making yearly contributions of $2,000 for the next 20 years until retirement. You expect these funds to earn 8 percent per annum during this period.

$$\text{Funds} \times \text{FV factor of 8\% for 20 years} =$$
$$\text{Funds at retirement} \times \text{Interest rate} = \text{Yearly amount}$$

$$\$20,000 \times 4.661^* = \$93,220 \times 0.08 = \quad \$7,457.60$$
$$\$2,000 \times 45.762^{**} = 91,524 \times 0.08 = \quad \underline{7,321.92}$$

Total yearly retirement income from IRAs $14,779.52

*FV factor of a single sum from Appendix A.
**FV factor of an annuity from Appendix C.

401(k) and Employment Pension Plans

Another source of retirement income is from tax-deferred pension plans, such as 401(k), 403(b), money purchase, and profit-sharing plans. Each type of plan has its own set of rules with regard to contribution amounts, employer matching, and plan withdrawals. As with IRAs, dollar contribution amounts are on a pretax basis, and the earnings on the contributed capital accrue on a tax-deferred basis.

To determine your retirement income from these plans, you would use the same types of calculations as shown in the IRA example.

Social Security

You can begin to collect reduced Social Security benefits at age 62 or, depending on the year that you were born, full benefits between ages 65 and 67. The easiest way to determine the exact amount of your yearly benefits is to request it from the Social Security Administration.

Home Equity

If you own a house and you are paying off a mortgage, you have an equity stake in the house. The amount of the equity is the current value of the house minus the mortgage balance. The equity amount will increase with every mortgage payment and over the years as house prices increase. At retirement if you sell your house and move into a smaller house or rent, you will free up money, which can then be invested to generate income. Another option is a reverse mortgage, where a bank will pay you a monthly amount and after the term is up you (or your heirs) can sell the house to pay the bank back. To quantify the amount of income generated from your home equity stake, you need to make several assumptions. The first is the current value of your house, and the second is the anticipated appreciation rate of your house. Currently, you are not taxed on the first $250,000 of the capital gains on the sale of a house if you are single, or $500,000 if you file a joint return. Assume that there are no tax consequences on these gains, although this is a large assumption as Congress is constantly making changes to the tax code.

For example, if you have a house that has been appraised at $300,000 and you have a mortgage of $125,000, you have $175,000 in equity ($300,000–$125,000). Assume that this equity will grow at 5 percent for the next 20 years until retirement, when you plan on taking out a reverse mortgage. The amount of retirement income based on these assumptions is:

$$\text{Equity} \times \text{FV factor of 5\% for 20 years} =$$
$$\text{Future equity} \times \text{Interest factor} = \text{Annual income}$$
$$\$175,000 \times 2.653 = \$464,275 \times 0.05 = \$23,213.75$$

Step 3: Determine Whether You Will Have Met Your Expected Needs in Retirement

Add up your total projected income in retirement and compare this to the anticipated amount needed in retirement. For example, if you anticipate that your yearly future needs will be $120,000, but you only come up with $100,000 a year from all your sources of savings, investment accounts, and retirement accounts, then you need to put aside greater amounts now to fund this shortfall.

You can use a computer or financial calculator to determine the additional yearly amount that you would need to save to make up a shortfall. Assuming that you have a $20,000 shortfall and you expect to earn 8 percent per year over the next 20 years until retirement, you will need to invest an additional $437.04 each year for the next 20 years.

You can use the future value of an ordinary annuity table to determine this, as shown below, or a spreadsheet program that has financial tables, such as Microsoft Excel.

$$\text{Future value of annuity factor at 8\% for 20 periods} \times \text{Annuity} = \$20,000$$
$$45.762 \times \text{Annuity} = \$20,000$$
$$\text{Annuity} = 20,000 \div 45.762$$
$$= \$437.04$$

Using Microsoft Excel, click on f^* in the top row of the toolbar. Highlight *financial* in the left box and *PMT* in the right box. A dialog box comes up where you can enter your information as shown in Figure 51.1.

Thus, if you have a shortfall, determine the extra payment amounts that you would need to invest to make up this shortfall.

FIGURE 51.1 Planning for retirement

Rate	8%
Nper	20
FV	$20,000
Type	0
PMT = $437.04	

How to Determine How Long Your Money Will Last in Retirement and the Amount of the Payment in a Systematic Withdrawal Plan

THE AIM OF MOST WITHDRAWAL PLANS is to have the retirement funds last through retirement. This means that you need to determine how much you can spend per year. If you spend too much you jeopardize the funding for your later years, as you could run out of money. Similarly, if you spend too little, you may not be enjoying the full comforts you can afford in retirement. Consequently, you need to determine how much money you can withdraw on an annual basis so that your funds will last you through your retirement.

Step 1: Determine Your Monthly and Yearly Needs

Assume, for example, that you will need $10,000 per month to live on during your retirement. You expect to receive close to $2,000 per month from Social Security and $3,000 per month from your pension plan. You would then need to withdraw $5,000 per month or $60,000 annually from your other sources, such as investments.

Step 2: Determine How Long Your Investment Funds Will Last

How long your investment funds will last you in retirement depends on several factors:

- The amount of your investment account
- Your withdrawal rate
- The rate of return earned on your investments
- The projected length of time of your retirement

Determine your withdrawal rate, which is the annual withdrawal divided by the total investment assets. For example, an annual withdrawal of $60,000 from an investment account of $800,000 is 7.5 percent.

$$\text{Withdrawal rate} = \frac{\text{Annual withdrawal}}{\text{Total investment assets}}$$

$$= \frac{\$60,000}{800,000}$$

$$= 7.5\%$$

With a 7.5 percent withdrawal rate, there is a good chance that the investment assets will be depleted in less than 20 years. A general rule of thumb is that a withdrawal rate of less than 5 percent can stretch retirement to 30 years. Of course, this depends on the rate of return earned on the investment assets. Table 52.1 lists different withdrawal rates and the lengths of time that investment assets will last, assuming an annual rate of return of 5.5 percent. A withdrawal rate that equals the rate of return means that you will never deplete your investment assets, as the principal will remain intact. You will be withdrawing only the interest earned on your investment assets. A 4 percent real rate of return (adjusted for inflation) means that retirement assets will not last as long with the same withdrawal rates.

TABLE 52.1 How long will your investment assets last?

Withdrawal rate*	Length of time of withdrawals*
12.8%	10 years
9.7%	15 years
7.3%	25 years
6.7%	30 years
5.5%	Indefinitely

Withdrawal rate**	Length of time of withdrawals**
8.6%	15 years
7.0%	20 years
6.1%	25 years
5.5%	30 years
4.0%	Indefinitely

*This example assumes a rate of return of 5.5% per annum on the investment assets.

**This example assumes a 4% real rate of return that is adjusted for inflation.

Step 3: Determine the Projected Rate of Return on Your Investment Funds

The composition of investment assets has a significant impact on the projected rate of return and, hence, length of retirement income. Traditionally, the greatest returns from financial investments over long periods of time have come from common stocks, followed by bonds, and then money market securities. The danger of investing all retirement funds in common stocks is that if there is a bear market, common stocks might underperform other financial investments, and there could also be an erosion of principal. A protracted bear market would affect the amount of withdrawals and the length of time that the retirement funds would last.

Another argument, besides the volatility of the stock market, against investing all retirement funds in common stock is that in retirement regular payments of income are needed. Bonds provide these payments, while common stock provides long-term growth for the portfolio. A diversified portfolio of investments consisting of stocks, bonds, and money market securities balances the trade-off between risk and return. Money market securities provide liquidity in the portfolio.

Your actual asset allocation plan depends on your individual personal circumstances, the amount of your retirement assets, your risk tolerance, the amount of funds you want to leave for your heirs, and so on. Stocks have returned around 7 percent per year over long periods of time, while bonds have earned around 4 to 5 percent. However, with the current low interest rates and bear market, you should be conservative in projecting your future rates of return on your retirement assets. Inflation should also be considered, as it erodes the future purchasing power of your withdrawals.

You should also have a plan for your withdrawals from your retirement assets. The composition of your withdrawals should come mainly from money market securities and regular income payments from bonds and stocks, without the bond and stock investments having to be liquidated. As you go along, however, you will need to liquidate some of these investments and convert them into money market securities for future withdrawals.

Step 4: Determine How Much You Can Withdraw over Your Projected Retirement Period

There are many Web sites on the Internet that have retirement calculators to determine how much you can withdraw over your projected retirement period. One such site is www.TrowePrice.com. In order to find the calculator on this Web site, click on the arrow Select a Tool and highlight *Retirement Income Calculator*. Enter your information to determine how much you can withdraw. On completion of your information, you will get an annual withdrawal amount based on your retirement assets, your asset allocation, and the number of years for your retirement. Each retirement calculator makes its own assumptions with regard to rates of return on stocks, bonds, and money market securities, and rate of inflation.

If necessary, you can always make changes to your withdrawal amounts to keep up with changing economic circumstances.

Worksheet 52.1 outlines the steps for determining your withdrawal amount.

WORKSHEET 52.1 How to determine your withdrawal amount

Step 1 Determine the monthly and annual income that you will need.

Projected income needs: Monthly _____ Annual _____

Step 2 Determine the withdrawal rate.

$$\text{Withdrawal rate} = \frac{\text{Annual withdrawal}}{\text{Total investment assets}}$$

$$= \frac{(\qquad)}{(\qquad)}$$

$$= \underline{\qquad}\%$$

Step 3 Determine the length of time that your retirement funds will last.

Compare your withdrawal rate to those in Table 52.1, using either the 5.5% return rate or the more conservative 4% real rate of return to determine the approximate length of time that your funds will last.

Withdrawal rate _____ Length of time of withdrawals _____

If the length of time is not sufficient, go to step 4.

Step 4 Determine how much you can withdraw over your projected retirement period.

Go to a retirement calculator on the Internet and enter your information. There are many websites that have retirement calculators, such as www.troweprice.com.

Enter your information to determine the amount that you can withdraw without depleting your retirement funds.

Monthly withdrawal _____ Annual withdrawal _____

Appendices

APPENDIX A: Compound sum of $1

n	1%	2%	3%	4%	5%	6%	7%	8%	9%	10%
1	1.010	1.020	1.030	1.040	1.050	1.060	1.070	1.080	1.090	1.100
2	1.020	1.040	1.061	1.082	1.102	1.124	1.145	1.166	1.188	1.210
3	1.030	1.061	1.091	1.125	1.158	1.191	1.225	1.260	1.295	1.111
4	1.041	1.082	1.126	1.170	1.216	1.262	1.311	1.360	1.412	1.464
5	1.051	1.104	1.159	1.217	1.270	1.338	1.403	1.469	1.539	1.611
6	1.062	1.126	1.194	1.265	1.340	1.419	1.501	1.587	1.677	1.772
7	1.072	1.149	1.230	1.316	1.407	1.504	1.606	1.714	1.828	1.949
8	1.083	1.172	1.267	1.169	1.477	1.594	1.718	1.851	1.993	2.144
9	1.094	1.195	1.305	1.423	1.551	1.689	1.838	1.999	2.172	2.358
10	1.105	1.219	1.344	1.480	1.629	1.791	1.967	2.159	2.367	2.594
11	1.116	1.243	1.394	1.539	1.710	1.898	2.105	2.332	2.580	2.853
12	1.127	1.268	1.426	1.601	1.796	2.012	2.252	2.518	2.813	3.138
13	1.138	1.294	1.469	1.665	1.886	2.133	2.410	2.720	3.066	3.452
14	1.149	1.319	1.513	1.732	1.980	2.261	2.579	2.937	3.342	3.797
15	1.161	1.346	1.558	1.801	2.079	2.397	2.759	3.172	3.642	4.177
16	1.173	1.373	1.605	1.873	2.183	2.540	2.952	3.426	3.970	4.595
17	1.184	1.400	1.653	1.948	2.292	2.693	3.159	3.700	4.328	5.054
18	1.196	1.428	1.702	2.026	2.407	2.854	3.380	3.996	4.717	5.560
19	1.208	1.457	1.753	2.107	2.527	3.026	3.616	4.316	5.142	6.116
20	1.220	1.486	1.806	2.191	2.653	3.207	3.870	4.661	5.604	6.727
21	1.232	1.516	1.860	2.279	2.786	3.399	4.140	5.034	6.109	7.400
22	1.245	1.546	1.916	2.370	2.925	3.603	4.430	5.436	6.658	8.140
23	1.257	1.577	1.974	2.465	3.071	3.820	4.740	5.871	7.258	8.954
24	1.270	1.608	2.033	2.563	3.225	4.049	5.072	6.341	7.911	9.850
25	1.282	1.641	2.094	2.666	3.386	4.292	5.427	6.848	8.623	10.834
30	1.348	1.811	2.427	3.243	4.322	5.743	7.612	10.062	13.267	17.449
40	1.489	2.208	3.262	4.801	7.040	10.285	14.974	21.724	31.408	45.258
50	1.645	2.691	4.384	7.106	11.467	18.419	29.456	46.900	74.354	117.386

n	11%	12%	13%	14%	15%	16%	17%	18%	19%	20%
1	1.110	1.120	1.130	1.140	1.150	1.160	1.170	1.180	1.190	1.200
2	1.232	1.254	1.277	1.300	1.322	1.346	1.369	1.392	1.416	1.440
3	1.368	1.405	1.443	1.482	1.521	1.561	1.602	1.643	1.685	1.728
4	1.518	1.574	1.630	1.689	1.749	1.811	1.874	1.939	2.005	2.074
5	1.685	1.762	1.842	1.925	2.011	2.100	2.192	2.288	2.386	2.488
6	1.870	1.974	2.082	2.195	2.313	2.436	2.565	2.700	2.840	2.986
7	2.076	2.211	2.353	2.502	2.660	2.826	3.001	3.185	3.379	3.583
8	2.305	2.476	2.658	2.853	3.059	3.278	3.511	3.759	4.021	4.300
9	2.558	2.773	3.004	3.252	3.518	3.803	4.108	4.435	4.785	5.160
10	2.839	3.106	3.395	3.707	4.046	4.411	4.807	5.234	5.695	6.192
11	3.152	3.479	3.836	4.226	4.652	5.117	5.624	6.176	6.777	7.430
12	3.498	3.896	4.334	4.818	5.350	5.936	6.580	7.288	8.064	8.916
13	3.883	4.363	4.898	5.492	6.153	6.886	7.699	8.599	9.596	10.699
14	4.310	4.887	5.535	6.261	7.076	7.987	9.007	10.147	11.420	12.839
15	4.785	5.474	6.254	7.138	8.137	9.265	10.539	11.974	13.589	15.407
16	5.311	6.130	7.067	8.137	9.358	10.748	12.330	14.129	16.171	18.488
17	5.895	6.866	7.986	9.276	10.761	12.468	14.426	16.672	19.244	22.186
18	6.543	7.690	9.024	10.575	12.375	14.462	16.879	19.673	22.900	26.623
19	7.263	8.613	10.197	12.055	14.232	16.776	19.748	23.214	27.251	31.948
20	8.062	9.646	11.523	13.743	16.366	19.461	23.105	27.393	32.429	38.337
21	8.949	10.804	13.021	15.667	18.821	22.574	27.033	32.323	38.591	46.005
22	9.933	12.100	14.713	17.861	21.644	26.186	31.629	38.141	45.923	55.205
23	11.016	13.552	16.626	20.361	24.891	30.376	37.005	45.007	54.648	66.247
24	12.239	15.178	18.788	23.212	28.625	35.236	43.296	53.108	65.031	79.496
25	13.585	17.000	21.230	26.461	32.918	40.874	50.656	62.667	77.387	95.395
30	22.892	29.960	39.115	50.949	66.210	85.849	111.061	143.367	184.672	237.373
40	64.999	93.049	132.776	188.876	267.856	378.715	533.846	750.353	1,051.642	1,469.740
50	184.559	288.996	450.711	700.197	1,083.619	1,670.669	2,566.080	3,927.189	5,988.730	9,100.191

APPENDIX B: Present value of $1

n	1%	2%	3%	4%	5%	6%	7%	8%	9%	10%
1	.990	.980	.971	.962	.952	.943	.935	.926	.917	.909
2	.990	.961	.943	.925	.907	.890	.873	.857	.842	.826
3	.971	.942	.915	.889	.864	.840	.816	.794	.772	.751
4	.961	.924	.888	.855	.823	.792	.763	.735	.708	.683
5	.951	.906	.863	.822	.784	.747	.713	.681	.650	.621
6	.942	.888	.837	.790	.746	.705	.666	.630	.596	.564
7	.933	.871	.813	.760	.711	.665	.623	.583	.547	.513
8	.923	.853	.789	.731	.677	.627	.582	.540	.502	.467
9	.914	.837	.766	.703	.645	.592	.544	.500	.460	.424
10	.905	.820	.744	.676	.614	.558	.508	.463	.422	.386
11	.896	.804	.722	.650	.585	.527	.475	.429	.388	.350
12	.887	.789	.701	.625	.557	.497	.444	.397	.356	.319
13	.879	.773	.681	.601	.530	.469	.415	.368	.326	.290
14	.870	.758	.661	.577	.505	.442	.388	.340	.299	.263
15	.861	.743	.642	.555	.481	.417	.362	.315	.275	.239
16	.853	.728	.623	.534	.458	.394	.339	.292	.252	.218
17	.844	.714	.605	.513	.436	.371	.317	.270	.231	.198
18	.836	.700	.587	.494	.416	.350	.296	.250	.212	.180
19	.828	.686	.570	.475	.396	.331	.277	.232	.194	.164
20	.820	.673	.554	.456	.377	.312	.258	.215	.178	.149
21	.811	.660	.538	.439	.359	.294	.242	.199	.164	.135
22	.803	.647	.522	.422	.342	.278	.226	.184	.150	.123
23	.795	.634	.507	.406	.326	.262	.211	.170	.138	.112
24	.788	.622	.492	.390	.310	.247	.197	.158	.126	.102
25	.780	.610	.478	.375	.295	.233	.184	.146	.116	.092
30	.742	.552	.412	.308	.231	.174	.131	.099	.075	.057
40	.672	.453	.307	.208	.142	.097	.067	.046	.032	.022
50	.608	.372	.228	.141	.087	.054	.034	.021	.013	.009

n	11%	12%	13%	14%	15%	16%	17%	18%	19%	20%
1	.901	.893	.885	.877	.870	.862	.855	.847	.840	.833
2	.812	.797	.783	.769	.756	.743	.731	.718	.706	.694
3	.731	.712	.693	.675	.658	.641	.624	.609	.593	.579
4	.659	.636	.613	.592	.572	.552	.534	.516	.499	.482
5	.593	.567	.543	.519	.497	.476	.456	.437	.419	.402
6	.535	.507	.480	.456	.432	.410	.390	.370	.352	.335
7	.482	.452	.425	.400	.376	.354	.333	.314	.296	.279
8	.434	.404	.376	.351	.327	.305	.285	.266	.249	.233
9	.391	.361	.333	.308	.284	.263	.243	.225	.209	.194
10	.352	.322	.295	.270	.247	.227	.208	.191	.176	.162
11	.317	.287	.261	.237	.215	.195	.178	.162	.148	.135
12	.286	.257	.231	.208	.187	.168	.152	.137	.124	.112
13	.258	.229	.204	.182	.163	.145	.130	.116	.104	.093
14	.232	.205	.181	.160	.141	.125	.111	.099	.088	.078
15	.209	.183	.160	.140	.123	.108	.095	.084	.074	.065
16	.188	.163	.141	.123	.107	.093	.081	.071	.062	.054
17	.170	.146	.125	.108	.093	.080	.069	.060	.052	.045
18	.153	.130	.111	.095	.081	.069	.059	.051	.044	.038
19	.138	.116	.098	.083	.070	.060	.051	.043	.037	.031
20	.124	.104	.087	.073	.061	.051	.043	.037	.031	.026
21	.112	.093	.077	.064	.053	.044	.037	.031	.026	.022
22	.101	.083	.068	.056	.046	.038	.032	.026	.022	.018
23	.091	.074	.060	.049	.040	.033	.027	.022	.018	.015
24	.082	.066	.053	.043	.035	.028	.023	.019	.015	.013
25	.074	.059	.047	.038	.030	.024	.020	.016	.013	.010
30	.044	.033	.026	.020	.015	.012	.009	.007	.005	.004
40	.015	.011	.008	.005	.004	.003	.002	.001	.001	.001
50	.005	.003	.002	.001	.001	.001	.000	.000	.000	.000

APPENDIX C: Sum of annuity for n periods

n	1%	2%	3%	4%	5%	6%	7%	8%	9%	10%
1	1.000	1.000	1.000	1.000	1.000	1.000	1.000	1.000	1.000	1.000
2	2.010	2.020	2.030	2.040	2.050	2.060	2.070	2.080	2.090	2.100
3	3.030	3.060	3.091	3.122	3.152	3.184	3.215	3.246	3.278	3.310
4	4.060	4.122	4.184	4.246	4.310	4.375	4.440	4.506	4.573	4.641
5	5.101	5.204	5.309	5.416	5.526	5.637	5.751	5.867	5.985	6.105
6	6.152	6.308	6.468	6.633	6.802	6.975	7.153	7.336	7.523	7.716
7	7.214	7.434	7.662	7.898	8.142	8.394	8.654	8.923	9.200	9.487
8	8.286	8.583	8.892	9.214	9.549	9.897	10.260	10.637	11.028	11.436
9	9.368	9.755	10.159	10.583	11.027	11.491	11.978	12.488	13.021	13.579
10	10.462	10.950	11.464	12.006	12.578	13.191	13.816	14.487	15.193	15.937
11	11.567	12.169	12.808	13.486	14.207	14.972	15.784	16.645	17.560	18.531
12	12.682	13.412	14.192	15.026	15.917	16.870	17.888	18.977	20.141	21.384
13	13.809	14.680	15.618	16.627	17.713	18.882	20.141	21.495	22.953	24.523
14	14.947	15.974	17.086	18.292	19.598	21.015	22.550	24.215	26.019	27.975
15	16.097	17.293	18.599	20.023	21.578	23.276	25.129	27.152	29.361	31.772
16	17.258	18.639	20.157	21.824	23.657	25.672	27.888	30.324	33.003	35.949
17	18.430	20.012	21.761	23.697	25.840	28.213	30.840	33.750	36.973	40.544
18	19.614	21.412	23.414	25.645	28.132	30.905	33.999	37.450	41.301	45.599
19	20.811	22.840	25.117	27.671	30.539	33.760	37.379	41.446	46.018	51.158
20	22.019	24.297	26.870	29.778	33.066	36.785	40.995	45.762	51.159	57.274
21	23.239	25.783	28.676	31.969	35.719	39.992	44.865	50.422	56.764	64.002
22	24.471	27.299	30.536	34.248	38.505	43.392	49.005	55.456	62.872	71.402
23	25.716	28.845	32.452	36.618	41.430	46.995	53.435	60.893	69.531	79.542
24	26.973	30.421	34.426	39.082	44.501	50.815	58.176	66.764	76.789	88.496
25	28.243	32.030	36.459	41.645	47.726	54.864	63.248	73.105	84.699	99.346
30	34.784	40.567	47.575	56.084	66.438	79.057	94.459	113.282	136.305	164.491
40	48.885	60.401	75.400	95.024	120.797	154.758	199.630	295.052	337.872	442.580
50	64.461	84.577	112.794	152.664	209.341	290.325	406.516	573.756	815.051	1,163.865

n	11%	12%	13%	14%	15%	16%	17%	18%	19%	20%
1	1.000	1.000	1.000	1.000	1.000	1.000	1.000	1.000	1.000	1.000
2	2.110	2.120	2.130	2.140	2.150	2.160	2.170	2.180	2.190	2.200
3	3.342	3.374	3.407	3.440	3.472	3.506	3.539	3.572	3.606	3.640
4	4.710	4.779	4.850	4.921	4.993	5.066	5.141	5.215	5.291	5.368
5	6.228	6.353	6.480	6.610	6.742	6.877	7.014	7.154	7.297	7.442
6	7.913	8.115	8.323	8.535	8.754	8.977	9.207	9.442	9.683	9.930
7	9.783	10.089	10.405	10.730	11.067	11.414	11.772	12.141	12.523	12.916
8	11.859	12.300	12.757	13.233	13.727	14.240	14.773	15.327	15.902	16.499
9	14.164	14.776	15.416	16.085	16.786	17.518	18.285	19.086	19.923	20.799
10	16.722	17.549	18.420	19.337	20.304	21.321	22.393	23.521	24.709	25.959
11	19.561	20.655	21.814	23.044	24.349	25.733	27.200	28.755	30.403	32.150
12	22.713	24.133	25.650	27.271	29.001	30.850	32.824	34.931	37.180	39.580
13	26.211	28.029	29.984	32.088	34.352	36.786	39.404	42.218	45.244	48.496
14	30.095	32.392	34.882	37.581	40.504	43.672	47.102	50.818	54.841	59.196
15	34.405	37.280	40.417	43.842	47.580	51.659	56.109	60.965	66.260	72.035
16	39.190	42.753	46.671	50.980	55.717	60.925	66.648	72.938	79.850	87.442
17	44.500	48.883	53.738	59.117	65.075	71.673	78.978	87.067	96.021	105.930
18	50.396	55.749	61.724	68.393	75.836	84.140	93.404	103.739	115.265	128.116
19	56.939	63.439	70.748	78.968	88.211	98.603	110.283	123.412	138.165	154.739
20	64.202	72.052	80.946	91.024	102.443	115.379	130.031	146.626	165.417	186.687
21	72.264	81.698	92.468	104.767	118.809	134.840	153.136	174.019	197.846	225.024
22	81.213	92.502	105.489	120.434	137.630	157.414	180.169	206.342	236.436	271.028
23	91.147	104.602	120.203	138.295	159.274	183.600	211.798	244.483	282.359	326.234
24	102.173	118.154	136.829	158.656	184.166	213.976	248.803	289.490	337.007	392.480
25	114.412	133.333	155.616	181.867	212.790	249.212	292.099	342.598	402.038	471.976
30	199.018	241.330	293.192	356.778	434.738	530.306	647.423	790.932	966.698	1,181.865
40	581.812	767.080	1,013.667	1,341.979	1,779.048	2,360.724	3,134.412	4,163.094	5,529.711	7,343.715
50	1,668.723	2,399.975	3,459.344	4,994.301	7,217.488	10,435.449	15,088.805	21,812.273	31,514.492	45,496.094

APPENDIX D: Present value of an annuity of $1 for n periods

n	1%	2%	3%	4%	5%	6%	7%	8%	9%	10%
1	.990	.980	.971	.962	.952	.943	.935	.926	.917	.909
2	1.970	1.942	1.913	1.886	1.859	1.833	1.808	1.783	1.759	1.736
3	2.941	2.884	2.829	2.775	2.723	2.673	2.624	2.577	2.531	2.487
4	3.902	3.808	3.717	3.630	3.546	3.465	3.387	3.312	3.240	3.170
5	4.853	4.713	4.580	4.452	4.329	4.212	4.100	3.993	3.890	3.791
6	5.795	5.601	5.417	5.242	5.076	4.917	4.767	4.623	4.486	4.355
7	6.728	6.472	6.230	6.002	5.786	5.582	5.389	5.206	5.033	4.868
8	7.652	7.326	7.020	6.733	6.463	6.210	5.971	5.747	5.535	5.335
9	8.566	8.162	7.786	7.435	7.108	6.802	6.515	6.247	5.995	5.759
10	9.471	8.983	8.530	8.111	7.722	7.360	7.024	6.710	6.418	6.145
11	10.368	9.787	9.253	8.760	8.306	7.887	7.499	7.139	6.805	6.495
12	11.255	10.575	9.954	9.385	8.863	8.384	7.943	7.536	7.161	6.814
13	12.134	11.348	10.635	9.986	9.394	8.853	8.358	7.904	7.487	7.103
14	13.004	12.106	11.296	10.563	9.899	9.295	8.746	8.244	7.786	7.367
15	13.865	12.849	11.938	11.118	10.380	9.712	9.108	8.560	8.061	7.606
16	14.718	13.578	12.561	11.652	10.838	10.106	9.447	8.851	8.313	7.824
17	15.562	14.292	13.166	12.166	11.274	10.477	9.763	9.122	8.544	8.022
18	16.398	14.992	13.754	12.659	11.690	10.828	10.059	9.372	8.756	8.201
19	17.226	15.679	14.324	13.134	12.085	11.158	10.336	9.604	8.950	8.365
20	18.046	16.352	14.878	13.590	12.462	11.470	10.594	9.818	9.129	8.514
21	18.857	17.011	15.415	14.029	12.821	11.764	10.836	10.017	9.292	8.649
22	19.661	17.658	15.937	14.451	13.163	12.042	11.061	10.201	9.442	8.772
23	20.456	18.292	16.444	14.857	13.489	12.303	11.272	10.371	9.580	8.883
24	21.244	18.914	16.936	15.247	13.799	12.550	11.469	10.529	9.707	8.985
25	22.023	19.524	17.413	15.622	14.094	12.783	11.654	10.675	9.823	9.077
30	25.808	22.397	19.601	17.292	15.373	13.765	12.409	11.258	10.274	9.427
40	32.835	27.356	23.115	19.793	17.159	15.046	13.332	11.925	10.757	9.779
50	39.197	31.424	25.730	21.482	18.256	15.762	13.801	12.234	10.962	9.915

n	11%	12%	13%	14%	15%	16%	17%	18%	19%	20%
1	.901	.893	.885	.877	.870	.862	.855	.847	.840	.833
2	1.713	1.690	1.668	1.647	1.626	1.605	1.585	1.566	1.547	1.528
3	2.444	2.402	2.361	2.322	2.283	2.246	2.210	2.174	2.140	2.106
4	3.102	3.037	2.974	2.914	2.855	2.798	2.743	2.690	2.639	2.589
5	3.696	3.605	3.517	3.433	3.352	3.274	3.199	3.127	3.058	2.991
6	4.231	4.111	3.998	3.889	3.784	3.685	3.589	3.498	3.410	3.326
7	4.712	4.564	4.423	4.288	4.160	4.039	3.922	3.812	3.706	3.605
8	5.146	4.968	4.799	4.639	4.487	4.344	4.207	4.078	3.954	3.837
9	5.537	5.328	5.132	4.946	4.772	4.607	4.451	4.303	4.163	4.031
10	5.889	5.650	5.426	5.216	5.019	4.833	4.659	4.494	4.339	4.192
11	6.207	5.938	5.687	5.453	5.234	5.029	4.836	4.656	4.487	4.327
12	6.492	6.194	5.918	5.660	5.421	5.197	4.988	4.793	4.611	4.439
13	6.750	6.424	6.122	5.842	5.583	5.342	5.118	4.910	4.715	4.533
14	6.982	6.628	6.303	6.002	5.724	5.468	5.229	5.008	4.802	4.611
15	7.191	6.811	6.462	6.142	5.847	5.575	5.324	5.092	4.876	4.675
16	7.379	6.974	6.604	6.265	5.954	5.669	5.405	5.162	4.938	4.730
17	7.549	7.120	6.729	6.373	6.047	5.749	5.475	5.222	4.990	4.775
18	7.702	7.250	6.840	6.467	6.128	5.818	5.534	5.273	5.033	4.812
19	7.839	7.366	6.938	6.550	6.198	5.877	5.585	5.316	5.070	4.843
20	7.963	7.469	7.025	6.623	6.259	5.929	5.628	5.353	5.101	4.870
21	8.075	7.562	7.102	6.687	6.312	5.973	5.665	5.384	5.127	4.891
22	8.176	7.645	7.170	6.743	6.359	6.011	5.696	5.410	5.149	4.909
23	8.266	7.718	7.230	6.792	6.399	6.044	5.723	5.432	5.167	4.925
24	8.348	7.784	7.283	6.835	6.434	6.073	5.747	5.451	5.182	4.937
25	8.442	7.843	7.330	6.873	6.464	6.097	5.766	5.467	5.195	4.948
30	8.694	8.055	7.496	7.003	6.566	6.177	5.829	5.517	5.235	4.979
40	8.951	8.244	7.634	7.105	6.642	6.233	5.871	5.548	5.258	4.997
50	9.042	8.305	7.675	7.133	6.661	6.246	5.880	5.554	5.262	4.999

Index